'An enjoyable paperchase after novelists, playwrights and poets who were once much read. Fowler's *Forgotten Authors* is a book packed with vignettes, amusements and new names to try' *Sunday Times*

'Discover brilliant-but-long-lost writers with this pocket-sized delight' *Emerald Street*

'Check out your local library or second-hand bookshop and you'll find that these are some of the best storytellers you've never heard of' *Irish Times*

'Glorious . . . A real treat' Bookbag

'A joy. Fowler has put in an awesome amount of research and clearly could have created a compelling list that was twice as long' *Scotsman*

'This considered foray into the backlists and backstories of 99 forgotten authors reminds us of how focused we are on the new and the novel. It's fascinating to ponder which of these writers will remain forever in aspic and which might one day be ripe for revival' *The Bookseller*

'A godsend for book lovers if you want to make new discoveries, explore the fertile past and have a yearning for quality and quirk.' Maxim Jakubowski, Crimetime

'What stands out is his wicked humor and witty one-liners . . . Fowler writes such compelling descriptions of seemingly superb books that have fallen through the cracks of history' Bookriot

Also by Christopher Fowler

THE BRYANT & MAY MYSTERIES

Full Dark House
The Water Room
Seventy-Seven Clocks
Ten-Second Staircase
White Corridor
The Victoria Vanishes
Bryant & May On The Loose
Bryant & May Off The Rails
Bryant & May And The Memory Of Blood
Bryant & May And The Invisible Code
Bryant & May – The Bleeding Heart
Bryant & May – The Burning Man
Bryant & May – London's Glory
(Short Stories)
Bryant & May – Strange Tide
Bryant & May – Wild Chamber

NOVELS

Roofworld
Rune
Red Bride
Darkest Day
Spanky
Psychoville
Disturbia
Soho Black
Calabash
Breathe
Hell Train
Plastic
Nyctophobia
The Sand Men

GRAPHIC NOVELS

Menz Insana
The Casebook of Bryant & May

SHORT STORIES

City Jitters
City Jitters Two
The Bureau of Lost Souls
Sharper Knives
Flesh Wounds
Personal Demons
Uncut
The Devil In Me
Demonized
Old Devil Moon

MEMOIRS

Paperboy   *Film Freak*

'Well researched and wide-ranging . . . *The Book of Forgotten Authors* is a bibliophile's treat written with verve and passion. It will have readers scurrying into secondhand bookshops in search of yellowing paperbacks' *Guardian*

'Invigoratingly down-to-earth . . . Bibliophiles will love revisiting the midlist of yesteryear' Kathryn Hughes, *Guardian*, The Best Biography and Autobiography Books of 2017

'Full of humour and pathos, Christopher Fowler's survey of authors who have fallen into obscurity is a bibliophile's dream' *Financial Times*

'A real gem, filled with old favourites and new discoveries, and written in a light, snappy, erudite tone, as satisfying as a full English breakfast at your local art-house café' Joanne Harris

'A sure-fire Christmas gift . . . charged with an irresistible passion for the world of the book' *Telegraph*

'A joyous saunter through the lives and words of yesterday's big names. Readers will love this fascinating book' Cathy Rentzenbrink

'A treasure trove of trivia . . . Excellent . . . This colourful compendium of literary lives should be read by anyone who loves books' *Evening Standard*

'A great memory jogger AND an intriguing pointer to some I haven't read. Perfect for the bedside table' Val McDermid

'This is wholly delightful. What a charming, brilliant idea from the great Christopher Fowler' Mark Gatiss

‘Christopher Fowler’s cherishable book is as quirky and mesmerising as one of his novels; his detailed, loving excavation of a slew of unjustly neglected writers will have the inevitable effect of sending readers in search of these intriguing lost names’ Barry Forshaw

‘The perfect gift for a book-obsessed friend or if you simply want to uncover a hidden gem’ *Stylist*, 50 unmissable books for autumn 2017

‘His services to rescuing other writers from oblivion deserve a medal . . . He has a wonderful talent, actually rather rare among critics, for conveying just what it is about a book that makes it worth reading’ Jake Kerridge, *Sunday Express*

‘It’s hard to believe that anyone who loves fiction of all genres wouldn’t be completely won over by this treasure-filled book about books’ *Irish Independent*

‘A sheer joy. This is a lovely but dangerous book as I’ve already added some new names to my wants list’ Sarra Manning, *Red Magazine*

‘He reevaluates the reputations of dozens of lost authors with a sharp eye for detail and a dry, mordant wit. He makes you want to rush to your nearest secondhand bookshop and start digging out some of these forgotten authors’ Andrew Wilson

‘If you’ve forgotten the voice of your generation, the brilliant Christopher Fowler’s *The Book of Forgotten Authors* will provide you with the necessary reminder’ *Spectator*

‘Full of delights and surprises and will have you hunting down lost masterpieces . . . Totally absorbing’ *Sunday Sport*

THE BOOK OF FORGOTTEN AUTHORS

Christopher Fowler

riverrun

First published in Great Britain in 2017 by riverrun
This paperback edition published in 2018 by

riverrun

an imprint of
Quercus Editions Ltd
Carmelite House
50 Victoria Embankment
London EC4Y 0DZ

An Hachette UK company

A CIP catalogue record for this book is available from the British Library

PB ISBN 978 1 78648 490 1
EBOOK ISBN 978 1 78648 491 8

10 9 8 7 6

Typeset by
Printed and b

Contents

Why Are Good Authors Forgotten? 1

1. Margery Allingham 5
2. Virginia Andrews 8
3. Charlotte Armstrong 11
4. Frank Baker 15
5. R. M. Ballantyne 18
6. Alexander Baron 21
7. Peter Barnes 24
8. Lesley Blanch 27
9. Kyril Bonfiglioli 30

The Forgotten Disney Connection 33

10. Ernest Bornemann 38
11. Pierre Boulle 41
12. Mary Elizabeth Braddon 44

13. Caryl Brahms 47
14. Pamela Branch 49
15. Brigid Brophy 52
16. Thomas Burke 55
17. Dino Buzzati 57
18. Patricia Carlon 60
19. Barbara Comyns Carr 62

The Forgotten (pre-Tarantino) Pulp Fiction 64

20. John Dickson Carr 68
21. Leslie Charteris 71
22. John Christopher 74
23. John Collier 77
24. Norman Collins 80
25. Richard Condon 84
26. Edmund Crispin 87
27. E. M. Delafield 90
28. Patrick Dennis 93
29. Raymond Durgnat 95

The Forgotten Rivals of Holmes, Bond and Miss Marple 98

30. Rosalind Erskine 107
31. Dr Christopher Evans 110
32. Jack Finney 113
33. Ronald Firbank 116

34. Peter Fleming 120
35. Lucille Fletcher 122
36. R. Austin Freeman 124
37. Michael Green 127
38. Peter Van Greenaway 130

The Forgotten Books of Charles Dickens 133

39. Robert Van Gulik 137
40. Thomas Guthrie 140
41. Charles Hamilton 143
42. James Hanley 145
43. Sven Hassel 148
44. A. P. Herbert 151
45. Georgette Heyer 154
46. Eleanor Hibbert 157
47. Harry Hodge 160
48. Sheila Hodgetts 163

The Forgotten Queens of Suspense 166

49. Polly Hope 175
50. Richard Hughes 180
51. Graham Joyce 182
52. Robert Klane 185
53. Thomas Nigel Kneale 188
54. Ronald Knox 191
55. Gavin Lambert 194
56. George Langelaan 197

The Forgotten Nonsense Writers 200

57. Noel Langley 206
58. Marghanita Laski 209
59. Michael McDowell 212
60. John McGlashan 215
61. Juliane Maclaren-Ross 218
62. Richard Marsh 220
63. Arthur Mee 222
64. Gustav Meyer 226
65. Margaret Millar 229

The Forgotten Booker Authors 232

66. Clifford Mills 236
67. Gladys Mitchell 239
68. Brian Moore 242
69. J. B. Morton 244
70. Peter Nichols 247
71. Bill Naughton 250
72. Emma Orczy 252
73. Edward John Moreton Drax Plunkett 254
74. Thomas Love Peacock 256

Forgotten For Writing Too Little –
and Too Much 259

75. Joyce Porter 266
76. David Pownall 268
77. Philippa Pullar 271
78. Barbara Pym 274
79. Richard Quittenton 276
80. T. Lobsang Rampa 278
81. Simon Raven 281
82. Maurice Richardson 284

The Rediscovered Forgotten Authors 287

83. Arnold Ridley 294
84. Tom Robbins 296
85. Cynthia Propper Seton 299
86. Idries Shah 301
87. Richard Shaver 304
88. Matthew Phipps Shiel 307
89. Peter Tinniswood 309

Lost In Translation: The Forgotten World Authors 312

90. Thomas Tryon 319
91. Arthur Upfield 321
92. Edgar Wallace 324
93. James Redding Ware 327
94. Keith Waterhouse 330
95. Winifred Watson 334

The Justly Forgotten Authors 337

96. Dennis Wheatley 343
97. T. H. White 346
98. Kathleen Winsor 349
99. Cornell Woolrich 352

The Last Word 355

Acknowledgements 359
Index 361

Where Were All The BAME Writers? 373

100. William Melvin Kelley 377

Why Are Good Authors Forgotten?

Absence doesn't make the heart grow fonder. It makes people think you're dead.

Come along to an authors' event some time and listen to the comments we get. Readers will say things like, 'I read one of your books when I was twelve,' or, 'I had no idea you were still going. You don't need the money now, surely?' or, 'My grandmother was a fan of yours, but then she'd read anything, not being able to get out.'

It doesn't stop there. One day you find a complete set of your books in a charity shop, suggestive of a house clearance after a death. You perform at a library on a rainy night where the audience is mainly interested in the radiator. Your publisher can never wait to get off the line. Your pants are older than your publicist. Finally you depart the world in penury, and *then* they republish your backlist to great acclaim.

Some years ago I attended a paperback fair in the basement of a dank Victorian hotel that reeked of stale breakfasts and dead salesmen, and found myself the only punter in a room of a hundred haunted-looking second-hand booksellers. It felt as if I was attending the wake of an unloved relative. As I loaded my arms with musty pocketbooks I wondered if popular writing was finally redundant. Last year I returned to the same hotel and had to queue for half an hour to get in. The fair was mobbed. Then I thought, Vinyl came back, maybe paperbacks are analogue nostalgia.

It's more than that. I realized that others also loved old paperbacks, as I had always done. At the age of ten I'd discovered a chain of seedy second-hand book stores called Popular Book Centres. They made their money from top-shelf smut and needed racks of yellowing paperbacks to make themselves look respectable. They were as useful as public libraries, only more disgusting.

The Popular Book Centre in Greenwich, South London, had windows coated in thick dust. It was run by a thin, unshaven man who looked like a kipper with sweating sickness. He watched me all the time in case I stole anything and operated a peculiar pricing system that valued racy covers over content.

As a result, I spent every Saturday morning searching through his randomly arranged racks, digging out lost treasures. When books are costed by their weight and whether they have a naked girl on the front you not only find great bargains, you lose all sense of quality control. Much of what I bought was dropped into the dustbin by my horrified mother, but some stayed with me forever.

It taught me that the life of a book really begins when a reader turns to the first page. The moment this happens, its fate is out of its creator's hands.

I hadn't intended to start remembering vanished novels, but as an inveterate keeper of notebooks I soon found myself jotting down titles, then adding descriptions. As I did so, the same question hung over each addition: why? If these books were any good at all, why were their authors forgotten?

It was the kind of question that intrigued Suzi Feay, the literary editor of the *Independent on Sunday*, who allowed me to do some exploring. I began with E. M. Delafield, the daughter of a count, whose charming diaries were once immensely popular. We began publishing their stories, then opened the question to readers – which once-popular authors would they recommend for rediscovery?

I hadn't been prepared for the deluge of suggestions that followed.

It seemed that everyone had a personal favourite. Authors I'd long considered to be household names had been wiped from the collective memory, and were ripe for a renaissance. Some were mainstream novels from the recent past that caused sensations in their time. The task of tracking them down became obsessive. Unlike musicians or film-makers, authors can vanish completely. Their print-runs can be pulped, copies misfiled, manuscripts lost, banned and burned. They can be ubiquitous, influential and massively successful only to disappear within their own lifetimes.

Sometimes authors became famous for a particular novel that touched a public nerve, but it was rarely the only thing they wrote. Others became so popular that you would see people carrying copies of their novels around wherever you went, yet within a year or two no one could recall the titles.

Real readers don't forget, and I relied on admirers to notify me about their favourite forgotten authors. Sometimes I was contacted by the widow or son of a lost novelist, who would help me uncover the reason behind the disappearance.

How did I gauge whether a popular author had become forgotten? First I read them, and if their books proved difficult to obtain I considered including them. Then I tested their names on a focus group of about twenty book-lovers, including agents, publishers, friends and relatives. If I drew blank looks (and some of these blank looks shocked me until I realized it was partly an age thing) I tried to uncover the reasons for their disappearance.

To whittle down nearly 400 possible entries into one manageable volume I had to leave out some absolute gems. I junked nearly all playwrights, poets, screenwriters and graphic novelists, and dumped personal indulgences. I reluctantly excised many SF pioneers, whose works would easily fill a separate edition on their own. The writers I removed were every bit as worthy as the ones I included. The final selection was designed to whet your appetite, offer new reading ideas and let you take another look at authors you thought you knew.

So, here are ninety-nine stories and a dozen essays about the men and women who reached for the moon, and found that it wouldn't always be there . . .

1

Margery Allingham

I thought carefully about including Margery Allingham, so let's address the problem right at the start. She's hardly ever out of print and there are readers who recognize her name even if they haven't read her. However, very few readers seem to have got to grips with her novels. The ones who do, often become passionate fans. Ms Allingham has her own society, which holds literary events throughout the year. For many years I had her wrongly pegged as an Agatha Christie knock-off, until I took time to properly read her prose.

What I discovered, and what I suspect everyone who becomes an Allingham fan discovers, is the extraordinarily varied richness of her writing. Some of her books are more straightforward than others, but at its best the prose is allusive, colloquial, witty, bravura stuff – a window to a London mindset that is now completely lost.

Allingham was born in Ealing, London, in 1904. She wrote her first crime novel in 1928 (like many writers of her era, she started young) and continued for the next forty years. She regarded the mystery novel as a box with four sides: 'a killing, a mystery, an enquiry and a conclusion with an element of satisfaction in it'. She also distinguished between her 'right hand writing', which she did for pleasure, and her 'left hand writing', which was commissioned.

Her detective is Albert Campion, aristocratic and unassuming to the point of vacancy, so ethereal that he vanishes altogether in the film version of her most famous novel. Campion is supported by a sidekick, of course, in this case Magersfontein Lugg, an unfeasibly large former cat burglar, various cops and an unusually smart wife, Amanda. Campion differs from Sir Henry Merrivale or Hercule Poirot by being probably the least annoying detective in crime fiction, matched only by Dorothy L. Sayers's genteel detective Lord Peter Wimsey and Ngaio Marsh's Roderick Alleyn.

The Golden Age crime writers led readers into closed worlds, the theatre, clubland, village life, London's brittle nightlife, and brought them vividly to life with an insider's eye for detail. *Coroner's Pidgin* is one of Allingham's best because of its wartime lowlife atmosphere.

The first time I read *The Tiger in the Smoke*, the book widely regarded as her masterpiece, I kept losing my place. The chase to track Jack Havoc, jail-breaker and knife artist, in the London fog is as densely confusing as the choking gloom through which he carves his way. There's a central image of a hopping, running band of ragtag musicians silhouetted in the murk that stays beyond the conclusion. It's a dark, strange read and possibly not the best place to begin, but such offbeat fun. For years, Allingham's books seemed to have completely vanished into one of her pea-soupers.

'I don't stick me 'ead into every nark's nest I 'ear of!' says one character, and you want to hear the book read aloud, possibly by Sid

James. Allingham's language is so colourful that it's best to keep a copy of Brewer's *Phrase & Fable* close by. Her exuberant early prose gave way to a more mature, elegant style but both are wonderful. Her short fiction is easier to find, but less evocative.

Allingham believed in the 'Plum Pudding Principle' – that every few pages the reader should be treated to a plum so that it's not all stodge. Reading *Look to the Lady* one can see that the Golden Age plan was to reduce books like stock, to boil them to a kind of thick broth of a language that tastes rich enough to satisfy and leaves you wanting to copy down the recipe.

After a while you start to see the influences of Allingham everywhere. I joined the TV series *The Avengers* at the start of the Emma Peel series, where strange plots were the norm – the field in which rain drowns people, the village where nobody dies but the cemetery fills up, killer nannies, houses that send you mad – and eventually realized that these were Allingham-style Golden Age plots transposed to the medium of television, something the *Avengers* writer Brian Clemens confirmed to me. All of which makes her well worth seeking out and sticking with.

2

Virginia Andrews

Allingham was an acquired taste, but Andrews proved instantly popular. Sometimes an author's work lives on, but this one actually lived beyond her death. Or rather, not – because the real Virginia Andrews has been forgotten and replaced by a ghostwriter called Andrew Neiderman, who has since penned a huge number of volumes (close to seventy by my count) in her name. Andrews's books did so well that her agent and publishers found it necessary to keep her alive and continue earning money. The Inland Revenue Service even argued that her name was a valuable, and therefore taxable, asset. There was an ugly lawsuit after the auditor spotted a ghostwritten Virginia Andrews book in a local store and realized it was not part of the taxed estate.

In the age of the brand, this publishing behaviour is becoming more and more the norm. We've had extensions of everything from Sherlock Holmes to *Pride and Prejudice*, because they come with a built-in readership and provide fan service. But let's go back to the beginning of the Andrews story.

Cleo Virginia Andrews was an American novelist born in 1923, in Virginia. She started out as an illustrator and portrait painter, a sedentary occupation chosen largely because she was crippled by arthritis supposedly stemming from problems compounded by an early fall. She lived most of her life in pain, and never found love. When she switched from commercial art to writing at the relatively late age of fifty-five, she first chose science fiction, then produced a novel called *The Obsessed*, which her publisher felt she should sex up and retitle.

The revised version, a perverse fairy tale marketed as a horror novel and now called *Flowers in the Attic*, appeared in 1979 and became a surprise bestseller. It's an airless, claustrophobic work, telling the story of four blonde, blue-eyed siblings, Cathy, Cory, Carrie and Chris, who are imprisoned in an attic by their mother and grandmother in order to gain an inheritance. Kept there for years, mentally and physically abused by their relatives, two of the children eventually fall in love and form a new family unit before escaping. In fact the twins, Cathy and Chris, have incestuous sex that's appallingly close to rape.

The siblings wreak revenge on their captors in the second novel, and subsequent sequels continue the style from new viewpoints. Throughout, gothic imagery is laced with all the trappings of suffocating Victorian melodramas; there are hidden identities, arsenic poisonings and outbreaks of religious hysteria complete with bouts of incest, arson and incarceration in madhouses, tied up in circular plots that cascade with retribution and resolution. It seems that the feverish hothouse atmosphere of life in the attic appealed to the temperament of teenaged girls, who clearly wanted to have their most macabre fears about sex confirmed, and bought the books in their millions.

It is impossible not to read the novels as a dark fable reflecting Andrews's own sense of physical imprisonment. She was the flower in the attic. The success of the books brought Andrews freedom – she could afford to travel, to make friends and have a better life.

Her hallucinatory stand-alone novel *My Sweet Audrina* explored similar child-rape themes in outlandishly lurid prose, but what still shines through is her ability to see the world through a child's eyes. She began another series, but soon these volumes were only 'inspired' by her voluminous notes as, by this time, Andrews had inconveniently died. It was a fact that the publisher could not hide from avid readers. The original books are psychologically unsettling and compellingly awful, whereas the pseudonymous volumes that were designed to keep the brand alive are merely extensions and variations on Andrews's themes. Neiderman, the ghostwriter, had proven a solid, prolific horror writer before he took on the role of the dead author, but the real interest in Andrews lies in her first volume, *Flowers in the Attic*. One could say it was the forerunner of all those Gothic YA novels that brought us the 'Twilight' series, but its subject matter now feels much more uncomfortable, especially in the light of Josef Fritzl and his ilk.

3

Charlotte Armstrong

The early books of Virginia Andrews prove once again that female authors are particularly adept at tightening the emotional thumbscrews. But although tales of psychological suspense were explored in Britain by Ruth Rendell and others, they arguably reached their peak in post-war America.

Charlotte Armstrong was born in the iron-mining territory of Vulcan, Michigan, and worked in the classified ads department of the *New York Times* before hitting her stride as a playwright and mystery writer. She adopted a second identity, Jo Valentine, and produced at least twenty-seven novels, using as her heroines (and anti-heroines) women at all stages of life. She had abandoned a detective series to start this new style of writing, which largely avoids the whodunnit angle to portray women locked in psychological warfare with the members of their extended families and male-dominated workforces. Naturally she deals with stereotypes of the time, but the thrill comes in seeing her constrained protagonists gradually become empowered.

Armstrong wrote for the TV show *Alfred Hitchcock Presents* and Hitchcock personally directed one of her stories. It's not hard to see why he chose to do so. She wrote a very specific kind of mystery, the female suspense tale, and it played well in a televisual format.

In a second-hand bookshop in Yorkshire I found one Armstrong novel that really lived up to its name. *Mischief* was written in 1951, and is a story that unfolds in 'real time', a one-sitting read that ratchets up a feverish level of tension by watching a single situation unfold.

Ruth and Peter are staying overnight at a big city hotel with their daughter, nine-year-old Bunny. Peter is in town to make an after-dinner speech, but at the last minute they are forced to find a new babysitter. The liftman seems trustworthy and as it's an emergency he offers the services of Nell, a girl he knows, so the couple go off to dinner leaving their daughter in her hands. However, the liftman suspects something about blank-eyed Nell that her employers don't know – she burned down her family home with her parents still inside . . .

When Nell loses her temper and is seen risking the child's life at a window, several hotel guests attempt to voice their concerns, but a series of miscommunications and complications merely serve to raise the stakes. This kind of simple idea, produced in bravura style, was for a while a mainstay of popular American suspense fiction, and the stories were often turned into teleplays in the USA. Sadly, the single-play series ended after advertising demographics showed that they garnered a lower loyalty factor from viewers than long-running soaps.

Mischief became a film called *Don't Bother to Knock*, and France's answer to Hitchcock, Claude Chabrol, directed two features from Armstrong's novels. *Merci pour le Chocolat* (based on Armstrong's novel *The Chocolate Cobweb*) starred Isabelle Huppert as a poisoner with unguessable motives, while *La Rupture* had Stéphane Audran as the victim in a murderous family drama. The latter was made in a year when Chabrol made three such films in France, for the suspense genre had belatedly become popular there too.

If you'd like to understand how suspense tales are constructed you could do no better than to pick up a copy of *Night Call*, in which Armstrong demonstrates again and again how to create an involving scenario from the very first paragraph of each story. A young woman buys a suspiciously cheap fur coat, then cannot prove her innocent involvement in its purchase. A husband and wife travelling through Mexico find themselves having to cross the border with a dead body in their car. In *The Other Shoe* a couple attending a wedding reception find themselves having to create an alibi for their whereabouts. The story involves an affair, a murder and a pair of fabulously impractical, highly incriminating shoes.

It's easy to see why the 1950s were the golden age of suspense. The middle classes had grown strong on their adherence to conservative values, but luxury and status came at a price. A song from the period, 'We've Got to Keep Up with the Joneses', suggests that it still wasn't enough to have a car and a pool; the ultimate status symbol was an oil well. But a kind of collective guilt about wealth clearly surfaced in the form of these worst-case scenarios, played out to their natural conclusions.

The transgressions in Armstrong's tales damage the status quo, so her stories are about putting things right. Her characters are women who still have black maids. Their doctors don't discuss their health problems in detail in order to spare their feelings, so they're encouraged to pop pills for a variety of stamina-sapping illnesses, real or imagined. Their friends and families watch them for signs of unusual behaviour. They are forever being observed by patrician guardians (including their suspicious husbands) who are forever warning them not to 'overdo' things. Their homes are oppressive hothouses in which they wilt and poisons flourish.

Armstrong unfailingly understood the motivation of her damaged characters and drew out suspense by crossing their paths with innocents. Her writing style exerts the same kind of grip Ira Levin always managed so effortlessly, although it must be said that sometimes you want to wring the necks of her protagonists for picking the one option that will get them into deeper trouble. But hey, bad choices make good stories.

At school Armstrong once voted for herself as class president, only to be caught out when she won the election unanimously; it's exactly the sort of thing that would happen in one of her stories. Championed by respected editors like Kirby McCauley, some of her short fiction was repackaged. About suspense writing, she said: 'I do believe that if you are any kind of a storyteller, you are not excused from looking all about you, as well as within . . . Boredom is forbidden you.'

Armstrong died in 1969. We'll get to other forgotten stars of suspense later, but she was the first I discovered, and so remains a favourite.

4

Frank Baker

Alfred Hitchcock had an eye for finding writers like Charlotte Armstrong whose material would work visually. But who wrote the story upon which he based his film *The Birds*? Before you say Daphne Du Maurier, consider this. Thirty years before Du Maurier's short story, Frank Baker wrote *The Birds*, in which London's inhabitants were mysteriously turned upon by avian predators. Although Baker's version was longer and much more ambitious, the stories are remarkably similar, and like Du Maurier, Baker was also living in Cornwall. Du Maurier was also Baker's publisher's cousin, so it seems reasonable that she got to hear of the book. This does not mean she stole it, of course. All authors unwittingly absorb ideas from one another.

So was it coincidence or something more? Baker's birds seemed more supernatural in origin, but the author was naturally upset and corresponded with Du Maurier, who sympathized. Hitchcock, who seems to have followed Baker's version more closely, ignored the likeable young church organist, who was persuaded not to pursue costly litigation against Universal Studios (he had only been earning a pound a week). Legal counsel reckoned he would not win the case, as the two stories were markedly different. Yet, for me, Baker's version – which sold fewer than 300 copies – feels closer to Hitchcock's style.

Baker was born in Hornsey, London and moved to St Just-In-Penwith, where he began to write. In 1935 his first novel, *The Twisted Tree*, was published. It told the story of a woman who gives birth to a child who turns out to be a monster, and was a peculiar choice for a man who sought the conformity of religious comfort.

Baker became a professional actor, and his training clearly gave him the ability to add a sense of the dramatic to his light-hearted writing. Although he was drawn to the whimsical, he always grounded his novels with recognizable characters and evocative locations. *Mr Allenby Loses the Way* (1946) reflected this curious mix of realism and fantasy. In it, a fat little shopkeeper leaves his family to discover his true magical identity. This morality tale of belief and the demands of social conformity is haunted by the war and by Baker's own self-doubts.

Of his fifteen novels, Baker's masterpiece is the enchanting and timeless *Miss Hargreaves*, which really deserves classic status. It tells the story of two friends on holiday in Ireland who are required to invent the titular lady in order to gain access to a church. News of their acquaintanceship with Miss Hargreaves reaches England and they are soon forced to explain how they met her. Attempting to reassure those at home that they haven't strayed, they slowly add details to her life, embellishing her backstory with the information that she is eighty-three years old and always travels with a cockatoo, a harp and her own hip-bath.

Back in England the lie rather runs away from them. Just as this lark gets out of hand they receive a telegram from Miss Hargreaves herself, informing them that she is coming to stay for an indefinite period and will be arriving on the afternoon train. A dilemma ensues: how can they explain who she is when they can't even understand why she exists?

It's a comedy about the creative imagination, the pressures of conformity and losing control over your inventions. *Miss Hargreaves* came to the London stage starring Margaret Rutherford, the living embodiment of the character and a good friend of the author. Sadly the outbreak of war put an end to a planned film version.

However, another novel of Baker's, *Lease of Life*, was filmed with Robert Donat, and *Miss Hargreaves* is available again in print. Other novels followed, along with three volumes of memoirs. But we'll never get a satisfactory answer about what happened to *The Birds*.

5

R. M. Ballantyne

What drew the Scots to literary tropicana? Did they just enjoy reading books in which nobody wore a jumper? Everyone in my class had read Edinburgh-born R. M. Ballantyne's novel *The Coral Island*, about three schoolboys marooned on a South Pacific island after a shipwreck. The testing experience improves the moral fibre of the shipwrecked schoolboys as they take on responsibility without adult supervision, an idea later upended by William Golding in *Lord of the Flies*, which explicitly referenced the original. At the time of writing, coral was greatly in vogue with Victorians, who used it in jewellery.

Three years after the successful publication of the book, Ballantyne brought the boys back for a sequel, *The Gorilla Hunters*, but this proved less popular.

One of ten children, Ballantyne hailed from a printing and publishing family. Arriving in Canada at the age of sixteen, he went to work for the Hudson's Bay Company, trading fur and eventually writing about his experiences.

The Coral Island was published in 1858, remained a hit for over a century and was translated around the world. It was considered appropriate for primary-school children despite blood-gushing descriptions of death and sacrifice. The book apparently exists in a peculiar sub-genre called 'Robinsonades', which were works inspired by Defoe's *Robinson Crusoe*. It's presented as a recollection, and is partly a tale of survival, partly action-adventure with pirates, missionaries and cannibals. However, Ballantyne never went to such an island and got his details wrong. It wasn't so much his description of peaceful Polynesians as cannibals that caused him a problem but his idea that coconuts had soft skins.

Mortified, Ballantyne resolved only to work from direct evidence in future, living with a lighthouse keeper and hanging out with Cornish tin miners, but this in-depth research made little difference to his work. For *The Coral Island* he also borrowed from others rather heavily, but he learned from his mistakes. Robert Louis Stevenson was strongly indebted to the novel for his own *Treasure Island*, and acknowledged him in his introduction.

Ballantyne wrote around a hundred books but this was his biggest success, proving that the life of the imagination may be more vivid than one drawn only on empirical evidence. In the same way, crime author H. R. F. Keating mostly wrote his India-set Inspector Ghote novels without visiting the sub-continent. One could argue that Ballantyne's dashing story of Jack, Ralph and Peterkin is overtly 'improving', piously Christian and imperialist but *The Coral Island* is a fascinating window to a lost world. The boys are a bit too good to be true and seem obsessed with their living arrangements, their attempts to create an aura of domesticity and the ceaseless cataloguing of nature, but these concerns reflect their British background. One feels that if a bunch of Victorians were really shipwrecked on a desert island they would immediately try to get some houses, a church and a post office up.

Still, Ballantyne can hardly be castigated for seeing a desert island as a paradise of opportunities rather than a primitive hell on earth. His book belongs to a time of empire builders, and it would be a curmudgeon indeed who belittles the lads' enthusiasm for their new life.

One other book in the author's backlist sticks out, and has an odd connection to the band Deep Purple. *The Butterfly's Ball and the Grasshopper's Feast* was the illustrated reworking of a poem about an insects' party where beetles, gnats, dragonflies and moths amuse themselves and even the wasp lays down its sting for a bit of a boogie.

The book was dazzlingly reinvented by psychedelic artist Alan Aldridge, who virtually designed the 1960s, from Warhol's *Chelsea Girls* poster to the illustrated Beatles lyrics. It was a huge hit and became a lush rock-opera concept album originally conceived for Deep Purple's Jon Lord, ending up with a starry cast of rock musicians who created something that sounds like a missing Beatles album. It was spun into a less magical animated cartoon.

6

Alexander Baron

Ballantyne may have been bothered by his spongy coconuts, but Alexander Baron had no such qualms. There's an experienced toughness to his prose that shines from every page.

It's hard for frontline war writers to show an objective sensitivity to their subject matter while fighting for their country. Baron is one of the most consistently underrated British novelists of the Second World War. A left-wing author and soldier who read Jane Austen in the bomb-craters of Normandy, he was interested in the psychological aspects of war, and wrote with unusual sympathy about the lives of ordinary women as well as squaddies, portraying them as essentially decent people caught in extraordinary circumstances.

Hackney-raised Alexander Bernstein was born towards the end of one world war and served in another. In the 1930s, together with his friend Ted Willis, he became a leading light in the Labour League of Youth (then affiliated with the Communist Party), but grew disillusioned with far-left politics after talking to fighters returning from the Spanish Civil War. Serving in the British Army's Pioneer Corps, he was among the first troops to land in Sicily during D-Day, and used the experience to write his first novel, *From the City, from the Plough*. The fictional story of soldiers of the Fifth Battalion, Wessex Regiment, in the build-up to D-Day was born from Bernstein's own experience. Today the novel is regarded as one of the most accurate and unsentimental portrayals of day-to-day military life ever written.

He followed this with *There's No Home*, about British soldiers waiting out a lull in the war. The third part of the highly acclaimed trilogy was *The Human Kind*, a series of linked vignettes that act as an overview of the entire war. The books benefited from being in the first wave of popular Pan paperbacks. *The Human Kind* was turned into a Hollywood travesty called *The Victors*, with Americans replacing the British war heroes.

Although he had been convinced by his publisher Jonathan Cape to change his name to Baron, the author now chose to write about the tumultuous lives of gamblers and prostitutes on the streets of the East End, and the Jewish migration to suburban 1960s North London.

The Lowlife and its sequel, *Strip Jack Naked*, brilliantly capture life on the streets. Baron's Jewish gambler anti-hero is a marvellous creation, aware of his own failings, unable to change and forever letting his family down – you get a sinking feeling every time he goes out gambling with the last of his money, and worse when he takes a naive, easily led and virtually penniless neighbour out to the dogs – but he's kind enough to give up an eye to a blinded boy who needs a corneal transplant.

Baron's epic novel of Edwardian Jewish gangs, *King Dido*,

remained his personal favourite and so it should be, for here is a tale that outlines, with infinite care and patience, the causal link between poverty and crime. It's a *Bildungsroman* with a working-class protagonist, an anti-hero who is all too human and decent, and its final postscript carries a tragic resonance that is utterly heartbreaking. It is one of the greatest and least-read novels about London ever written, arguably an East End version of *Les Misérables*.

This post-war work was proof that serious literature could also be popular, and the shy, courteous Baron (whose failure of nerve once prevented him from attending his own launch party) now switched to film and TV. He was a regular writer on *Play for Today*, and subsequently adapted classics like *Jane Eyre*, *Vanity Fair* and *Sense and Sensibility* for television.

His elegant style and warm sense of humanity secured a reputation that's now starting to enjoy a revival. Happily, a few of his books are once more available after years in the wilderness.

7

Peter Barnes

In the 1960s new British writing flourished, especially in the theatre. Rising labour costs eventually forced up seat prices, which meant that theatre chains needed certain houses to stage sure-fire hits that would pay for new plays. As one impresario put it, 'Five nights of the Nolan Sisters will buy you one performance of *Equus*.' As a consequence, great theatrical authors are now more in danger of being forgotten than most novelists.

Plays become ephemeral if they fail to enter repertoires. The shock of their experience fades, and only the scripts remain. Samuel French was an American entrepreneur who founded a play-publishing business with a British actor-manager in 1859. He soon became the most important theatrical publisher in England. At the time of his death in 1898 almost all renowned English playwrights of the present and recent past had been represented by his company.

For the rest of its life in Covent Garden French's bookshop was a great hangout for penniless writers and actors. The staff would let us sit on the floor reading all day and never chuck us out. Tiny Elena Salvoni used to run a nearby restaurant called Bianchi's, and encouraged writers to lurk there, knowing we would bring a certain louche, argumentative charm to the place. Whenever it looked like we couldn't afford to stay there any longer she would stroll past the table and surreptitiously stick a bottle of cheap plonk on it so that we wouldn't leave.

I rather think that French's and Bianchi's did more for the struggling author than any creative-writing course. But I digress. There were certain playwrights who became idolized by writers and actors-in-training, and for many years Peter Barnes came close to the top of that list. Barnes is still misunderstood by critics seeking easy tags; his work was elaborately constructed, intellectually rigorous and controversial, his language exact and demanding. It must also have been a bugger to memorize.

Barnes was born in Bow in 1931, but his parents soon moved to a geriatric coastal town to run an amusement arcade. Appropriately, his writing links death and jokes to create a dark carnival atmosphere. A part-time theologist, film critic and screenwriter, Barnes was one of the great proponents of anti-naturalism, a dazzling response to the dreary kitchen-sink novels and plays of the fifties.

At a time when Monty Python was reconfiguring comedy, a number of authors, including Peter Nichols, John Antrobus and Alan Bennett, started incorporating surrealism, disjunction and Pirandello-esque antics into their work. Barnes wrote *The Ruling Class*, a strange, disturbing satire about power that nominally concerns a mad earl and his identification with Christ. Asked how he knows he's Jesus, his lordship replies, 'It's simple. When I pray to him I find I'm talking to myself.' A film version with Peter O'Toole was brave but problematic.

Barnes proved too uncomfortable for middle-class audiences, never more so than in *Laughter!*, a horrifying but deeply moral comedy about office workers providing the paperwork for crematorium chimneys in Auschwitz, who are forced to realize their complicity.

Beloved by serious theatre actors like Guinness and Gielgud, Barnes later softened a little to write period comedies and monologues (perhaps because he became the father of triplets in his seventies), but not before turning out *Red Noses*, one of the few slapstick comedies set during the time of the Black Death. For this raucous tale of a troupe of performers touring afflicted French villages, he won a well-deserved Olivier award.

Barnes's screenplay for the film *Enchanted April* secured an Oscar nomination, and his history plays became more naturalistic, although he was always capable of dazzling *coups de théâtre*. He wrote, 'Write what you know is good advice for journalists. I write what I imagine, believe, fear, think.' To read his intense, rarely performed plays now is to see how far the theatre of ideas has lately fallen.

Would-be writers should read playscripts to understand that conversation is not dialogue, and that serious themes can be explored via outrageous, apocalyptic situations. The crime writer Ngaio Marsh was so influenced by Pirandello's *Six Characters in Search of an Author* that she used it as a template for a novel, *Death and the Dancing Footman*. Plays can teach writers how to condense ideas and allow for multiple interpretations, and Barnes is one of the best.

8

Lesley Blanch

From Chiswick, London, to the remotest regions of the world, the glamorous Blanch was another writer drawn to the exotic, but for once it was a woman who ventured into the world of the almost exclusively male traveller.

Born to idle and unconventional parents, she fell in love with the idea of exotic travel after an unnamed friend – possibly a lover of her mother's – visited their house with wild tales of his journeys overseas. He instilled in her a passion for all things Russian, especially the writings of Alexander Herzen, who once said: 'I am truly horrified by modern man. Such absence of feeling, such narrowness of outlook, such lack of passion and information, such feebleness of thought.' He would deserve a separate entry in this book.

Blanch studied at the Slade in the early 1920s and took up scenery design, making murals, costumes and book jackets for the publishing house Faber. She also designed a poster for the London Underground before becoming the features editor of the UK edition of *Vogue* between 1937 and 1944. She was a fine caricaturist, with a sharp eye for colour and line. The society photographer Cecil Beaton became a lifelong friend. But she wasn't about to settle down.

An attraction to the artistic side of high society manifested itself as her second marriage to a French diplomat resulted in extensive travel and friendships with film stars. Her husband left her for the ill-fated actress Jean Seberg, who was hounded by the FBI for her support of the Black Panthers.

Working for the Ministry of Information, Blanch had a rather good war. Of the Blitz she said: 'Every day was possibly your last . . . It was a free-for-all for me and my kind. A lot of women were loyally waiting for their man to come back, but I didn't have any particular tie-up.'

She was now known in royal and Hollywood circles and, although she kept her top-tier contacts, had become fascinated by the Middle East. She didn't start writing until she was fifty, presumably when she stopped being a Jezebel. Her first book became her most famous. In *The Wilder Shores of Love* she explored the lives of four extraordinary women: Isabel Burton, who supported her husband Sir Richard Burton, sharing his adventures; Lady Jane Digby, the aristocrat whose scandalous life spanned continents and who died as the wife of a young Arab sheik; Isabelle Eberhardt, the explorer who dressed as a man, converted to Islam and drowned in a flood at twenty-seven; and Aimée Dubucq de Rivéry, who was kidnapped by pirates and given as a gift to a Sultan in the Ottoman Empire.

The theme of the book was, unsurprisingly, women escaping the boredom of convention, but as Blanch continued to travel and write she set other volumes in far-off lands, her personal favourite being *The Sabres of Paradise*, a history of imperialist Russia in the early nineteenth century.

It could be argued that women like Blanch were free to travel and express themselves only because they had the financial security and the connections to do so, but she was a fine, spirited writer with an eye for telling detail and an ability to understand the ambitions, flaws and passions of her subjects. Her accounts are crammed with fabulous stories of love and war, and became hugely influential. She is particularly regarded as being ahead of her time in the way she attempted to bridge the Christian West and Islamic East. Although she eventually divorced her second husband, she kept his name because, she said, in France it improved her place at table.

Blanch believed that learning how to deal with pain was the most important thing in life. She wrote twelve colourful volumes packed with the kind of details that could only be picked out by someone with an original eye. She also produced a cookbook, *Round the World in Eighty Dishes*, including a useful tip about what to do if you've over-salted a meal – add a potato. She died in 2007 one month short of 103. What an innings!

9

Kyril Bonfiglioli

Imagine a politically incorrect combination of Bertie Wooster, Falstaff and Raffles, and you get an idea of this author's fictional hero. He appeared in (almost) four of Bonfiglioli's books, and is a marvellous invention.

The author was born to an English mother and an Italian-Slovenian antiquarian-book-selling father in Eastbourne, on the south coast. After fifteen years as an art dealer in Oxford, an experience that clearly provided the background for his books, he became the editor of small science-fiction magazines, although his own writings showed little interest in that direction. All other biographical information about Bonfiglioli – that he was an expert swordsman, a good shot and a teetotaller, for example – was at least partially wrong. Luckily, we now have his second wife's biography, *The Mortdecai ABC*, to thank for the facts.

Before his first book, *Don't Point That Thing at Me*, has even started, Bonfiglioli warns, 'This is not an autobiographical novel. It is about some other portly, dissolute, immoral and middle-aged art dealer.' In fact, the first line is: 'When you burn an old carved and gilt picture frame it makes a muted hissing noise in the grate – a sort of genteel fooh – and the gold leaf tints the flames a wonderful peacock blue-green.'

This is his snobbish, cowardly, dandy art thief, Charlie Mortdecai, speaking before fencing a Goya and attracting the murderous attention of several governments. Mortdecai is a delicious creation who, accompanied by his thuggish sidekick Jock, outrages the art-world dullards of the 1970s as he heads towards comeuppance and a disgraceful cliffhanger of an ending.

Mortdecai returned (with no explanation whatsoever for the precipitous season-end interim) in *After You with the Pistol*, *Something Nasty in the Woodshed* and three-quarters of *The Great Mortdecai Moustache Mystery*, which was published posthumously, having been finished by the literary mimic Craig Brown, an act of forgery which Bonfiglioli would surely have adored.

His only other work is the hilarious period romp *All the Tea in China*, which features a scurrilous Dutch ancestor of Mortdecai's. Everyone agrees that Bonfigioli should have become world famous. The sad truth was that, although his joyous books would have you believe otherwise, he lived in various states of poverty and alcoholism, and died of cirrhosis.

However, his wife Margaret told me that her husband's party piece was removing shirt buttons with a sword, and a friend of Kyril's, at the Gordon Highlanders Depot where they met, said he had taught him knife throwing, fencing and how to fry peas in Worcestershire sauce, so there's a real basis in the tall tales. Margaret also pointed out that he could shoot a sixpence from the bravely held-out thumb and forefinger of a visiting French art dealer, standing at the far end of a large room.

Bonfigioli's novels aren't ordinary enough to be simple crime capers; they're scabrous, witty, packed with demanding intelligent jokes, rude in the very best sense. He never found the right fans in his lifetime, but has become a true cult hero. Sadly, a horrible film version called *Mortdecai*, starring the entirely inappropriate Johnny Depp, failed to capture the salty charm of his writing – but then it's hard to see how it ever could have. Some writers belong to the page alone.

The Forgotten Disney Connection

When I was a child it seemed the only available family films at the cinema were all made by Walt Disney. As we know from the somewhat sentimentalized film *Saving Mr Banks*, Uncle Walt was good at persuading authors that he could turn their treasured works into films, but Pamela Travers was not his only conquest (she was hardly his conquest at all, forever complaining about the poor quality of the *Mary Poppins* movie).

Nobody now remembers the Swiss beekeeping pastor Johann David Wyss, but in the late eighteenth century he was so impressed by Defoe's *Robinson Crusoe* that he wrote a book for his children which would act as an adventure and a series of life lessons. *The Swiss Family Robinson* is the tale of an ordinary family who become shipwrecked on an uninhabited tropical island and christen it 'New Switzerland'.

This chronicle of survival against pirates, wild animals and the elements went on to become a beloved classic and the most memorable thing about Switzerland apart from Toblerones and euthanasia, but it's the Disney version with John Mills that sticks in the mind, and readers of a certain age will not be able to see an ostrich without thinking of the film's animal race. Jules Verne wrote a direct sequel, *The Castaways of the Flag*, which no one I know has ever read.

Wyss wasn't the only author to reach a wider audience because of Disney. Fred Gipson was a journalist who wrote for the *Daily Texan*. His novel *Old Yeller* was filmed in 1957 and became a massive hit for the studio. The sentimental story of a fourteen-year-old boy left in charge of a homestead, helped only by the titular stray dog, packed out cinemas everywhere with sobbing children. Disney traumatized a generation in the scene where faithful Old Yeller gets rabies and has to be shot. Gipson somehow managed to write two sequels, *Savage Sam* and *Little Arliss*, but he never topped the original.

Felix Salten was a Jewish Hungarian-Austrian author whose books were banned by Hitler. He sold the film rights to his most famous work, *Bambi*, for $1,000. Although he also wrote a sequel to his biggest hit, Disney used two of his unconnected further works for the basis of his films *Perri* and *The Shaggy Dog*. Before he began writing animal stories, Salten was the anonymous author of an erotic novel about a Viennese prostitute. That didn't come out in the *Bambi* publicity.

The beloved *Dumbo*, hastily made to bail out the studio after the disaster of *Fantasia*, was created by author Helen Aberson for a novelty toy called 'Roll-A-Book' which never took off, unlike its big-eared elephant star. And *Song of the South* was structured from stories collected by Joel Chandler Harris, but remained unreleased on home video for many years because the song 'Zip-a-Dee-Doo-Dah' echoed the racist folk song 'Zip Coon'.

Walt Disney's main concern was to fill cinemas with entranced ankle-biters and their parents, but to do this he had to bowdlerize the original source material of his films to suit American tastes, so Bambi's species was altered to one that could be recognized by native audiences.

Until the late 1960s Disney continued to search Europe for novels he could adapt. *Lottie and Lisa* was the second most famous novel by the German author and satirist Erich Kästner (his first was *Emil and the Detectives*, also filmed by Disney). It told of two reunited identical twins who switch places to help their parents' respective marriages, and was filmed by Disney as *The Parent Trap*, starring the once ubiquitous Hayley Mills. It managed three sequels and a remake with Lindsay Lohan.

Margery Sharp's best-known book was rewritten by Disney but it made her wealthier and more famous than she would otherwise have been. *The Rescuers* concerned a pair of rodent agents for the Prisoners' Aid Society of Mice, sent on a mission that involves the daring rescue of a Norwegian poet and the thwarting of an evil Persian cat called Mamelouk. Sharp cared deeply about words. She especially liked 'tureen' and 'vermin', the soft opening V of 'velvet', 'violets' and 'voluptuousness'. She said: 'I absolutely believe it is fatal ever to write below your best, even if what you write may never be published.'

Perhaps the oddest Disney film to be based on a book was 1943's *Victory Through Air Power*, propaganda created from a non-fiction bestseller by the Russian aviation pioneer Alexander P. de Seversky.

Starting with a comical history of flight, its images become increasingly sinister and aggressive as bombers take to the air.

According to my reckoning, out of the eighty Walt Disney features produced over two decades (the 1950s and 1960s) only nineteen were *not* based on novels. Disney reimagined works by an astonishing array of authors, including J. M. Barrie, Robert Louis Stevenson, Lewis Carroll, Eleanor Porter (*Pollyanna*), Johnston McCulley (*Zorro*), Alois Podhajsky (*Miracle of the White Stallions*), Sheila Burnford (*The Incredible Journey*) and Gordon Buford (*The Love Bug*). Jules Verne's *The Children of Captain Grant* was retitled *In Search of the Castaways* as a star vehicle for Disney favourites Hayley Mills and Maurice Chevalier.

After Disney's death the adaptation habit continued. Nineteen eighty-one's *The Fox and the Hound* was the studio's most expensive animated film to that date, and was based on a novel by Daniel P. Mannix. Harking back to the style and themes of *Bambi*, it surprisingly flopped but is now considered a classic. By the time we get to the present day only a tiny handful of Disney films are produced from original works. Most now stem from park attractions, TV shows, remakes or time-weathered traditional sources. *Frozen*, *very* loosely based on Hans Christian Andersen's 'The Snow Queen', brought the studio full circle; back in 1940 Disney's second feature was *Pinocchio*, after the fairy tale by Carlo Callodi.

So, did Uncle Walt ruin great novels by trampling subtlety and replacing it with American philistinism? Certainly his version of the Hundred Acre Wood in *Winnie-the-Pooh* seemed more like Central Park, and his film of T. H. White's *The Sword in the Stone* was a thrown-together travesty, but he drew huge numbers of new readers to relatively rare works, and sometimes perfectly captured the spirit of the original novels. *Lady and the Tramp* was based on *Happy Dan, the Whistling Dog* by Ward Greene and feels so much like a literary source directly transcribed to film that it should have come with chapter headings.

There were disasters too; Mark Twain's *A Connecticut Yankee In King Arthur's Court* became *Unidentified Flying Oddball*, and let's not mention the animated high-concept mess *Treasure Planet*, but many superb authors with only local readership unexpectedly found themselves basking in worldwide adoration.

10

Ernest Bornemann

'Never have two girls; have three. Two are too much.' So said sexual prodigy Bornemann. Born in Berlin in 1915 and raised as a Communist, he quickly developed wide-ranging interests. At ten he saw African musicians in Paris, who fired his fascination with new music forms. An intensely curious young man, he described himself as 'sexually mature at fourteen, politically mature at fifteen, and intellectually mature between fourteen and sixteen'.

He escaped from Germany in 1933 by posing as a member of the Hitler Youth going to Britain as an exchange student. Becoming fascinated with jazz theory, he wrote an encyclopaedia of jazz at twenty-five. I think it was at this point that I started to hate him.

In 1940 he was deported to Canada as a German national, then worked for the BBC. He became an expert in ethnomusicology, film-making, psychoanalysis, social anthropology and later (famously) sexology. He wrote screenplays for Alfred Hitchcock (seemingly a rite of passage for all young writers of the time) and Carlo Ponti, worked as a scriptwriter for Orson Welles in Morocco, composed a jazz opera and wrote plays. His script *Tremolo* was directed by Yul Brynner in 1950 and proved the biggest TV hit of the year. His murder mystery movie *Bang! You're Dead* had the unusual setting of a US army camp for bombed-out civilians. Further novels followed.

After this lunatic life he settled down in a tiny, isolated Austrian village.

But let's rewind to Bornemann arriving in Britain as a teenager. Granted political asylum, he anglicized his name to Cameron McCabe and wrote the book for which he became famous (at least, within certain circles), an extremely confident, wildly messy meta-novel called *The Face on the Cutting-Room Floor*, published before he was twenty.

It's a murder mystery unlike anything previously seen in Britain, once described by literary crime expert Julian Symons as 'a dazzling, unrepeatable box of tricks – the detective story to end all detective stories', but also pegged by Jonathan Coe as 'a brilliant nineteen-year-old's roar of frustration at the limitations of the genre which he has chosen for himself'. The book is certainly frustrating, insolent and exhausting, the work of a prodigy, not least because when Bornemann arrived he barely spoke a word of English. What's most miraculous, of course, is that it got published at all.

While British mystery authors were still rattling teacups and finding bodies in libraries, Ernest's prose was like free-form jazz, slangy, lightning fast, impressionistic, fractured, or as he described it, 'a finger exercise on the keyboard of a new language'. There are mis-steps; some passages are so banal that they feel like American noir parodies; others are brilliantly haunting.

The story involves a starlet found dead in an editing suite, and is a melody quick-cut into ever-changing jive forms. The opening is straightforward enough – was it suicide or murder? – but three suspects confess and it transpires the whole event was filmed. However even this is smoke and mirrors for what is to come, as the plot becomes a tesseract, changing form depending upon the angle at which you view it, and concluding with a treatise on the form itself.

Traditionalists felt cheated because of the way in which the novel somersaults halfway through, defying all expectations, but critics loved it, even though the publisher had to hide the author's identity until 1974. It ran through many editions but was refused publication in America, possibly because Bornemann was a Communist. At eighty he killed himself over a love affair. You've got to adore him for that alone.

11

Pierre Boulle

As you can see from Ernest Bornemann, sometimes the lives of authors are as exciting as their books. This French novelist trained as an engineer, working on British rubber plantations in Malaya.

He became a secret agent, aiding the resistance movements in China, Burma and French Indochina, met a married woman who became the great love of his life, and was captured by Vichy France loyalists on the Mekong River, where he was forced into hard labour. During this period he kept a diary on scraps of paper. Later, despite being decorated as a war hero, he found himself down and out in Paris. Moving in with his widowed sister, he began to write from his collected scraps.

The first two attempts amounted to nothing, but Boulle's third novel became a multi-million global bestseller. *The Bridge over the River Kwai* was a fictionalized account concerning the Allied POWs who were forced to build the notorious Death Railway. The book was a powerful amalgam of the author's memories, but was attacked by survivors who felt it misrepresented the facts (Boulle pointed out that he had created a fictional main character, but this was overlooked). The main point of controversy was over a plot-point that saw the Allied senior officer at Kwai collaborating with the enemy. Besides, this was a British story, dammit, and how dare a Frenchman come along and tell it?

David Lean's Oscar-winning film version starred Alec Guinness, and was credited to Boulle because its screenwriters, Michael Wilson and Carl Foreman, had been blacklisted by the House Un-American Activities Committee as Communist sympathizers. Boulle accepted an Oscar with the shortest speech in the academy's history: '*Merci.*' The film won seven 1957 Oscars, despite tampering with the story. In the book the bridge is not blown up, but Hollywood needed an uplifting climax.

For nine years Boulle continued writing with moderate success, and then struck gold a second time. Working with his usual translator Xan Fielding, he produced *Monkey Planet*, which was hailed as a masterpiece of suspense and satirical intelligence. A parable of scientific speculation and inverted evolution, it was reissued as *Planet of the Apes*, and filmed in 1968 with heroic plank Charlton Heston. Four sequels followed, along with a TV series, reboots, comics, cartoons and parodies.

However, Boulle's book is radically different to the filmed version. Its most iconic scene – the Statue of Liberty on the beach – is missing and the story has a twist ending which in fact is somewhat closer to the much-derided Tim Burton remake.

Boulle had written a sequel called *Planet of the Men*, but it was turned down in favour of an inferior studio version, *Beneath the Planet of the Apes*. The films benefited from the first appearance of related marketing, as toys, games and licensed clothing became popular with teens, and 'Apemania' gripped viewers. Boulle was reportedly staggered by this sudden late success, having (rightly, it turns out) considered his original book unfilmable.

There is a school of writing in France that's rather overlooked: one of simplified prose and clear narrative progression. It's a style adopted by modern writers like Amélie Nothomb, which may explain why Agatha Christie is so admired there, and Boulle adopted this style for his novels. He continued to produce long-form fiction, short story collections and non-fiction, living out a full and happy conclusion to a life that had contained so much drama and hardship.

12

Mary Elizabeth Braddon

In 1835, London's Soho was chaotic, squalid and rough. There are authors whose lives mirrored their novels, none more so than Braddon, who was born there. Taken away by her mother, who walked out of her marriage due to her husband's infidelities (a very daring thing to do at that time), Mary went on the stage, where she took to playing matronly roles even when she was young in order to support the pair of them. At the age of six she was given a writing desk, and it sparked the desire to write. With Britain's burgeoning youth addicted to penny dreadfuls, she soon began churning out serials teeming with lurid incident.

It was wearying work packing every episode with escalating drama, so Braddon turned to novels, by which time she was living in her married publisher's home with her mother, acting as stepmother to his five children and delivering six more of her own while his actual wife languished in an insane asylum.

If not quite bigamy, it was close enough, and real life found a strong echo in her first and most sensational 'sensation' novel, *Lady Audley's Secret*, which was published in serial form in 1862.

Braddon's bigamous heroine dumps her child, shoves her first husband down a well, nearly poisons the second one and burns down the hotel that's housing her other male friends. Reading her now, I find some of what she says almost indecipherable: 'Self-assertion may deceive the ignorant for a time; but when the noise dies away, we cut open the drum, and find it was emptiness that made the music.'

Lady Audley's Secret is packed with classic Victorian anxieties and echoes the sensational real-life case of Constance Kent, throwing traditional images of blissful domesticity and dedicated motherhood into confusion. Is Lady Audley insane, faking madness or acting deceitfully in a proto-feminist attempt to wrest control of her life, as is current fashionable thinking?

Other puzzles abound in the plot, which blurs the lines between gender and class and asks questions about Victorian identity. But there's strong evidence to suggest that Braddon had not thought greatly about any of this; the last third of the serial was written in under two weeks, and she may have been simply channelling the spirit of the times.

As a result, it's hard to know what exactly she thought of her villainess/heroine, although one suspects she had a kindlier eye than her critics, who weren't happy that the literature of servants had been dragged into the main house. Certainly it was the greatest success of her eighty-plus novels, most of which have utterly vanished, the last being written in 1908.

Fame brought the author material wealth, but also brought

disaster; when her partner's wife died in the asylum the funeral was hushed up, but letters of condolence were accidentally sent to the house, and the staff walked out upon realizing that Mrs Braddon was not the first wife but a 'bigamous' mistress. In a twist the author could not have foreseen, the scandal of her novel had been reproduced in her life.

Happily, Braddon was subsequently married and went on to edit her own magazines. Her books were adapted many times, not always with her permission, but she remained successful and carried on with charity work until her death. It was written of her that 'Miss Braddon is a part of England; she has woven herself into it; without her it would be different. This is no mere fanciful conceit. She is in the encyclopaedias; she ought to be in the dictionaries.' An association celebrating her life and works exists to this day.

13

Caryl Brahms

How did the English cheer themselves up during wartime? One of the ways was by turning to the eleven sprightly comic novels of Caryl Brahms and her sidekick.

Caryl (née Doris Abrahams) Brahms and 'Skid' Simon (né Simon Skidelsky) met in a hostel and shared the same ridiculous sense of humour. First they wrote captions for David Low's political cartoons in the *Evening Standard*, then they graduated to crime novels. She had been born into a Sephardic Jewish family in Croydon. Her writing partner had been born in Manchuria. She trained as a musician and wrote ballet criticism. He was a genius bridge player, winning tournaments, writing books on card systems and becoming the bridge correspondent of the *Observer*, when there were such things.

A Bullet in the Ballet (1937) was the result of a delayed meeting and a conversation over a cup of tea. Brahms did the ballet bits and Skid wrote the parts that involved detection. A dancer is shot in the head during a production of *Petrushka*, and Detective Inspector Quill, 'the Scotland Yard Adonis', is dispatched to uncover the killer, only to find that the *corps de ballet* is filled with vipers. The novel's first line is, 'Since it is probable that any book flying a bullet in its title is going to produce a corpse sooner or later – here it is.' If you can't spot who the murderer is by the novel's mid-point you must be holding the book upside down, but this is not to be read for the originality of its plot; the characters are the thing, and the authors' sense of silly fun, as if they were writing to amuse themselves and by accident amusing others.

It was followed by a ballet-themed sequel the following year, called *Casino for Sale*. Both feature the high-living impresario Vladimir Stroganoff, a hilarious creation who deserved his own series. Curiously, my edition of *A Bullet in the Ballet* suggests that I might also enjoy reading *A Survey of Russian Music*, which may be an indication of the thoroughness of Brahms's research.

Envoy on Excursion is a European farce with Nazis, somewhat akin to *The Lady Vanishes*, and *Six Curtains for Stroganova* concludes the set with the same characters. Farce should never outstay its welcome, and all the books are short but packed tight with merriment.

You can't teach an author lightness of touch; it's something innate, born from viewing the world with a sense of resigned amusement. Two further novels deserve mention: the delightful, much imitated Shakespearean tale *No Bed for Bacon*, and *Don't, Mr Disraeli*, which famously includes every Victorian literary cliché you can think of. And in case you wonder whose books Brahms and Simon pinched bits from, they thoughtfully provide a list.

Brahms went on to write my favourite biography of Gilbert & Sullivan, *Lost Chords and Discords*, which refreshingly damns as well as praises them. Her biography was entitled: *Too Dirty for the Windmill*.

14

Pamela Branch

It's a crime to be talented and die young; the beautiful, glamorous mystery writer Pamela Branch succumbed at forty-seven after years of suffering cancer, and her work was quickly forgotten. She was born on her parents' tea estate in Ceylon, went to RADA, married, learned Urdu, trekked the Himalayas, trained racehorses and moved to a twelfth-century Greek monastery. As one does.

Back in post-war London she lived a chaotic existence in tiny, dark flats with a slobbery boxer dog and a husband, Newton, who failed to find his footing as a writer and became an alcoholic film censor. Yet their existence was devil-may-care and full of laughter, which explains the tone of her bizarre, deliciously funny novels. Although set in the bleak world of austerity Britain, there's something perversely joyous about their ramshackle construction. Branch will happily give you an insight into the mind of a murderer but is just as likely to do the same with a horse.

The Wooden Overcoat is unlike anything I've ever read, although at a push you could describe it as P. G. Wodehouse meets *The Ladykillers*. What happens when someone is murdered in a houseful of murderers? The Asterisk Club in Chelsea provides a home for wrongfully acquitted felons, so when a corpse turns up in their midst they at least know how to deal with it. Except they don't. Like Hal's poor mother in Joe Orton's *Loot*, the corpse is hoicked around, making its way from wardrobe to riverbed until a second cadaver propels the scenario into high gear. Our merry murderers are unfazed by arsenical poisonings or the thought that they might require a bone-saw and a steamer trunk to deal with the problem, because they're really far more concerned about themselves, and the devious rats that keep stealing the soap in their boarding house.

The second volume, *Lion in the Cellar*, reaches such heights of madness that no synopsis can do justice to the plot. Suffice it to say that a machine gun, an axe and the Chamber of Horrors all feature, and the characters include drunk bartender Mr Tooley, who has a phantom marmoset attached to his neck, and George Heap, the Silk Scarf Strangler, who can't abide the sight of blood. Volumes three and four are slightly weaker but still treasurable. A fifth and final volume appears to have been carelessly misplaced forever.

Pamela and Newton drove about town in an old taxi while she used to mail out blood-smeared postcards and boxes of poisoned chocolates from her characters. The mysteries earned her comparisons to Evelyn Waugh, and would have made wonderful Ealing comedies thanks to their subversive, madcap charm. Although virtually unknown in her native country, this most English and anarchic of writers has found new fame in America. Surprisingly few biographical details have survived, always an indication that the author was having too good a life to be bothered with chronicling such things. Open her books and hear her laughter.

15

Brigid Brophy

If Brophy survives in the collective memory it's probably as much for her tireless campaigning as for her novels. Her commitment to causes worth fighting for was forged in the 1960s: feminism, pacifism, vegetarianism, Public Lending Right, pornography and the Vietnam War all came within her sights and rarely found a more apposite spokesperson. But she was an even better writer.

Released from her studies at Oxford for outrageous behaviour (hurrah!), she came down with nothing but her intellect and caused a splash with her slender first novel, *Hackenfeller's Ape* (issued with a brilliantly rude cover that turns its typography into a phallus), about a scientist studying a rare London Zoo monkey.

I prefer her elegantly written London roman-à-clef, *The King of a Rainy Country* (1956), which tells the story of bisexual Susan and her 'not quite' boyfriend in drizzly Tottenham Court Road. Most of her novels are out of print, including *The Snow Ball*, which concerns a baroque, erotic New Year's Eve party, but the most fascinating, *In Transit*, has now returned.

It's a wonderfully playful confection set in a nameless airport lounge ('one of the rare places where twentieth-century design is happy with its own style'). Waiting for a flight, Evelyn Hillary O'Rooley suddenly loses any sense of gender, and the unsuccessful, hilarious tests she/he performs to get to the truth are filled with puns, puzzles, meta-fiction moments of awareness and surreal situations that include a dyke revolution at the baggage carousels. The result is an examination of language that reads as if someone had crossed Virginia Woolf's *Orlando* with B. S. Johnson or even J. G. Ballard, and while experimental, is extremely entertaining. 'I can't find anyone who will teach me the rules,' complains the hero/ine. 'So how can I make sure of breaking them?'

The paperback has wicked Allen Jones cover art and is truly cultish, known and loved by a few, not yet adopted by bandwagon-jumpers. Brophy was an enemy of novelistic naturalism, which she regarded as a (re)invention by Victorian writers and no longer appropriate in the twentieth century. If painting could undergo a revolution from the figurative to the abstract thanks to the invention of photography, why could not prose? In this respect she became part of a 1960s revolution in which non-naturalistic prose experimentation very nearly gained a populist foothold – it certainly did in films and on TV – but the movement was killed off by the neo-Victorian popular narrative fiction of the following decade.

Brophy's non-fiction added more jigsaw pieces to her psyche, with her championing of the neurasthenic novelist Ronald Firbank (on whom, more later). The penetrative biography *Prancing Novelist* is her greatest non-fiction work, and should have helped to restore his lustre. The fact that she also wrote a biography of Aubrey Beardsley explains her aim, to draw attention to artifice and the 'fictionality of fiction'.

The 600-page volume on Firbank is much more than a biography, though; it is a powerful defence of prose fiction at a time when she felt it was particularly under threat.

In 1967 Brophy flung a pot of ink in the public face with *Fifty Works of English Literature We Could Do Without*, a bracingly healthy argument in favour of dumping everything from *Hamlet* to *Jane Eyre* that's smashing fun now that shock and outrage have subsided.

Brophy was diagnosed with multiple sclerosis and wrote about her deteriorating health in *Baroque 'n' Roll*. Ahead of her time during publication, she now deserves rediscovery.

16

Thomas Burke

His short story 'The Hands of Mr Ottermole', a somewhat overwrought reworking of the search for Jack the Ripper, was voted the best mystery tale of all time by critics in 1949, but Burke was a writer of fantasies who has been utterly forgotten. His prose was often purple, but his story is interesting.

Eltham, Burke's South London home, was built for the middle classes, but its houses became run-down while he was still young. His family moved in an attempt to find respectability, and Sidney, now called Thomas, fabricated his past so completely that nobody knew what to believe.

What we do know is that in 1915, when he was twenty-nine, he got *Nights in Town: A London Autobiography* published, and in it was a chapter called 'A Chinese Night, Limehouse', supposedly based on factual reportage. The following year he expanded on this with a collection of melodramatic short stories called *Limehouse Nights*. Mystifyingly, respected reviewers were ecstatic and accepted what they read at face value. Burke said it was 'a tale of love and lovers that they tell in the low-lit Causeway that slinks from West India Dock Road to the dark waste of waters beyond'. It had a Chinese hero called 'The Chink' and revealed rather too much information about Burke's own predilections, being full of voluptuous, pure young girls, predatory Chinamen and corporal punishment.

Burke insisted he had grown up in the East End, where he had 'sat at the feet of Chinese philosophers who kept opium dens to learn from the lips that could frame only broken English, the secrets, good and evil, of the mysterious East'. He quickly became regarded as an expert on the Chinese living in London.

There was only one thing wrong with these biographies: they were nonsense. The 'Yellow Peril', an idea that lasted for decades, was built around fantasies of white women being abducted into sexual slavery by sinister Chinamen, but there were only a few streets in Limehouse, where the Chinese ran rather ordinary shops, mainly grouping themselves together for protection from thuggish locals.

Thanks to Burke, Sax Rohmer and M. P. Shiel's *The Yellow Danger*, visitors to Limehouse went looking for brothels and opium dens, where, of course, someone was more than happy to take their money from them, so they thrilled to melodramatically staged street fights.

Burke's tales were given further credence by D. W. Griffith, who filmed his 'The Chink and the Child' as *Broken Blossoms*. The idea of the now long-vanished neighbourhood operating as London's home of exotic vice and white slavery has somehow managed to linger to this day.

In 1937 Burke published a map of London's public urinals, noting in particular their sexual possibilities.

17

Dino Buzzati

It's surprising how many vanished authors have managed to survive in their short fiction rather than their novels, even though their full-length works received plaudits on publication. Dino Buzzati (1906–72) is obscure even by bibliophiles' standards, so it's nice to be able to include him here, because he is an extraordinary writer.

A painter, poet, playwright, editor and journalist, Buzzati found fame with the publication of *The Tartar Steppe*, a disturbing novel reminiscent of Camus, about a young soldier appointed to a far outpost, where he awaits inundation by barbarians, sensing that they daily grow nearer. The novel, which damns the dogmatic military mindset, denies the reader the satisfaction of a final explanation, and in doing so captures the elusive contours of our real lives.

Buzzati completed five novels, comics, a graphic novel, a number of plays and a still-popular children's book about bears in Sicily, but discerning editors can cherry-pick from his three slender volumes of pungent short stories. One or two reprints have also found their way into present-day English language collections. Buzzati's greatest strength lay here, in a kind of Italian magical realism that heightened the simple and practical with laterally glimpsed disturbing events. Often he uses a kind of spiralling repetition to heighten the discomfort of his unfortunate characters.

In 'Seven Floors', a businessman with a minor ailment is admitted to a hospital in which each floor denotes a different severity of illness, the ground level being reserved for those about to die, an event signalled by the closing of the window shutters. By a series of apparent accidents and clerical errors, the hero soon finds himself being shunted down floor by floor . . .

In 'Just the Very Thing They Wanted', a touring couple visit a small town and find themselves denied the most basic human rights: the need to sit down, to drink, to rest, to gather their strength.

In 'The Elevator', from his collection *Restless Nights*, a lift takes its occupants on a journey far below the bottom of the building, but instead of producing a standard hellish tale of the fantastic, Buzzati uses the situation to frighten his leading character into an honest declaration of love.

There's a disconcerting touch of Buñuel in his prose, wherein we imagine people marching down long roads in bright sunlight towards unknown futures. Buzzati also owes a considerable debt to Kafka, working in a school of writing that extends to Magnus Mills today. Character details are lightly sketched, but situations are painted with great clarity.

Perhaps because translation forced his language into a specific type of universal English, his writing feels timeless. As a creative polymath he rarely returned to the same subject matter, but much of his prose exhibits the same sense of unease. If he has a recurring theme, it's to do with man's wilful inability to control his own destiny. Buzzati's characters tend to paint themselves into corners. Most of his tales are extremely brief but linger in the mind long after you've turned the page.

Buzzati received international acclaim, and *The Tartar Steppe* was published in over twenty languages, but how could you promote such a multi-talented writer overseas? Fifty-one of his stories were gathered in a single (untranslated) volume, *Il Colombre*, but finding any works in English without paying a fortune for them is a labour of patience. A small collection of stories was recently available on the internet for around $250.

18

Patricia Carlon

Buzzati sketched out disturbing scenarios in just a few sentences. When it came to putting women in dangerous situations and wringing tension from them, Patricia Carlon was up there with another Patricia: Highsmith. Born in 1927 in Wagga Wagga, New South Wales, she wrote nerve-racking novels with strong Australian themes, but was unable to find a publisher for them locally.

Happily, UK publishers Hodder & Stoughton picked up her best work – she produced fourteen novels between 1961 and 1970, starting with *Circle of Fear* – and brought them out to great acclaim. An American publisher discovered her novels by chance in a London bookshop, and an Australian did the same in New York, so her books eventually appeared in her native country forty years after she had become a success in Britain. Her writing was intelligent, hard-hitting and unsentimental, her prose deceptively simple, but there was something odd about it . . .

The Whispering Wall is a fairly typical example of her work. In it the elderly heroine, Sarah, is confined to her bed by a stroke while a sinister group of individuals plot against her. They assume that because she can't communicate she doesn't understand, but she is only too aware of their intentions and is determined to foil their plans. Her only ally is a girl traumatized by rape. The narrative has an atmosphere of claustrophobic menace, and is excruciatingly intense. In *Hush, It's a Game*, a little girl is locked in a kitchen by her babysitter, who is murdered. Then the murderer realizes that there's someone else in the apartment . . .

This ability to sustain tension to an unbearable degree would have made her perfect for adaptation by Alfred Hitchcock, who came to the rescue of so many of these authors, but Carlon was in the wrong time and place. She never married and lived alone, right next door to her parents in suburban Sydney. She refused all publicity and only communicated with her publishers by letter. By this time her agent had noticed an obvious theme running through her books – all of her heroines experience a strong sense of isolation.

You only have to look at the keywords in Carlon's titles to grow suspicious. 'Hush', 'Silence', 'Unquiet', 'Whispering' . . .

A little more research revealed the reason for this theme. Carlon had been deaf since the age of eleven, and understood all too well what it was like to feel lonely and unable to communicate to others, so she recreated the sensation in her books, producing variations on a theme that never actually included deafness.

She eventually received the recognition she deserved in her homeland, and her books were republished in the UK. Often such biographical details give us an insight to the author's mindset, and so we look out for the clues behind the words.

19

Barbara Comyns Carr

The pocket-sized *Lilliput* is usually considered (if anybody considers it at all anymore) to be the sort of magazine you would have got if the British had been the first to produce *Playboy*: a quirky Bloomsbury amusement for clubbable gentlemen. Each cover featured a man, a woman and a terrier, and inside were tasteful photographs of naked ladies interspersed with fiction from a portfolio of genuinely superb authors. It was responsible for bringing these writers to wider audiences, one of whom was Carr (née Bayley).

Edwardian by birth, she trained as an artist and married one, and although they were well-connected within London's artistic community her husband proved incapable of making a living or, indeed, of being faithful. Broke and desperate, Carr fell in with a black marketeer, hopping from flat to flat as the money ran out. She repaired pianos and bred poodles to make ends meet, sold antiques, drew advertisements, tried anything to stay afloat. But when her fortunes continued to decline, she took a job as a cook in a country house and began to write stories for her children.

Carr's luck changed when she met civil servant Richard Comyns Carr (who worked in Whitehall with Kim Philby and was tarred with the rumour of also being a spy). Her childhood autobiography, *Sisters by a River*, was serialized in *Lilliput* magazine under the title 'The Novel Nobody Will Publish'. She wrote about impoverished artistic days in *Our Spoons Came from Woolworths* and later about happier times shuttling to Barcelona in *Out of the Red and into the Blue*. Although she published eleven novels in all, *The Vet's Daughter*, an Edwardian fairy tale of unremitting gloom, stood out strongest, and plays like a precursor to Stephen King's *Carrie*.

Alice is the daughter of an animal-torturing vet who beats her and his wife. I seem to remember he also keeps a parrot in the lavatory and sells puppies to a vivisectionist. Alice's mother dies of her injuries and is replaced by tarty barmaid Rosa. The innocent girl survives an attempted rape and becomes the companion of a lonely old lady who once tried to hang herself, the rope-marks remaining upon her neck. There's a suggestion that Alice escapes into a fantasy world to avoid further abuse – or does she really learn to levitate?

When Rosa and her father discover her occult powers they see the commercial possibilities of exhibiting her, and arrange for a display to take place on Clapham Common, setting the scene for a final terrible tragedy. Graham Greene admired this mixture of innocence and ominous fantasy, and the book was a hit. Although quite why Sandy Wilson, the camp composer of *The Boy Friend*, thought it would make a cheering subject for a musical is anyone's guess. Mind you, he also squeezed a show out of John Collier's controversial *His Monkey Wife*, so anything's possible.

The Forgotten (pre-Tarantino) Pulp Fiction

I recall buying a copy of *Black Wings Has My Angel* by Lewis Elliott Chaze in a fantastically disreputable bookshop on a stretch of the Holloway Road, North London, the sort of area where charity groups hand out mismatched shoes to alcoholics.

The UK edition had the kind of cover you needed to pick up: a tough blonde in a red skirt and slip, pointing a gun, dragging a guy along with her as a hostage. The caption read: 'She had the face of a madonna and a heart made of dollar bills!' Like many other writers of his era, Chaze was a great admirer of Hemingway's style. His prose was snub-nosed and nail-hard. It didn't waste time with fancy descriptions, but felt authentic and was full of local colour.

Black Wings is the story of Tim Sunblade, who escapes from prison to stage the perfect heist. There's just one snag: it'll take two to pull it off. Unfortunately, his taste in women steers him to the one girl he should really stay away from.

Virginia is a hooker, a 'ten-dollar tramp' whose lavender eyes light up when money is mentioned. After the crime is committed, the cash changes Virginia into 'a candy-tonguing country club Cleopatra who nested in bed the whole day long and thought her feet were too damned good to walk on'. Their love-hate relationship causes them to find the flaws in one another that will doom them. Chaze's peers knew that the novel was more than just a pulp, it was *the* pulp, the best example of a noir outside of James M. Cain.

Old pulp paperbacks provided shops like the one on Holloway Road with a legitimate business front while they sold under-the-counter pornography. The stock was not chosen by book-lovers but by bottom-rung businessmen who had found a cheap commodity which could be pitchforked into a room and cleared fast. The pulp authors – very few of whom ever achieved recognizable name status – had the ability to draw aside a curtain and let us glimpse a less wholesome alternative to library fiction. Pulp writing wasn't intellectual but it had atmosphere and pungency, and often revealed a kind of innocence we were fast losing.

It was an equal opportunity employer too; while males could read about fast cars and faster girls, females could lose themselves in romantic novels in which saturnine sea captains 'compromise' gently protesting women. A great many pulp writers were simply bad and fast, churning words to fill post-war demands, but once in a while someone rose above the genre's mediocrity. The pulp writers of the past sometimes produced brilliant short fiction because they wrote to live and wrote so much.

Veering between hardboiled noir and science fiction, Fredric Brown accidentally made himself memorable, and became the connoisseur's choice for his shocking plot twists and misplaced clues.

His short stories were humorous, dark, fantastical and paradoxical, and had unusual titles like 'The Cheese on Stilts', 'The Discontented Cows', 'Heil, Werewolf' and 'Thirty Corpses Every Thursday'. His story 'Arena' became one of the original episodes of *Star Trek*.

Sometimes he sold the title before writing the story. He was prolific, but according to his wife he hated writing and especially plotting, for which he had an unusual talent.

Brown launched a series of pulp thrillers, the first of which, *The Fabulous Clipjoint*, won an Edgar Allan Poe Award, granted by the Mystery Writers of America. There were stranger novels, like *Here Comes A Candle*, an experimental novel told through alternating media formats, *The Far Cry*, which dissected a spiritually barren marriage and featured an explosive ending, and *The Screaming Mimi*, about an alcoholic journalist looking for a killer, which was filmed by Dario Argento as *The Bird with the Crystal Plumage*.

Within the pages of trashy magazines like *Startling Stories* it was possible to stumble across novels like Brown's inventive *What Mad Universe*, which featured an alternative New York where inter-galactic flight is developed due to advanced sewing-machine technology. Brown would pack every bug-eyed-monster cliché into jungle journeys featuring Arcturian spies and seven-foot-tall purple moon-monsters.

About the process of writing, Brown remained controversial. He said: 'There are no rules. You can write a story, if you wish, with no conflict, no suspense, no beginning, middle or end. You have to be regarded as a genius to get away with it, and that's the hardest part: convincing everybody you're a genius.'

The value of pulp fiction has been reassessed and rises according to market demands. It has become niche, and therefore desirable once more – but this time it's also the books themselves which have become appealing as decorative artefacts.

20

John Dickson Carr

Sometimes authors simply fall out of favour with the public because they relentlessly pursue a single theme. Pennsylvania-born John Dickson Carr (1906–77) hit upon the ultimate mystery, the murder that takes place in a hermetically sealed space, and wrote variations that increased in ornate complexity, with cliffhanger chapter ends and solutions that still have readers face-palming in equal measures of frustration and annoyance. Yet there's something undeniably satisfying about Carr's work, even at its most abstruse. It's like watching a trainspotter write down serial numbers: it's obsessive behaviour but you can't help admiring the dedication.

Writing prolifically under a number of pseudonyms (including 'Carter Dickson') Carr became one of the greatest American writers of Golden Age mysteries. Although his plots stretch credulity far, far beyond snapping point, therein lies their great pleasure. His sleuth Dr Gideon Fell, fat and rumpled, with a cape, canes and a monocle, was modelled on G. K. Chesterton, and Sir Henry Merrivale, blustery, noisy and Churchillian, is parodied in Anthony Shaffer's play *Sleuth*.

Sadly, we live in a time where there is no patience for barmy British sleuths who uncover insanely complex murders, and Dickson Carr wasn't remotely interested in offering his readers realism or relevance. Instead he provided cases that involved witchcraft, automata, eerie disappearances, snowstorms, impossible footprints, a hangman's ghost, keys on bits of elastic, knives that pop out of ceilings, corpses that walk through walls, a victim who dives into a swimming pool and vanishes. He combined an infectious joy with a powerful sense of the macabre, and once announced: 'Let there be a spice of terror, of dark skies and evil things.'

After marrying an Englishwoman called Clarice Cleaves, he moved to England and produced a string of classics, including *The Judas Window*, in which he suggests that every room in London has a window only a murderer can see, and his masterpiece, *The Hollow Man*.

This latter novel involves a Transylvanian legend about being buried alive and is generally regarded as one of greatest locked-room mysteries ever written. A murderer kills his victim and literally vanishes, reappearing in the middle of an empty street to strike again, with watchers at either end who see nothing, and no footprints appearing in freshly fallen snow. The book has a famously jaw-dropping double-plotted denouement. The beauty of Carr's fixation is that you don't even wonder why anyone would go to such ridiculous lengths to commit murder. Wouldn't a conk on the head do? For Carr the plot isn't just the thing, it's *everything*, and most of the characters are ambulatory board-game figures being shunted according to the author's master plan.

Although he is regarded as a pulp writer, most of Carr's output possesses the reliability of finely crafted clockwork. His writing is exotic, antiquarian, gruesome, steeped in gothic imagery and yet filled with a sense of Wodehousian slapstick. It's the extreme single-mindedness that often makes it so enjoyably silly.

In 1949 Carr had a great success with the authorized biography of Sir Arthur Conan Doyle, then turned to writing historical whodunnits. He created legions of fans who have kept his name alive on the internet, even if his books are as impossible to discover as the methods of his murderers. The problem for Carr collectors is that no two volumes appear to have been designed at the same time. Given the hermetic nature of his writing, I imagine the idea of a matching set, preferably ones with abstruse clues hidden on the covers, would be very appealing to his fans.

21

Leslie Charteris

The urbane creator of the quintessentially English stiff-upper-lipped hero, The Saint, certainly had paperbacks in grubby second-hand shops, although he probably wouldn't have been very pleased about it. Charteris was half-Chinese, born in Singapore in 1907. His experiences working on a rubber plantation, in a tin mine, as a gold prospector, fairground carnie, bus driver, pearl fisher, bartender and professional bridge player gave him experiences he later used (I should hope so, too).

Changing his name from Bowyer-Yin to Charteris (chosen from a phone book), he introduced The Saint in his third novel, *Meet – The Tiger!*, when he was just twenty, and went on to write nearly a hundred Saint adventures.

The Saint was Simon Templar, an unknown entity with no family or home who uses the names of Catholic saints as his false identities. Handsome and debonair, he's the world's greatest thief, but uses his powers against despots and villains, although the police are forever trying to put him behind bars. He leaves a calling card at the scenes of his crimes, comprising a stick figure with a halo. In the early books he battled white slavers, arms dealers and Nazis. Charteris also wrote the scripts for the globally syndicated Saint comic strips. On radio, Vincent Price played the character between 1947 and 1951.

Driven to succeed and make a name for himself, Charteris became one of the earliest members of Mensa, and invented a pictorial sign language called Paleneo. Travelling to Hollywood, he turned his hand to screenwriting and produced scripts for films such as Deanna Durbin's *Lady on a Train* and George Raft's *The Midnight Club*. However, he was excluded from permanent residency in the USA because the Chinese Exclusion Act prohibited immigration for people of '50% or greater' oriental blood.

Founding his own fan club for the Saint books, Charteris eventually grew tired of writing the stories and handed them over to the SF writer Harry Harrison, editing a number of further volumes.

If The Saint is remembered now, it's mainly for the TV series featuring frozen-faced Roger Moore (who occasionally broke the fourth wall to address viewers). Moore moved so stiffly through the absurd plots that he appeared to have an ironing board up his jacket. Later, *The Return of the Saint* featured the more characterful Ian Ogilvy. The iconic theme music used on TV actually began in the 1930s in the RKO Saint films. Val Kilmer's portrayal in Philip Noyce's 1997 film was a hit despite the muddled script's divergence from the books.

It's a credit to the author's skills that a character who was little more than a cardboard cutout could become so frequently adapted.

One would be tempted to suggest that the time for blank, emotionless adventurers has passed. The Saint books are steadily coming back into print. You can't keep a good halo down.

22

John Christopher

Every doomy teenager at some points feels as if they're part of the last generation. Pessimistic literature is almost a genre in itself, but it was unusual in so-called young adult novels before the arrival of dystopian dramas like *The Hunger Games*.

John Christopher was ahead of the curve, and is the genre's true pioneer. If the name's not familiar, try Stanley Winchester, Hilary Ford, William Godfrey, William Vine, Peter Graaf, Anthony Rye or his birth-name, Sam Youd. Was there ever an author with so many pseudonyms? He was Lancastrian by birth, and Youd was an old Cheshire name. As he averaged four novels a year, the adoption of other identities became necessary to prevent reader fatigue.

As a schoolboy Christopher loved serious science fiction and produced his own magazine, 'The Fantast'. After serving in the Second World War he pursued a writing career and was granted a scholarship to do so, back when such things were not uncommon. His first novel, *The Winter Swan*, was produced at the age of twenty-seven, but

SF was about to enter its great golden years, and he wrote *The Year of the Comet*, followed by his best work, *The Death of Grass*, in 1956.

In this dark, post-apocalyptic novel, a virus kills off plant-life, causing worldwide famine after it infects East Asian rice crops. America imposes a quarantine, and the novel follows an engineer and a civil servant as they battle their way across an England descending into complete anarchy. The book is written in a clean economical style and presents a moral conundrum: what would you sacrifice to justify your own survival?

Christopher's novel was published by Michael Joseph, who had scored repeated successes with John Wyndham, another apocalyptic SF writer. *The Death of Grass* touched a raw nerve, appearing at a time when the idea of nuclear Armageddon was posing a very real threat to the nation's peace of mind. The first of the Aldermaston marches, in which tens of thousands protested against the H-Bomb, was just two years away. Unlike other apocalyptic books of the time (and there were quite a few), this one ends badly. It was published in the USA as *No Blade of Grass* and subsequently filmed by Cornel Wilde. Christopher did not bother to sit through the new version. The book is rightly regarded as a modern classic, unlike Christopher's *The Little People*, which featured – and there's no easy way to put this – Nazi elves.

A decade later Christopher began writing SF for teenagers, at the time a rather far-sighted move, and produced his best-remembered series, the 'Tripods' books, starting with *The White Mountains*. These were created as a trilogy but later expanded to include a fourth volume, and tell the story of alien walking machines that stride through the devastated English countryside tackling resistance groups. There's a clear nod to H. G. Wells's *The War of the Worlds*, the difference being that here people have come to accept the totalitarian rule of the Tripods until one young rebel fights back. As in *The Hunger Games* and the Harry Potter books, there's an enforced sporting event that carries grave consequences for mortals. A *Tripods* TV series was subsequently made and is fondly remembered.

Christopher wrote several late novels dealing with global catastrophe. *The World in Winter* features the Earth descending into barbarism as the Northern hemisphere freezes solid, and has evocative images of ice-swept London. With Africa offering the only hope of survival, the ugly thought of colonization returns. *A Wrinkle in the Skin* has an unlikely premise – devastating worldwide earthquakes – but Christopher is more interested in the psychological aspects of dealing with disaster. In *Empty World* we have an unstoppable plague wiping out all adults, leaving children to cope with a new world order.

Rereading them now, what strikes me is that Christopher's novels are more human and morally complex than those that followed. Even in the worst dystopias, where there are traps to be negotiated at every turn, there are still adventures to be had and pleasures to be found. It's what the young do best.

23

John Collier

For those of a certain age, John Collier was simply 'the window to watch', as the ubiquitous TV commercials for the menswear store once proclaimed. The other John Collier is far more interesting, an English writer who became famous for his wonderful short stories. Since his family couldn't afford more than a rudimentary education for him, Collier was privately educated at home by his uncle, who was a novelist. He spent much of his time in art galleries, and fell under the influence of the Sitwell family, who wrote and edited light poetry. He loved the intensity of poetic imagery, but failed to produce satisfactory verse, instead writing a novel, *His Monkey Wife*. This satire about an explorer who marries an intelligent chimpanzee is an extremely odd way to kick off a career, from his choice of the schoolmaster hero's name, Alfred Fatigay, to his idiosyncratic style. Here's how it was described: 'a strange book . . . an emotional melodrama, complete with a Medusa villainess, an honest simpleton of a hero, and an angelic if only anthropoid heroine, all functioning in the two-dimensional world of the old Lyceum poster or the primitive fresco . . . where an angel may outsize a church, and where a man may marry a monkey on a foggy day.'

Two more novels followed: the dystopian *Tom's A-Cold: A Tale*, and *Defy the Foul Fiend; or, The Misadventures of a Heart*, both of whose titles reference *King Lear*. Around them formed a body of uniquely sardonic short stories, often written for the *New Yorker* magazine. They were collected in many volumes, one of which, the Edgar-winning *Fancies And Goodnights*, was reprinted in 2003.

In some ways, Collier feels like a natural successor to the cynical Edwardian master of tales-with-a-sting, H. H. Munro, better known as 'Saki'. His simple, sharp style brought his tales colourfully to life with a hint of brimstone. 'The Devil, George and Rosie' starts: 'There was a young man who was invariably spurned by the girls, not because he smelt at all bad but because he happened to be as ugly as a monkey.' In one of his most famous stories, 'Evening Primrose', a failed poet bids the world farewell and moves into a department store, only to find that others have also moved there to escape the world. In this enclosed society everything natural is man-made, and what can be seen from the windows is compared to store products by those who have lived too long inside; ice is like vinyl, trees are like broken umbrellas. It was filmed for television as a play with a number of Stephen Sondheim songs in 1966. Another story, 'Green Thoughts', about a man-eating plant, became the basis for the film *Little Shop of Horrors*, also made into a musical. What is it about great short-fiction writers and musicals?

Collier was married to a silent movie actress and moved to Los Angeles, where he contributed to many films and TV shows. His tales often had a fantastical element, and some were adapted for *Alfred Hitchcock Presents*, a format they fitted perfectly. He contributed to screenplays for *The African Queen*, *Sylvia Scarlett* and *I Am a Camera*, the basis for *Cabaret*, but within a decade of working in Hollywood, his output – typically – became much less original and interesting.

Collier was his own harshest critic, and once said, 'I sometimes marvel that a third-rate writer like me has been able to palm himself off as a second-rate writer,' but there is no one quite like him. In 1972, *The John Collier Reader*, a collection of almost fifty first-rate stories selected by the author, was published to fresh acclaim. How could you not love an author who writes a story entitled 'Night! Youth! Paris! And the Moon!' Perhaps because he is so unclassifiable, Collier's books are still hard to locate.

24

Norman Collins

Writing is a wonderful outlet for personal passions. In 1929, when he was just twenty-one, writing for the *News Chronicle* (a newspaper that had the good taste to employ several of our chosen ninety-nine authors), Collins wrote a lovely piece called 'London from a Bus Stop', in which he watched the city from the top of a double-decker bus and noted how its residents behaved. The piece was simple but affecting, because Collins was one of those people who was naturally interested in the daily lives of others. He was a populist, a bit of an ethnographer and therefore well suited to writing, but these days we remember him better for his other career, first running BBC Radio's Light Programme (which had grown out of popular entertainment for the forces), launching iconic shows like *Housewives' Choice*, *Woman's Hour* and *Dick Barton – Special Agent*.

Collins saw nothing wrong in appealing to the widest audience, and once castigated T. S. Eliot for complaining about the growth of television. A story could please people and make the same legitimate point as a piece appealing to the intelligentsia, he argued.

Collins was also the literary editor of the *Daily News*, which Dickens had edited. He later became one of the major figures behind the establishment of the Independent Television network in the UK, which was the first organization to break the BBC's broadcasting monopoly when it began transmitting in 1955. Having co-founded ATV, he continued in the medium, always noting the number of TV aerials he saw above houses. However, parallel to his main career, Collins wrote sixteen books, one of which became a huge success.

Born in Beaconsfield, Buckinghamshire, Collins had started out as an editorial assistant at the Oxford University Press, publishing his first volume, *The Facts of Fiction*, at twenty-five. It seems if you were born at the start of the twentieth century, you had a shot at getting published at an early age.

Unusually, Collins wrote his most successful novel in the middle of his career. *London Belongs to Me* is a sprawling 700-plus-page story in the style of Dickens, and is one of the great city novels, now considered a modern classic. It follows the fortunes of the down-at-heel tenants of No.10 Dulcimer Street, Kennington, South London, a lodging-house sub-divided into flats; there's the lonely landlady looking for love and meeting instead a charlatan 'Professor of Spiritualism'; Connie the ageing seen-it-all Soho hostess who comes homes each night on the 4 a.m. tram; the world-weary Mr Josser who manages to symbolically smash his cheap retirement clock; the doomed, adenoidal Mr Puddy who lives on tinned food; and young mechanic Percy, who gets involved in stolen cars and deepening trouble. They're barely scraping by in 1939 London, but the narrative is also joyful and packed with gruesome period detail. It was made into a decent film starring Richard Attenborough.

A sequel of sorts, in a more minor key, *Bond Street Story* follows the lives of employees of a department store that seems suspiciously like the real-life Fenwick's. A few of his other novels are available once more, including *The Bat That Flits*, in which a research assistant in bacteriological warfare uncovers a sinister plot.

My favourite Collins novel is a colonial story of secrets, lies and endless ineptitude among Africans and the English. *The Governor's Lady* has an appropriate opening image of a slow-turning ceiling fan that is losing its bearings so that it will probably come down, killing people and smashing everything. As the lovesick pen-pusher Harold falls for the older and racier governor's wife, he allows a situation to develop that will destroy his world. Yet the cleansing conclusion of a scandal revealed is denied to the reader; like everything else in this tainted, artificial life, it is kept under wraps by those with vested interests.

This and another novel, *Flames Coming Out of the Top*, reveal a fascination with life in the tropics as experienced by weak-chinned Englishmen who are not sent out as heroes but as observers. He delineates the English attitude to foreigners thus: 'He grouped together all those nationalities with whom he had been brought closely into contact under one comprehensive and unflattering heading of unreliability.' Or as one character explains, it's their country and you mustn't let them remember it.

These books place him alongside Somerset Maugham, Evelyn Waugh and William Boyd, while his London novels give him the air of a less cynical Patrick Hamilton. Yet Collins remains by far the least respected of any of these writers, probably because he was more vocal than any of the others about his populist beliefs.

In his two stylistic extremes, the domestic realities of down-at-heel London and an imaginary colonial outpost, Collins shows us his greatest strength: a willingness to expose the fault-lines of his characters without condemning them. His cynicism is always tempered by an innate humanity.

25

Richard Condon

When in 1970 John Lennon announced, 'The dream is over', he caught the mood of the times. Nationwide cynicism had replaced optimism as the twin catastrophes of military incompetence and state corruption brought America to its knees, inspiring some of the most jaundiced prose of the twentieth century.

Condon was a sharp-witted Hollywood agent and copywriter who gazed out at this world of lost ideals and decided to delineate it. It soon became obvious that he wasn't concentrating on his day job, so his boss shaved a little off his wages each month, then fired him, handing over the details of a Mexican bank account and the keys to a house by the ocean where he could write.

It was a far-sighted act of generosity, if not exactly altruism; the pair worked for United Artists, after all. But as a result, *The Manchurian Candidate* was born. It was Condon's second book and caused a sensation, the title entering the English language to mean someone who's been brainwashed. The story of a soldier unwittingly programmed to become an assassin was published four years before J. F. Kennedy's death, and gained added resonance from the idea that Lee Harvey Oswald might have been exposed to similar psychological trauma. It has further relevance today, and John Frankenheimer's 1962 film was remade with Denzel Washington and Meryl Streep in 2004, proving that the tale could easily fit different eras.

The Manchurian Candidate should have ensured that Condon remained on bookshelves, but he also wrote the four-volume crime saga *Prizzi's Honor*, with the first part subsequently filmed. Sadly, at the time of writing, the quartet has utterly vanished. To my mind, Condon was a better writer than Mario Puzo, but *The Godfather* took the crown in mafia tales.

Condon was a satirist who turned what could have been an unbearably bleak outlook into something rich and frequently hilarious. His instantly recognizable and occasionally exhausting style pitches the reader into a fast-moving, complex and often lurid sequence of events. An arch-trickster, Condon sometimes prefaced his novels with quotes from *The Keener's Manual*, a fictitious work, then used real names in his plots. His densely detailed prose featured so many cascades of professions and obsessions that they must surely have inspired Bret Easton Ellis's lists in *American Psycho*, to the same polarizing effect.

Political satirists are generally unbeloved and under-appreciated by their critics. *An Infinity of Mirrors*, a grim downward spiral through Nazi-occupied Paris, won few new readers. *Mile High*, about gangsters and the rise of Prohibition, shows the author at his peak but had the disadvantage of reaching publication just as *The Godfather* appeared.

Condon selected big targets and aimed high; his committed, connected prose has sadly fallen from fashion with today's introspective readership, but his sexily packaged paperbacks still turn up. And in the last few weeks of writing this I've started to hear his name being bandied about once more, this time by coffee-shop hipsters. Could it be that Condon is finally *fashionable*?

26

Edmund Crispin

If you love an author, it's always a shame when you know you can pull their entire output from your bookcase with one hand. But to Robert Bruce Montgomery, working under the pen-name of Edmund Crispin, quality took precedence over quantity.

Montgomery was the organist and choirmaster of St John's College, Oxford. This spirited, funny man turned to composing movie music and wrote, of all things, six scores for the *Carry On* films. If you listen carefully to them, you'll spot musical allusions which are more amusing than anything in the one-note scripts. He was also an important critic and editor, but best of all he wrote the Gervase Fen books, eleven delicious volumes, all but one of which were produced between 1945 and 1951.

The first set the tone for what was to follow. Fen is Professor of English Language and Literature, 'cherubic, naive, volatile, and entirely delightful', and assumes that the reader can keep up with him as he spouts literary allusions while cracking crimes. The books are fast and fun, their hero charming, frivolous, brilliant and badly behaved. When investigating, Fen tends to dive into pubs, play word games or start singing badly, anything rather than stick to the job at hand. Sometimes he even winks at the reader by making jokes about his publisher.

In the first Fen story I read, the lanky don hijacks a philosophy lecture by noisily cracking walnuts and then loudly telling his own tale, which is far more interesting. In *The Moving Toyshop* a poet visiting Oxford discovers the dead body of an elderly woman lying in a toyshop, and is promptly whacked on the head. When he comes to, he finds that not only has the body vanished but the toyshop has disappeared, and has been replaced with a grocery store.

During the subsequent investigation, Fen imagines titles for Crispin's novelized version while tied up in a cupboard. "'*Fen Steps In*,' said Fen. '*The Return of Fen. A Don Dares Death (A Gervase Fen Story). Murder Stalks the University. The Blood on the Mortarboard. Fen Strikes Back*.'" Then, to pass the time, he lists unreadable books, including *Tristram Shandy* and *The Golden Bowl* (a view with which I find it hard to disagree).

The character becomes such a joy to be with that you usually don't care much about the crime, but the solutions are outrageously ingenious, entirely possible and correctly implausible. The last book is weakest, written as Montgomery finally succumbed to drink; he was clearly having too much fun, but thankfully he put an awful lot of it on paper too. Why isn't he better known? He's certainly a lot more enjoyable than the Golden Age's stuffier aristo detectives. Perhaps that's the problem, though; some prefer their whodunnits to be dry, logical, serious and straightforward, like crossword puzzles. Others have complained about patronizing attitudes to women, rather an unfair exercise given the age of the books. Crispin's Fen represents the detective as an erudite man of letters, and crimes are simply puzzles to be solved. Agatha Christie's tales were aggressively anti-intellectual and crueller for it; hers was a world where confirmed bachelors committed suicide out of shame. Fen is far more humane and forgiving.

27

E. M. Delafield

The English sense of humour is almost impossible to deconstruct (as you'll know if you've tried to explain *Viz*, *Abigail's Party* or anything by Alan Bennett to a non-English speaker). There's a kind of amused resignation about Delafield's work, which I first discovered via a beautiful American edition. Her real name was Edmée Elizabeth Monica de la Pasture; she was the daughter of a count, and an immensely popular and funny writer. She enlisted as a nurse in the First World War and as an ARP worker in the Second, and worked on a Russian collective farm. But hardly any of her thirty-plus publications can be found on bookshelves. Why did her popularity wane?

Delafield's take on life is dry and quintessentially English. Her five most famous books are autobiographical; *The Diary of a Provincial Lady* chronicles her daily life as she tries to run a family and handle the housekeeping while maintaining a modicum of dignity. Written in deceptively relaxed shorthand, it's a Pooterish masterpiece of twentieth-century humour that shows how easily

Delafield could communicate unspoken feelings of embarrassment and annoyance.

Quotation is virtually impossible, as the gentle humour builds through the account of the year, but here she is at tea: 'Lady B asks me how the children are, and adds, to the table at large, that I am "A Perfect Mother". Am naturally avoided, conversationally, after this, by everybody at the tea table.' Here she is on wartime black-outs: 'Serena alleges that anonymous friend of hers goes out in the dark with extra layer of chalk-white powder so as to be seen, and resembles the Dong With The Luminous Nose. (Query: Is it in any way true that war very often brings out the best in civil population? Answer: So far as I am concerned, Not at all.)'

In *The Provincial Lady in Wartime* we get an idea of what it was like to continue daily life during the Blitz, but the same sense of amused observation percolates through even these dark times. Invited to Lady B's London flat, Delafield is told that Lady B would love to offer her a glass of water, but it's the servants' night off and she doesn't know where they keep it.

Perhaps Delafield's charms are not suited to coarser times. One publishing house did her no favours a few years ago by shovelling four volumes of the diaries into one dense, ugly paperback prefaced with a foreword explaining why we should not find the books amusing at all. In America, facsimiles were printed with the original delightful drawings, and found a new audience that was prepared to appreciate Delafield's qualities of grace, endurance and quiet optimism.

The Diary of a Provincial Lady was eventually serialized for radio in the UK, but her other novels, such as *Zella Sees Herself*, *The War*

Workers, *Consequences* and *Gay Life*, remained virtually lost for years. The diaries are elegant comedies of manners (Kate Atkinson has channelled some of this resigned attitude in her marvellously English novels) but she could also be very dark.

For Delafield wasn't just the 'Provincial Lady'. She also tackled lesbian feelings, real-life murder, alcoholism, family cruelties, adulteries and betrayals. Her short story 'They Don't Wear Labels' shows how easy it is to misread signs in relationships, and its final throwaway paragraph, with its horrific image of a Christmas tree ornament, stayed with me for a long time after closing the book. Her reasonable voice seems currently out of favour, but thankfully she has survived to await discovery by a new generation of fans.

28

Patrick Dennis

Sometimes authors render themselves invisible; the vagaries of fashion killed this one off. After his greatest success he left the writing profession to become a butler, working for the CEO of McDonald's, and never admitted to having once been a publishing phenomenon.

Like much else about him, Dennis's name was an invention, along with another *nom de plume*, Virginia Rowans. He was actually Edward Everett Tanner III, born in Chicago in 1921, and nicknamed Pat as a child after the Irish heavyweight boxer Pat Sweeney. Married with two children, he began writing at the age of thirty-two, but *Oh What a Wonderful Wedding!* and *House Party* didn't make much of a splash.

So he penned a sparkling new novel, first suffering rejections from fifteen publishers before someone accepted it. *Auntie Mame* was a smash. It lasted 112 weeks on the bestseller list and was filmed with Rosalind Russell, then turned into a stage musical by Jerry Herman and filmed again in that form with Lucille Ball.

The story of an introverted boy, Patrick, sent to live with an eccentric bohemian relative, has touches of Graham Greene's *Travels with my Aunt* but is lighter in tone. Mame shows Patrick how to live life to the fullest, but the boy is taken away from her and grows up to become a small-minded snob, so his aunt steps in once more and reminds him how to enjoy life again, mainly by wrecking his forthcoming marriage to a ghastly fiancée (so perfectly caught in the first film version that it's impossible to forget her nasal intonations).

Dennis's next two books were also hits, with the result that he became the first writer to have three books on the *New York Times* bestseller list simultaneously. He created two odd *faux*-memoirs filled with staged photographs: the risqué *Little Me*, the story of Belle Poitrine, a kid from the other side of the tracks who ends up on board the *Titanic*, and *First Lady*, about a girl who accidentally becomes the president's wife. Two further novels ended up as TV sitcoms.

Dennis belatedly came out on the Greenwich Village gay scene, and as the disillusioned 1970s arrived his delightfully caustic comic fables became an irrelevance. Despite his liberal credentials – Mame sets up a home for unmarried mothers next door to the racist, anti-Semitic parents of her nephew's girlfriend – his character's creed, that 'life's a banquet and most poor bastards are starving to death', didn't sit well in the age of Watergate.

The wheel turns, though. *Little Me* also reappeared as a stage musical (clearly the highest accolade a popular novel could have in America). It boasted a *tour de force* central role and was performed by the great Sid Caesar. The books finally came back into fashion. Mame had the last laugh.

29

Raymond Durgnat

Serious film critics are more embattled than ever before, largely due to the egalitarianism of the internet which has allowed anyone to write extensively and knowledgeably about film. Durgnat, however, was a unique voice. Born in London to Swiss parents, he became one of the very first post-graduates of film in Britain. With Thorold Dickinson, the director of *Gaslight*, acting as his mentor, Durgnat started to write for the major film publications, although he fell out with *Sight & Sound* after editor Gavin Lambert left for Hollywood, accusing the magazine of elitism, overt politicization, snobbery and pretentiousness, charges which still arise against it today. To be fair, *Sight & Sound* is the only serious film criticism magazine in the UK, and remains there because it's the house magazine of the British Film Institute. We tend to treat film criticism with mistrust, and it maintains a niche readership. Although our own studios are full, that's mainly because our skilled technicians are rented out to Hollywood. The British studio system was sold off over two decades as Hollywood vertically integrated from production to exhibition, and most of us have forgotten that there was once a thriving, healthy homegrown industry here.

Thankfully, Durgnat was there to chronicle the glory years. He believed that film was a populist medium at which Americans excelled, feeling that it had the power to speak to all classes, being especially suited to working-class audiences and sensibilities, so he wrote an enlightening series of books on the subject.

The Crazy Mirror is a brilliant study of American comedy, from the crude early slapstick of Chaplin and Lloyd to comedies of social observation in the fifties. *Films and Feelings* examined the emotional power of the moving image, but he also tackled the dynamics of sexual freedom portrayed on film. He wrote film biographies of Robert Bresson, Hitchcock, Luis Buñuel, Samuel Fuller, Michael Powell, King Vidor and Greta Garbo, all illuminating and highly readable.

To my mind his most passionate book is *A Mirror for England*, which studies British films in the post-war years, from an era of austerity to one of affluence. Here, he looks at how the British way of life was portrayed on film, veering between stoic contentment and idealistic anger.

Fair-minded but with the clarity of well-reasoned opinion, Durgnat took a scalpel to the middle classes in a way that no film critic ever had before. He saw no aesthetic difference between the Hammer horrors and the films of Noël Coward, and his findings changed perceptions. It's the challenge of a critic to make you see something from a missing perspective.

In *A Mirror for England* Durgnat points out the misogyny of *Jason and the Argonauts* through its dominant father-figures and its sinister whispering goddess, 'rising like a cobra from the sea', and he explores the idea that Hammer's Transylvania-set fables, which he championed at a time when they were attracting hate mail from outraged right-wing journalists, were actually about the state of England itself, caught between censorious indignation and a desire to modernize. Once you regard Dracula as an avatar for social change, tearing through the remnants of Victorian society, it's hard to go back and see a tall bloke with fangs.

Like David Thomson (whose bizarre book *Suspects* knits all of film noir's main characters into a single cohesive world), Durgnat was part of an elite British group that added something to the experience of seeing film. He never lost the power to surprise. In the year of his death he published a masterpiece.

A Long Hard Look at 'Psycho' breaks down every single shot of Hitchcock's film, explaining its use of *mise-en-scène,* showing what it references and why it has been placed there. His observations and opinions take us inside the images themselves, so that the effect is like seeing a film in extreme slow motion. It's probably the closest we could ever get to being inside a director's head. Along the way he touches on everything from teen violence to parallel worlds and phallic symbolism. This and *A Mirror for England* are now available once more, and deserve to be read by anyone who is remotely interested in cinema.

The Forgotten Rivals of Holmes, Bond and Miss Marple

It's not hard to see why Sir Arthur Conan Doyle struck a chord with writers who wanted to emulate him. His stories were well constructed, easy to read and evocative of a very specific time and place, and his consulting detective inspired many to tackle further stories beyond the accepted canon. Adrian Conan Doyle picked up his father's mantle, accompanied by John Dickson Carr (who I imagine did most of the heavy lifting) for *The Exploits of Sherlock Holmes*, based on twelve unexplained cases mentioned by Holmes.

Conan Doyle's litigious son fell out with biographer Hesketh Pearson over the publication of a supposedly missing Holmes short story, but soon the barriers came down and everyone had a bash at them. Conan Doyle's style is incredibly easy to mimic, and the rules surrounding the structure of the stories mean that any professional writer with a mind to it can make a decent fist of producing them.

So we get Philip Jose Farmer's *The Adventure of the Peerless Peer* and Loren D. Estleman's *Dr. Jekyll and Mr. Holmes* and *Sherlock Holmes vs. Dracula*. Anthony Boucher, a talented American mystery writer in his own right, went so far as to create new stories under the name of Holmes.

Nicholas Meyer added Sigmund Freud to the psychological mix in his highly regarded novel *The Seven-Per-Cent Solution* and its lesser-known follow-ups *The West End Horror* and *The Canary Trainer*. Meyer's family moved in rarefied intellectual circles (at the age of eight the boy found himself seated next to Albert Einstein at dinner). Meyer caught the true Victorian tone of the originals so that his cases transcended mere pastiche.

Arthur Reeve created 'the American Sherlock Holmes' in his character Professor Craig Kennedy. There were eighty-two stories published between 1910 and 1918. Reeve wrote movies for Harry Houdini and, like Conan Doyle (also a friend of Houdini's), investigated phoney spiritualists. He later became a crusading anti-racketeer.

The new Holmes volumes came thick and fast – and continue to do so. Books were dedicated to Irene Adler, the Baker Street Irregulars, Mrs Hudson, Inspector Lestrade, Mycroft Holmes and Dr Watson. Holmes has squared off against Jack the Ripper in a thousand different scenarios, and has been sent onto the deck of the *Titanic* and into outer space.

From Doctor Who to the Muppets, from Basil Rathbone to Benedict Cumberbatch, everyone has tackled Conan Doyle's creation, but what's often overlooked is that the author himself contributed to the non-canonical stories, with 'The Field Bazaar', 'The Lost Special', and 'The Man with the Watches' featuring an unnamed sleuth who is most likely intended to be Holmes. Then there's a play written with William Gillette that contains the first mention of the phrase 'Elementary, my dear Watson' . . .

The writers' choice for truly smart Holmes pastiches remains Kim Newman, particularly for *Professor Moriarty: The Hound of the D'Urbervilles* and his delicious 'Mysteries of the Diogenes Club' volumes.

The nation went into mourning when it heard that Arthur Conan Doyle was not planning to write any more Holmes adventures, so the young American writer August Derleth wrote to Conan Doyle and rather cheekily asked if he could take over the series. Holmes's creator declined the offer, but the undeterred Derleth set about writing his own version, and assonantly christened him Solar Pons.

Derleth had built his reputation by being the first publisher of H. P. Lovecraft, and added to the Cthulhu mythos himself, founding publishing body Arkham House, but he was also a *pasticheur*. His Holmes parodies were blatant swipes. Dr Watson was replaced by Dr Parker, Mrs Hudson by Mrs Johnson, Mycroft by Bancroft, and instead of residing at 221b Baker Street, Pons was based at 7B Praed Street. But Derleth cleverly added a detail that prevented his series from being a straight steal of another author's work: Pons existed in Holmes's world. Pons knew all about Holmes, and was not his exact contemporary, operating in a later timeframe.

The Pons stories also crossed over with plot devices from other authors, including William Hope Hodgson, Lovecraft and Sax Rohmer, creating a tangle of literary tropes similar to those used by Alan Moore and the TV series *Penny Dreadful*. Derleth tackled Conan Doyle's mentioned-but-missing cases and went on to add other star sleuths into the mix, including Hercule Poirot, The Saint and W. Somerset Maugham's agent Ashenden in a kind of steampunk style that has since become an extremely popular sub-genre of fantasy. He also wrote many more stories featuring his detective than Conan Doyle managed.

When Derleth died in 1971 his character was in turn picked up by another author, Basil Copper, who explored Pons's 'missing cases' just as Derleth had done with Holmes's, as well as adding his own original tales, so that we have pastiches of pastiches. He also rearranged the stories into a correct chronology and removed glaring Americanisms that were the result of Derleth not having visited London. Several societies and magazines, including the Praed Street Irregulars and the *Solar Pons Gazette*, were dedicated to the memory of the pastiche sleuth, and further Pons tales were written by yet other authors, so that this strange self-reproducing homage continues to infinity.

As a footnote, I had a number of Holmes stories published, and thought I'd discovered a new angle when I told one tale from Mrs Hudson's point of view, only to find that there were dozens of similar tales already in print. Holmes has a worldwide grip; recently I spent an entertaining evening with the Argentinian Sherlock Holmes society and the Holmes writers of Madrid. I have a feeling we got drunk and had a fight, but I was told this was entirely usual when Latin Holmes fans got going.

Sir Arthur Conan Doyle isn't the only author to inspire rivals. Agatha Christie continues to expand in sales, with millions sold around the world each year (Poirot has proven popular in India). W. H. Auden pointed out that traditional crime fiction rewrites the creation myth: the snake is expelled, and Adam and Eve return to a state of innocence; or rather the snake, having been found guilty, stumps off to the library and shoots itself. What no one has adequately explained is why Christie leapt over her rivals in sales, and rivals there were aplenty.

Patricia Wentworth's heroine was a retired governess turned private eye, the incorrigibly nosy Miss Maud Silver, a character very like Miss Marple, who insinuated herself into upper-class households because she was 'known in the circles of society'. Somehow, between the prize marrows and potted chutney she interfered with police procedure enough to catch brutal murderers, whereas in the modern world she'd be banged up for obstructing justice. There are sinister undercurrents in Wentworth's thirty-two books that reflect the hypocritical morality of the period, but she couldn't keep romance out of her stories; usually a young couple's love is threatened by an inconvenient corpse, perhaps because one of the lovers is being charged with murder. In comes Silver, full of her horrible Little England opinions ('A really dreadful young man – quite like one of those spivs you hear about in the papers'), always spying on people ('I had to go into Sefton's for some buns and saw them with my own eyes!'), endlessly knitting or moaning about foreigners ('In Spain the trains don't run on time and the plumbing doesn't work').

Elizabeth Daly was purportedly Christie's favourite mystery writer, and it's easy to see why. She took the bloodless whodunnit to an extreme distance, turning every crime into an analytical puzzle that could be viewed through field-glasses. Her bibliophile detective is the literary and sophisticated Henry Gamage, a New York consultant who authenticates rare books (an obvious qualification for solving murders), and if the rest of her cast tends to be sketched in, her period NYC settings are superbly evocative. However, her plots feel as if they were constructed with the aid of an Ordnance Survey map and surgical tweezers.

Poke about in a good second-hand bookshop and you'll find shelves full of charming almost-Poirots. Anthea Fraser's 'Shillingham Police' novels sport titles based on lyrics from the folk song 'Green Grow The Rushes, O', and Hazel Holt created the gentle and very English 'Mrs Malory' series, but perhaps Caroline Graham turned out to be Christie's chief rival, even though her 'Chief Inspector Barnaby' series has only run to a measly seven volumes.

A TV series based on her books was originally adapted by Anthony Horowitz to become *Midsomer Murders*, the ghastly long-running series involving convoluted crimes in picturesque fictional Somerset villages. Shock international success brought longevity to the show, meaning that these thatched-cottage hellholes developed a murder rate five times higher than the Bronx in the 1970s.

Conan Doyle and Christie ultimately stayed ahead of their rivals; their murder motives are clear, and solutions are clean-cut. Christie's neatly structured but skeletal novels remain open to reinterpretation, while Conan Doyle's tales are undemanding atmospheric diversions. Although both authors used what were then contemporary settings, they accrued new readers in future decades who were drawn to period detail. It is, however, selective detail: the late Victorian milieu of foggy London, not collapsing empire; the roaring twenties of flappers and lords, not indentured poverty; the thirties of Riviera cocktails, not Jarrow marchers.

Thanks to Holmes and Watson (and Poirot and Hastings), writers have invented their own detective duos. The reason for this is expedience: it's hard to have a lone detective talking to himself. A sidekick, preferably a ninny to whom everything has to be explained, gives him someone to play off against.

The married writing team of Frances and Richard Lockridge created the married detectives Mr and Mrs North. They were probably inspired by Dashiell Hammett's only 'Nick & Nora' novel, about married fast-talking sleuths. The fact that they were betrothed allowed them to be saucier with one another, and Nick and Nora went on to star in six *Thin Man* films as well as (inevitably) a stage musical. William and Audrey Roos did something similar, developing a couple of smart New York sophisticates bouncing plenty of witty banter back and forth as the bodies pile up.

Two once-famous but now lost mystery writers teamed up to create a pair of memorably offbeat characters. Craig Rice (a woman) and Stuart Palmer have all but vanished, which is a shame as they created the scarecrow-like teacher Hildegarde Withers and her hard-living sidekick John J. Malone. The couple appeared in six novelettes (a long short story length fashionable in the 1960s) collected into one volume, *People vs. Withers & Malone*, and fourteen novels, in which Miss Withers gets a new sidekick. The mysteries are wacky, oddball but fair-play. The prolific Rice once wrote a novel using her own children as sleuths. Lawrence G. Blochman came up with one of the more unusual pairings: Dr Coffee and his Hindu assistant Dr Mookerji were early forensic detectives.

As writers left the shadows of Conan Doyle and Christie they became braver. Sometimes their detectives weren't even human. Lilian Jackson Braun came up with reporter Jim Qwilleran and his two smart Siamese cats, who somehow manage to help him solve crimes and not just stare at blank spots on walls. Surprisingly, their cases are well-written and fun.

James Bond was quick to develop copycats, too. At the height of 'Bond Mania', in the mid-1960s, a number of other espionage writers emerged, some as good or better than 007. One of these, described rather damningly by the *Sunday Express* as 'the adults' Ian Fleming', was William Haggard, the pseudonym of Richard Clayton. He produced thirty-three novels, twenty-five of which featured Colonel Charles Russell of the (fictional) British Security Executive. Haggard lacked Fleming's snooty dilettantism, and was better at creating subtle layers of political intrigue. As the series progressed he gained stature and popularity, and the books began to extend their range to include exotic locations and sexier set-ups.

But there was a problem: Haggard, a former Indian civil servant and British establishment figure, was middle-aged by the time he started producing novels. His experience gave him an appealing air of cynicism and some strongly held opinions about the British government, particularly in its strained relations with big business, but it also meant that he was heavily drawn to characters who spent their lives manoeuvring themselves around the political system. The public wanted Bond wandering into the Monte Carlo Casino with a fag on and a martini in an upturned hand. Gunplay and continental sex made for tartier adventures, but weren't really Haggard's field. His plots were first-rate, his world-weary characters were slyly intelligent and manipulative, but ultimately a great many scenes consisted of men arguing in dingy offices.

In *The Unquiet Sleep*, a popular Valium-like drug is found to have devastatingly addictive qualities, and a parliamentary official is linked to its parent company. Colonel Russell finds each level of government involvement murkier than the next, in contrast to Fleming's approach, which leaves world domination to a few egotistical madmen. Haggard treats his women with more respect, too. Loyal wives and sensual lovers they may be, but they are also investigators and heroines with lives of their own. As for exoticism, try his character Miss Borrodaile, the elegant black-clad ex-French resistance fighter with a steel foot.

By the time Haggard wrote *The Power House*, his publishers had cottoned on to the Bond effect, and the paperback cover featured an alarming décolletage perched over a pile of roulette chips. His writing requires attention, but there are rewards for modern readers, especially in the sixties scenes that explore the sleazy private lives of civil servants. Sometimes the rivals transcended their sources.

Meanwhile James Bond remains with us, more due to the persistence of Eon Films than to Fleming's books; few people now recall that in *Goldfinger* Bond's car races around the miserable English coastal resort of Herne Bay, not Switzerland.

30

Rosalind Erskine

Sometimes I stumble across a strange old paperback, investigate the author and discover something even more tantalizing hiding behind the words. In 1962, Rosalind Erskine's slim pink-and-black novel *The Passion Flower Hotel* caused a sensation and became a bestseller. It was very much a product of its era, when sexual barriers were falling – at least for the upper classes – and the time was ripe to make fun of the sexual revolution.

It tells the story of Bryant House, an exclusive private girls' school, where the sixth-formers find themselves unable to meet boys and learn about sex. Over at Longcombe School for Boys, the same problem exists. The solution is still shocking: the girls set up a brothel in the school basement, with a menu of categories and prices (the saucy bill of fare was featured on the book's cover).

At the time of the book's publication it was virtually impossible for pupils in private schooling to mix sexes, unless you counted events like the annual opera, where schools teamed up merely to provide the right gender balance. The original St Trinian's films had already tackled the tricky subject of schoolgirl sexuality, albeit in a discreetly suggestive way, and the Passion Flowers of Bryant House riotously smashed down the walls. The book spawned two inferior but successful sequels, a sleazy, terrible, German-made film and, inevitably, a West End musical, this one with a lush Bond-like score written by John Barry. Although the subject matter is frank, the narrative is charmingly innocent.

One of the book's biggest selling points was its author, fifteen-year-old Rosalind Erskine, apparently being educated at just such a school. Misinformation abounded about her – was she boarding at Roedean under an assumed name? Was there actually such a brothel? How did she smuggle the book out and find a publisher? Had she put her school career at risk by doing so?

The answer is of course not, because she didn't exist. 'Rosalind' was Roger Erskine Longrigg, the creative director of an advertising agency, who had recognized that the time had come for a smartly written erotic comic novel. The book is a joyful and oddly naive romp, but would have risked opprobrium had it been published under a male identity. Interestingly, the fictional Bryant House finds an echo in Longrigg's own school, Bryanston. They must have been thrilled.

Longrigg was a Scot from a rather upper-class military background who published two books about his experiences in the ad game, *A High-Pitched Buzz* and *Switchboard*. Recently unearthed, they now feel like the British answer to *Mad Men*. Longrigg went on to write fifty-five novels under eight different names, choosing a male or female persona appropriate to each work. His prose is sparkling and epithetical, and his career stayed buoyant for decades.

He was married to the novelist Jane Chichester, about whom I can find nothing.

Later, writing as Domini Taylor, Longrigg produced the 1983 novel *Mother Love*, which was filmed for television with Diana Rigg and David McCallum. He also wrote about fox hunting and horse racing, and proved pretty successful at any subject to which he turned his attention. But he'll be best remembered for the saucy Passion Flowers and their bill of sexual fare. The jazz-influenced John Barry album, which captures the naive tone of the book rather well, is still available.

31

Dr Christopher Evans

Throughout the twentieth century a surprising number of short-fiction anthologies were bestsellers. Some became legendary; Herbert Van Thal's *Pan Book of Horror Stories* comprised some thirty volumes produced over as many years. Alberto Manguel's immense *Black Water* and *White Fire* gathered together the greatest international fantastic fiction, much of it translated for the first time. Hugh Greene edited *The Rivals of Sherlock Holmes*, rediscovering the best Victorian detectives, while Michel Parry's *The Rivals of King Kong* introduced a host of rampaging giant creatures. Editors like Peter Haining and Stephen Jones clocked up hundreds of titles between them.

There have been anthologies of betrayals, revenges, lovers, trains, houses, black humour, even one concerning swimming pools printed on waterproof paper. I could always find dozens in second-hand book fairs, but with the end of the format they became scarce and went to collectors.

Dr Christopher Riche Evans was not an editor by trade, but he managed to create two of the most extraordinary anthologies ever published. Evans was fascinated by the idea that the more we behave like machines, the more they behave like us. He was a British computer scientist, experimental psychologist and writer, and when he was asked by Panther Books to create an anthology, he assembled a group of authors who could highlight his theme.

Evans was born in Wales in 1931. He joined the National Physical Laboratory in his twenties and wrote about a coming computer revolution, in which he predicted that microchips would transform world communications. His only other authored book apart from *Cults of Unreason* was *The Mighty Micro: The Impact of the Computer Revolution*, was successfully turned into a six-part TV series, but tragically Evans died before it could be published and the series transmitted. The enemy of pseudoscience, Evans was also fascinated by the ways in which the human brain and its electronic equivalent might interact. Could computers replicate consciousness, and eventually learn to dream?

Authors appear to have an obsession with flying. Evans was another passionate flyer and former RAF pilot whose thoughts turned to the links between humans and artificial intelligence. In 1969 these ideas coalesced into the anthology *Mind at Bay*, in which he suggested that the phantoms inhabiting our minds were about to take a new electronic form. What, he wondered, was the intersection between circuitry and imagination?

The first book gathers together eleven pieces complete with essays concerning our deepest hopes and fears. The stories are remarkable, covering everything from the fear of cancer, loneliness and going mad to the possibilities of the future, surveillance, paranoia and the likelihood that we would see an escalation of war in our lifetime.

Mind at Bay was a hit and spawned an even better sequel, *Mind in Chains*. This time, Evans explored a more cerebral frontier, providing a virtual survival manual for the world to come. In it, he balanced several classic pieces by established authors and juxtaposed them with extreme experimental writing.

Two electrifying pieces stand out. In 'The Dreams of the Computer' Evans sets out to confuse and disorientate a computer by deliberately misprogramming it. The computer eventually suffers a nervous breakdown and hallucinates. In 'Anxietal Register B' John Sladek (who really deserves his own entry here as one of the wittiest and most experimental SF writers) challenges the reader by providing a sinister form which must be filled in. The questions become increasingly intrusive, offensive and disturbing, and the form proves virtually impossible to complete.

These touchstone volumes had elegantly disturbing matched covers and became unlikely bestsellers.

In 1974, Evans published *Cults of Unreason*, in which he demolished a variety of woo-woo religions, along with Eastern mysticism and UFO sightings. His argument was that people turned to such systems when they were failed by theologies mired in outdated dogma, although his outright dismissal of yoga as a therapy is harder to take.

What makes a great anthology is a great editor, someone who can construct a volume so that each tale adds to the book's overall theme. I purchased these when I was still the kind of schoolboy who never lost his cap, and suspect they were my introduction to a more surreal, subversive world. I probably went into my stroppy years immediately after reading them.

32

Jack Finney

Not all of the writers championed here are easy reads. Some appear because they were game-changers, and don't deserve to be forgotten. I wanted to include Finney because of his prose, which is simple, light and pleasurable. Finney was a generous-spirited everyman who could make you believe in the most unlikely things because he always worked to win readers over.

In his short story 'I Love Galesburg in the Springtime' he carefully describes the town before bringing in a phantom trolley car that puts out a fire. Galesburg protects itself by drawing upon its own past, and you believe it because of the loving descriptions that foreground the situation. There's a touch of post-war rural folksiness about him.

Finney was born in 1911 in Milwaukee, Wisconsin, and led a fairly uneventful life, working for an advertising agency in New York, starting a family and moving to Los Angeles. His first story, 'The Widow's Walk', was published as the result of a contest in *Ellery Queen's Mystery Magazine*, and his first novel brought instant fame. *The Body Snatchers* hinges on such a powerful idea that it has been frequently filmed since publication in 1955. Alien invaders take over humans while they sleep, removing their emotions in preparation for a new world, but how can we tell who's been turned? And is a life lived without passion any worse than one full of pain and disappointment? The central theme of identity loss has come to stand for McCarthyism, fascism, militarism and the pressures of the modern world.

Finney was also fascinated by time travel, and in *Time and Again* (1970) he utilized old photographs of New York to help explain how his hero Morley practises self-hypnosis to travel back to 1882 and prevent a disaster from happening. The book's premise was subjected to a barely acknowledged 'homage' in the film *Somewhere in Time*, but there's talk of the original resurfacing as a movie. Just before his death, Finney published a sequel, *From Time to Time*, involving the *Titanic*, which left room for a third part that cannot now be written.

Time travel is a theme Finney repeatedly returns to, and *About Time* gathers together his short fiction on the subject. Here the tone is sentimental and elegiac. Stories like 'Second Chance' say it all; the narrator wants to turn back the clock to a simpler, gentler time and undo the mistakes that were made. The fact that Finney always adopts an amiable first-person narrative seems to suggest that he's projecting his own desires onto his heroes.

Some of his gently nostalgic novels remind me of Ray Bradbury, but Finney was also drawn to tales of heists, as in the casino robbery *5 Against the House* and the shipboard raid *Assault on a Queen*. My personal favourite is *The Night People* (1977) in which a group of friends form a club that stages elaborate practical jokes on the public after dark, only to find their increasingly risky behaviour getting out of hand.

Finney's many fine short stories have never been gathered in a complete edition, but paperbacks sometimes turn up at book fairs.

33

Ronald Firbank

In a world that praises commonplace prose for its realism, it's important to have Arthur Annesley Ronald Firbank. In some ways he is the most important writer to be featured in these pages, firstly because he changed the way in which we experience words, second because he was ignored in his own lifetime, and continues to be treated as a ridiculous footnote to avowedly 'serious' literature.

Firbank, born in 1886, had an eccentric narrative style that was more than just an extension of his personality; he sought a new language for fiction. Firbank unchained the novel from cause and effect, but few noticed his pioneering achievement at the time.

For a man who wrote so much about society, he was never comfortable in it, being too alcoholic, inarticulate, strange and effete. Nevertheless, Firbank provides a natural and conscious stepping stone from Oscar Wilde to T. S. Eliot. He became a cult figure, which by his reckoning meant that he was read by a dozen clever people, but his work faded from even this attention. He personally paid for the publication of all but one of his books.

These slim novels appeared in the aftermath of the First World War, but reflect nothing of the time. *The Flower Beneath the Foot* takes place in a vaguely Balkan state, and is as exotic as a poisonous orchid. 'Whenever I go out,' the king complains, 'I get the impression of raised hats.' 'Raised hats?' 'Nude heads, Doctor.' You have to work at understanding his distilled prose, which it is best to read aloud.

These were not the scribblings of a ninny, but of an intense writer keen to explain the art behind the artifice. He wrote: 'I think nothing of filing fifty pages down to make a brief, crisp paragraph, or even a row of dots!' Instead of fiction's building blocks (and all their superfluous bridges – a habit only developed in Victorian literature) he chooses seemingly light but texturally complex images arranged in mosaics with the gaps as important as the language. This was also a trick used by experimentalist B. S. Johnson.

This deeply shy, wispily neurasthenic author handwrote his manuscripts on postcards and taught an important lesson: that conversations need not sound real to be truthful. Firbank's prose condensed worlds while leaving much unsaid, in a way that is finally almost fashionable. Asked for his opinion of literature, he admitted that he adored italics; a typically oblique Firbankian remark. His books contain party chatter consisting of disconnected words and phrases, much as a child might actually perceive them, with sentences trailing off and the speaker unidentified. Indeed, it feels as if we are in the room, overhearing sections but not all, just as we would in life. Infamously, one chapter comprised nothing but eight identical exclamations of the word 'Mabel!'.

Firbank's novels were scribbled in hotel rooms heavy with flowers, but at dinner parties he was seen to consume but a single grape or pea. He sounds the least proactive writer of all time, having once pointed out that 'The world is so dreadfully managed, one hardly knows to whom to complain', but, in a typical paradox, was the opposite. He fought hard to be published and found more success in America where the bravery of his new form was better valued.

As I mentioned earlier, Brigid Brophy wrote an immense study of the author, being one of the few people who understood what he was on about. She points out that he grew up into 'an air still electric after the storm about Wilde'. Firbank took Wilde's style to its logical conclusion, doing away with naturalistic fiction altogether to create a body of work pointing the way to something entirely new. In doing so he managed to replicate the exact experience of hearing conversation.

His masterwork, *Caprice*, is the gauziest book ever written: blow on it and it will dissipate; odd topics are started and drift away, and absolutely nothing happens. It is resolutely determined to avoid anything like a clockwork Victorian plot.

Being artificial is exhausting work and can make for exhausting reading, but Firbank is an example of a timeless author who should not be forgotten because he is unique, and because he might have changed fiction forever.

Unsurprisingly, Firbank was drawn to the sexually exotic. His novel *Valmouth* is about (as much as it's *about* anything) a black masseuse who moves into a prim English coastal spa resort, and despite displaying his unique form of literary camp is also filled with images of flagellation, bondage and transvestism. It features bizarre characters like the hundred-year-old Lady Parvula de Panzoust, and inspired a British musical, clearly a rite of passage for all books which are entirely unsuitable for adaptation. Several cast albums have been produced, making this the most popular success of Firbank's novels, probably because it was given a narrative.

This is something the British have always clung to in fiction, whereas they were able to accept that painting and music in the twentieth century needed to metamorphose into the abstract. Only fiction was left behind. If Firbank had been taken seriously perhaps it would have made the leap into a more subconscious form. He died at forty, just before the publication of his tenth and final novel.

34

Peter Fleming

This is the story of the other Fleming. Peter was the eldest of four brothers, one of whom became the creator of James Bond. Born into a world of privilege, Peter went to Eton and Oxford and decided to be an adventurer, not a career category open to many. During the Second World War he served with the Grenadier Guards, and was awarded the OBE before returning to Oxfordshire squiredom. He had also married the actress Celia Johnson, and must have had to put up with a lot of *Brief Encounter* jokes, but we're particularly concerned with the period just before the war, when he began travel writing.

In 1932 Fleming replied to an advertisement in the personal columns of *The Times* that read: 'Room Two More Guns – Exploring and sporting expedition under experienced guidance, leaving England June to explore rivers central Brazil, if possible ascertain fate Colonel Percy Fawcett.' If it sounded like something from an Evelyn Waugh novel, it really was. The resulting travelogue, *Brazilian Adventure*, became regarded as a classic, and is filled with wandering-off natives, recriminations, foot-rot, revolting bugs and a race against another expedition.

Fleming became a special correspondent for *The Times*, crossing from Moscow to Peking through the Caucasus, the Caspian, Samarkand and Tashkent. He boarded the Turksib Railway and the Trans-Siberian to Peking at a time when travelling could still be called an adventure (i.e. it might end in death), eventually recounting the tale in *A Forgotten Journey*. After that he headed for India.

Although he was a decent writer like his brother, Peter was also the product of his time and class, and therefore the master of condescending snobbery. Beijing was dismissed as 'lacking in charm', Shenyang 'suburban', Moscow like 'a servant's quarters'. But his writing also contained genuinely sharp insights, although his political analysis was weak. His was not the modern mode of travel; he usually started by being introduced to ambassadors. Still, we occasionally need writers like this, who turn up at foreign ports with papers of introduction to the consulate. Not everyone has to represent the *vox populi*.

Later Fleming wrote accounts of historical events in lands through which he had travelled, *The Siege at Peking*, *Bayonets to Lhasa* and *The Fate of Admiral Kolchak*. In his memory, the Royal Geographical Society established the Peter Fleming Award for projects that seek to advance geographical science. After his brother Ian's death he looked after the 007 rights company, Gildrose – now there's a film title they haven't used yet. Incidentally, Stephen Winkworth's hilarious history of *The Times* personal columns, *Room Two More Guns*, tells the tales of those who answered classified ads, and is less available than Fleming.

35

Lucille Fletcher

'She crumpled at his feet in a heap of lavender chiffon,' wrote Violet Lucille Fletcher, a writer working in the defiantly male genre of noir suspense.

She was born in Brooklyn in 1912, and went to a very ordinary high school where she won the regional competition of the National Oratorical Contest. For this she received an all-expenses-paid trip to South America, a prize of $1,000 and an opportunity to compete for the national championship. (At school I came first in a literature competition. I won a pot.)

Thus was Fletcher set on a literary path. She became a publicist and aspiring writer at CBS, and while there met her future husband, the soundtrack composer Bernard Herrmann. They married in 1939 but very nearly failed to make it to the altar; Fletcher's parents objected to her marrying a Jewish man and Herrmann was legendarily abrasive (still, their marriage lasted sixteen years, only ending when Herrmann had an affair).

Lucille began writing stories for magazines, and two years later Bernard wrote the music for her broadcast story 'The Hitch-Hiker'. At that time radio and novels had a fluidity between them, so that although she particularly loved writing for radio, an idea developed for one medium could easily cross into the other.

Both she and her husband were drawn to hard-boiled thrillers, but it was unusual for a woman to make a name for herself in this field. She saw it quite simply: 'You bury the secret, lead the reader down the path, put in false leads and throughout the story remains completely logical.'

If only it was that simple. She wrote *Sorry, Wrong Number* as a novel, a play and a film for Barbara Stanwyck, about a woman who overhears a murder plot on a crossed line. It was a smashing success, described by Orson Welles as 'the greatest single radio script ever written', and won awards. Fletcher's great strength was placing everyman characters in desperate situations that inexorably spiral out of control. Her prose was tough and stripped of unnecessary detail, ratcheting suspense. One reason for this was her radio training; she had to bridge the sense of suspense so that it lasted across commercial breaks.

Fletcher wrote many plays and ten suspense novels, including *Eighty Dollars to Stamford* in 1975, about a cab driver who is duped by a beautiful blonde into being in the wrong place at the wrong time. It's an electrifying one-sitting read filled with noir tropes, including a discredited hero on the run from the cops and a missing femme fatale, and you can almost hear Herrmann conducting the score as you race to the jaw-dropping twist ending. Her books are the kind you slam satisfyingly shut at the end, only to find that your tea has gone cold.

36

R. Austin Freeman

Beware the author who follows in the wake of a bestselling series, for he will surely be forgotten. Sherlock Holmes spawned many imitators, including R. Austin Freeman's charming mysteries, set in the Edwardian era. Freeman's Dr Thorndyke was no mere copycat, though. He is a barrister and man of medicine who, armed with his little green case of detection aids, sets out to solve puzzles that would scarcely interest today's police: a collapsed man who later vanishes, an ingeniously forged fingerprint, a crime scene more interesting than the act that occurred there.

His books began as homages (Thorndyke has his own Watson, named Jervis) but quickly developed their own unique style. Freeman was a doctor, and used his training more believably than Conan Doyle. He understood the tangled workings of the courts and advances in science such as the forensic power of X-rays, and incorporated them into his stories.

In *The Eye of Osiris*, an Egyptologist vanishes from a watched room and must be presumed dead in order for his will to reach probate – but the will in question has a bizarre clause which makes it impossible to honour. Like W. S. Gilbert before him, Freeman takes great delight in outlining the peculiar properties of paradox. 'A man cannot deposit his own remains,' cries Thorndyke in exasperation, as he deals with recalcitrant jurors, bovine policemen and potty witnesses.

Freeman frequently used Egyptian themes. He also reckoned to have invented the opposite of the whodunnit, the 'inverted mystery', the How-Will-He-Be-Caught? puzzle, in 1912, in the collection *The Singing Bone*. About it he says: 'I devised, as an experiment, an inverted detective story in two parts. The first part was a minute and detailed description of a crime, setting forth the antecedents, motives, and all attendant circumstances. The reader had seen the crime committed, knew all about the criminal, and was in possession of all the facts. It would have seemed that there was nothing left to tell, but I calculated that the reader would be so occupied with the crime that he would overlook the evidence. And so it turned out. The second part, which described the investigation of the crime, had to most readers the effect of new matter.'

As a result the Dr Thorndyke stories lack Holmes's sense of atmospheric mystery, but Freeman is more thorough when it comes to technical detail – 'The Man with the Nailed Shoes' hinges entirely on a study of footprints, *The Eye of Osiris* has a lengthy examination of embalming processes, and the puzzle set in 'The Magic Casket' has an obscure metallurgical anomaly in its solution.

Freeman's dialogue exchanges are more freewheeling and sarcastic than Doyle's. 'I am a confounded fool!' says a character, as the reason for a corpse's finger being severed dawns on him. 'Oh, don't say that,' says Jervis. 'Give your friends a chance.'

Freeman treats criminals in a more balanced manner than the Holmes creator. His working-class characters – particularly in *Mr Polton Explains*, are decent, skilled and hard-working, but are still crushed by the system. However, in comparison to Conan Doyle, Freeman suffers in the building of suspense; his preference for exploring the nuts and bolts of criminal cases over the development of a tense atmosphere keeps him firmly behind the master.

Despite this, his thirty-odd books are certainly worth rediscovery, and can prove very addictive to those possessing a scientific turn of mind. Lately there has been a bit of a grass-roots movement among fans to return Dr Thorndyke to his rightful place.

37

Michael Green

Humour is an unrewarded genre; publishers like their fiction to have gravitas, which wins awards and looks important. As the comic Tony Hancock once pointed out, 'People take you more seriously when you stop getting laughs.' The paradox of comedic writing is that it's rarely taken seriously or regarded as important. Humour is disdained by those who are without it and rarely ages well. Comics will tell you that slapstick travels, but wit does not. Still, part of every bestseller list always consists of those slender one-joke volumes you find stacked by the checkout.

There was once no getting away from Michael Green. His books were everywhere. The Leicester journalist was involved with amateur dramatics and enjoyed rugby, hobbies that inspired two guides, *The Art of Coarse Acting* (also turned into a series of successful plays) and *The Art of Coarse Rugby*. Rather than being juvenile, they appealed to the concerns of the middle-aged suburban man. These bestsellers expanded to include other sports, and a funny account of one man's battle with his house in *The Art of Coarse Moving*. The idea of one's home becoming a source of mounting anxiety has long proved popular in novels like Jay Cronley's *Funny Farm*, Betty MacDonald's *The Egg and I* and *Mr Blandings Builds His Dream House* by Eric Hodgins.

Green's biographical books included recollections of his press days, *Don't Print My Name Upside Down*, and the memoirs *The Boy Who Shot Down an Airship* and *Nobody Hurt in Small Earthquake*.

While Green is remembered as a fairly eccentric newspaperman who once started the printing presses to run off his own edition, only to find that he couldn't stop them, nothing in his mild-mannered volumes quite prepares you for his classic, *Squire Haggard's Journal*, which, along with W. E. Bowman's *The Ascent of Rum Doodle*, is a one-of-a-kind volume that requires nothing more than a little knowledge of history and a sense of humour to appreciate.

The journal began as a series of columns and is a bawdy parody of a late-eighteenth-century gentleman's diary. Amos Haggard is a Hogarthian grotesque, chugging Madeira, horsewhipping servants, rogering prostitutes, evicting paupers and discharging his pistols at anything foreign. To avoid unpaid debts and an impending duel he escapes to the country, embarking on an unscheduled Grand Tour that allows him to behave in an indecent fashion towards the crowned heads of Europe. In the process, he reveals the origin of the Little Englander in all his sclerotic, xenophobic horror. The diary is obsessed with demises and unusual diagnoses, including 'Putrefaction of the Tripes' and 'Death from Windy Spasms', and whether by accident or design somehow manages to capture the flavour of the times more succinctly than many more carefully researched biographies.

When a writer is free to have fun with a topic the results sometimes yield pleasant surprises, and Squire Haggard can be seen as a precursor to Blackadder. The book has deservedly been republished.

38

Peter Van Greenaway

No, not the one who directed *The Draughtsman's Contract*. This author was a lawyer-turned-novelist who wrote topical, political, satirical thrillers. At his best he combined popular fiction with a rare passion and erudition.

Van Greenaway started in the style he very much developed as his own over the next two decades. His first novel, *The Crucified City*, was an allegorical thriller about the aftermath of a nuclear attack, and a pilgrimage to Aldermaston that took place at Easter. This kind of almost-SF novel, which extrapolated present-day concerns into future consequences, was very much in vogue in the 1960s. It often combined a big theme, like the misuse of science or runaway government control, and a rogue human element.

He could work in a lighter vein, too. *The Destiny Man* concerns a ham actor who seizes a last chance for stage fame when he discovers a lost Shakespeare play left behind on a train. There is a crime involved, but the novel's impetus derives from knowing that the hero – who has wangled sole rights to the play's performance – is going to turn the event into a hideous fiasco when he tries to rise to the role's challenge. Van Greenaway even has the nerve to create chunks of the bard's missing play from scratch, and pulls them off with enormous panache. The ending is a surprise and too delightful to be given away here.

The Man Who Held the Queen to Ransom and Sent Parliament Packing, published in 1968, describes a very British Victorian coup, played lightly for laughs, while scoring some nice points about British statesmanship. Van Greenaway excelled at cynical satire and wordplay, and we mere humans rarely come out well, especially when we're pitted against monkeys (in *Manrissa Man*) or killer mice (in *Mutants*).

In Van Greenaway's prescient political thrillers, terrorism was a recurring theme. Astoundingly, *Take the War to Washington* involved a group of Vietnam veterans who crash a passenger airliner into the Pentagon and launch a series of terrorist attacks on tall buildings in the USA in order to wreck the nation's international status, ending its financial dominance.

Van Greenaway was popular enough to see his books packaged as mass-market paperbacks, and his paranormal suspense thriller *The Medusa Touch* was filmed starring a wildly overacting Richard Burton. The book further developed his interest in individuals taking control of their lives by any means necessary, but this time he added a pseudo-scientific aspect that reflected the concerns and the righteous anger of the seventies. The lead character was a disturbed author with a 'gift for disaster' who survives a violent attack by an unknown assailant. While he hovers in a state between life and death, flashbacks reveal that he can influence events and remove people who stand in his way with the power of thought. Van Greenaway turns his hero's ability to cause telekinetic catastrophes into a powerful moral tool that reflects the anti-establishment mood of the time.

The author's peculiar talents were suited to the period in which he wrote but somehow transcended them, so that the books are still intriguing. His collections of short stories are pithy and sharp, and showcase some of his most stylish writing. At the time of writing, they're still nearly all out of print.

The Forgotten Books of Charles Dickens

There was once a comedy sketch from Monty Python precursor *At Last the 1948 Show* in which annoying bibliophile Marty Feldman tried to buy a copy of *Rarnaby Budge* by Darles Chickens, but no – I'm talking about the actual Charles Dickens, author of such books as *The Haunted House*, *Mugby Junction*, 'The Battle of Life', 'Going Into Society', 'Doctor Marigold' and 'A Message From The Sea'. Wait, haven't you heard of those?

Great writers tend to have their leading works repeatedly cherry-picked from the canon until we only remember those volumes. *Jane Eyre* always trumps Charlotte Brontë's *Shirley* and *Villette*, and Conan Doyle may have written one of the most gruesome stories of all time in 'The Case of Lady Sannox' but he'll always be the Sherlock Holmes man, just as J. M. Barrie became the Peter Pan man and A. A. Milne the Winnie-the-Pooh man. Robert Louis Stevenson was a literary superstar in his short lifetime, but it didn't guarantee immortality for much of his best work, which is macabre and sardonic. His exotic fables were inspired by his own travels in the South Seas, and 'The Bottle Imp' is the greatest genie-in-a-bottle story because of the dilemma it imposes upon its owner. Daphne Du Maurier was forever associated with *Rebecca* while her brilliant short fiction was often overlooked (her ungathered stories are still turning up even now). And after various versions of *Wolf Hall*, Hilary Mantel may find herself remembered as 'the Henry VIII writer', which would do her dazzling back catalogue a great disservice in years to come.

The same happened with the astoundingly prolific Dickens, who wrote short-story collections, non-fiction, children's works, supernatural tales, sketches, dramatic monologues, Christmas fables and a dozen collaborative works. To complicate matters, some books had excerpts removed to be tailored into individual stories. Let's not even go into his poetry, plays, essays and journalism.

The charming *A Child's History of England* is so chatty and informal that it probably provided a blueprint for today's hugely successful 'Horrible Histories' series. His chapter on Henry VIII begins: 'We now come to King Henry the Eighth, whom it has been too much the fashion to call Bluff King Hal or Burly King Henry and other fine names, but whom I shall take the liberty to call, plainly, one of the most detestable villains that ever drew breath.' No mincing words there.

Mugby Junction is a collaboration compiled by Dickens in which stories ranging from the eerie to the comic are interwoven around a bustling train station. Half of the eight stories are written by Dickens himself.

When the narrator sees a deserted house from his railway carriage in *The Haunted House*, he ignores local legends and takes up residence with a group of friends. The resulting multi-part Dickensian novel has contributions from Elizabeth Gaskell and Wilkie Collins among others. Dickens often wrote with Collins, but does that make his stories 'impure' and therefore less canonical? It seems odd that we should face annual remakes of *A Christmas Carol* while 'A Christmas Tree' and the 'Mrs Lirriper' Christmas stories are overlooked.

Popularity was the worst thing that could have happened to *A Christmas Carol*. After performances by Dickens himself, a long history of bowdlerization eventually led to the Muppets, by which time the story's fierce sense of social injustice had been somewhat diluted in favour of dance routines with cloth frogs.

There were other Dickens Christmas books, 'The Cricket on the Hearth', 'The Battle of Life', 'The Chimes' and 'The Haunted Man and the Ghost's Bargain', which failed to ignite the public imagination in the same way. Does this mean they were simply not as good?

Like Scrooge's transformation, the stories usually feature a character who has a change of heart. In 'The Chimes', Toby is a ticket porter (a delivery man) whose low self-esteem, placed there by the selfish rich, is restored to respect by midnight bells on New Year's Eve. In 'The Cricket on the Hearth', a married couple with a wide age difference are brought from suspicion to happiness by their guardian angel, a cricket, and the plot features subterfuge, disguise, a miserly toymaker and a blind girl. 'The Battle of Life' has no supernatural element and a truncated ending that disappointed readers. It concerns the romantic sacrifices made by two daughters, and fails to convince.

'The Haunted Man and the Ghost's Bargain' is far more interesting: a story about memory and humility, and the healing power of the Christmas season. Redlaw is a chemistry teacher visited by a phantom double who bestows on him the gift of forgetting painful memories. But it comes with a catch: anyone else who comes into contact with him will also lose their memory. When the gift is inevitably passed on it has tragic consequences, and must be reversed by someone whose pained remembrance proves the source of their goodness. The lesson here is that it's important to remember past sorrows and wrongs, so you can forgive those responsible and unburden your soul, and mature as a human being. The story was staged with the creation of a technique called 'Pepper's Ghost', a theatrical illusion using angled plate glass to make a person appear, become transparent and vanish.

It's clear that, in *A Christmas Carol*, all of the elements which were to feature in the other Christmas tales are present in the right order and proportion. An embittered miser, a dead child, a lowly humble employee, phantoms and a joyful Christmas reformation work more satisfyingly as a human story, even though Dickens's intention was to sugar-coat a bitter pill about the injustices of British society.

Dickens's less visible works are not out of print but have been collected too often in different formats, so that tracking them down without duplication was pretty tricky work until electronic formats arrived. His multiple-author works are patchy but still have very enjoyable sections.

39

Robert Van Gulik

At the start of the twentieth century, authors like Sax Rohmer (real name: Arthur Ward) were penning tales of imperial adventurers battling 'Yellow Peril' conspirators, amidst a prevailing fear that the Chinese were inherently criminal by nature. As we've seen, Thomas Burke fabricated his life to include this strain of fevered exoticism. Ward was actually attacked for his racial stereotyping at the time of publication, and now the novels are dismissed as absurd, colourful escapades reminiscent of the exploits of Indiana Jones.

Counterbalancing these stories were the erudite Judge Dee novels, created by Robert Van Gulik and written with more of an insider's touch. Van Gulik grew up in the Netherlands and Jakarta, before joining the foreign office to begin a lifetime of roaming the Far East. By the time he became the councillor of the Dutch embassy in Washington he was long established as an orientalist, a diplomat and expert player of the guqin, a delicate seven-string musical instrument rather like a zither.

Although he also wrote essays and short stories, Van Gulik remains best known for his excellent Chinese mysteries. These comprise some fourteen novels and short-story volumes chronicling the career of a stern but fair-minded judge, based on a real-life seventh-century Chinese detective called Di Renjie. Interestingly, the tales first found fame in oriental editions, before being translated into English in 1957.

Judge Dee is a magistrate who appears omnipotent and infallible, a fair-minded patrician whose adventures translate well to a Western readership. Of course, there were differences between Chinese and Western fiction, one being that a criminal's identity was known from the outset and rarely revealed at the end. Another was that morals and motives often remained opaque in early Chinese books, whereas in the West we like to be provided with clear-cut reasons.

The construction of the long Judge Dee novels is unusual. They take the form of several interwoven cases, and follow the traditional style (now itself forgotten) of Chinese detective stories. Despite the fact that he added elements from the much later Ming dynasty, Van Gulik was greatly concerned with accuracy, and created a detailed career timeline for his main character, adding his own graceful illustrations and maps to help readers understand the pattern of the judge's world.

As a magistrate, Dee was allowed up to four wives, so his personal life is complicated. What's more, several of the plot strands are based on real-life cases. In *The Chinese Nail Murders* one of the investigations is based on an event outlined in a thirteenth-century manual of jurisprudence and detection.

Elaborate, subtle cruelties abound within these tales; there are headless corpses, lake phantoms, corrupted monks, terrible murders, attacks by brigands, puzzles, clues and mysterious scrolls to be deciphered, but all these elements and events are informed by the decency of the clear-eyed judge, whose understanding of human nature extends beyond thoughts of formal retribution.

Best of all, the stories feel authentic because they are filled with simple descriptions of everyday Chinese life, the sights and sounds of a lost time lovingly recreated by a scholar who was immersed in the culture of the period. The books were acclaimed at the time of publication, and the first Judge Dee novel, *The Chinese Maze Murders*, was republished to find a new generation of fans. The rest have followed suit, most notably in an elegant set produced by the University of Chicago press.

40

Thomas Guthrie

Once you've seen the comic possibilities of the world in which you live it's very hard to unsee them, and this can lead humorous writers to be regarded with suspicion. Guthrie tried to be a serious novelist, but the public insisted on regarding him as a humorist. The son of a military tailor, he was born in a swanky part of Kensington in the middle of the nineteenth century. He gave up the legal profession to write, adopting the pseudonym F. Anstey after a printing error favoured his middle name.

His novel *The Giant's Robe* concerned a plagiarist, ironically something of which he was himself accused, but it was as a master parodist and satirist that he went to work for *Punch* magazine, becoming a mainstay there for many years (writing pieces like *Mr. Punch's Pocket Ibsen*).

Guthrie's greatest ability was to portray the fantastic in everyday terms. As a result, his comic novels bore the test of time and have worn well. The first, *Vice Versa*, concerns a magic stone brought back from India that allows a father and son to switch bodies, granting them a better understanding of each other. This idea of a magical stone or potion was very popular at the time, and W. S. Gilbert frequently tried to foist it on the distinctly unimpressed Arthur Sullivan. Guthrie's book has been filmed at least five times and many other versions, such as *Big*, *Freaky Friday* and *18 Again!* repeated the original's high-concept premise, not always acknowledging Guthrie.

Many of Anstey's works contain fanciful elements employed to gently poke fun at modern (i.e. Victorian) life. He wrote some serious fiction like *The Pariah*, about class prejudice, and *The Statement of Stella Maberly*, about schizophrenia, but to my mind, the best of his novels is the charming satire *The Brass Bottle*.

The plot concerns untried architect Horace Ventimore, who runs an errand for his girlfriend's father and ends up purchasing an old bottle at an auction. Upon uncorking it, he encounters a grateful old genie who grants him a series of wishes, each of which places him in a disastrous situation. The author takes great delight in poking fun at the provincialism of the Victorian middle classes: they complain about the horrible taste of the exotic banquets created by the genie; they worry about the cost of having a dazzling Arabic palace replace their dark terraced house; they fret about what the neighbours will think when a golden chariot turns up in the street; and after the genie suggests that Horace should ditch his priggish fiancée for an alluring Arabian princess, it's hard not to agree.

When Horace's future father-in-law is transformed into a one-eyed mule, the family seem more concerned about the damaged furniture. It's surprising just how many authors from this period jumped from tales of provincial domesticated life to ones filled with exotic orientalism, but unlike Guthrie, they rarely did both in the same novel.

Many film versions of *The Brass Bottle* followed, the most famous featuring Barbara Eden, who parlayed the role into the anodyne TV series *I Dream of Jeannie*.

41

Charles Hamilton

He was one of the most prolific authors in history, but hardly any of his books can now be found – why have you never heard of him?

Owen Conquest, Martin Clifford, Ralph Redway, Winston Cardew and Peter Todd were authors with something in common: they were all alter egos of the writer Charles Hamilton, born into a large family in 1876. Tales of schooldays and derring-do filled the pages of two Edwardian story papers, *The Gem* and *The Magnet*, and Hamilton excelled at them.

For the next thirty years, Hamilton churned out several thousand adventures about cowboys, firemen, coppers and crooks. It was estimated that he wrote 100 million words (that's the equivalent of 1,200 average-length novels). He used a great many pen-names, and in the process of writing schoolboy excitements had to create over a hundred schools in which all his heroes could study. We know there were definitely more than 5,000 short stories, and although they were extremely popular with the young at heart, Hamilton was critically ignored.

The Gem and *The Magnet* had a tried fiction formula and stuck to it: fair play, decency, teamwork, respect and discipline bonded groups of like-minded chums whose vicariously thrilling exploits never included smoking or gambling, unlike their creator's own fondness for the tables at Monte Carlo. Public-school settings meant that adults could be dispensed with (aside from the presence of the odd teacher), allowing for readers' wish-fulfilling fantasies. But the papers became outdated. Readership declined and paper shortages led to their demise. What was Hamilton to do?

In 1946 he claimed back one of his most popular characters from Amalgamated Press, who had kept all the rights to his stories, and began a series of hardback books under the name Frank Richards. His salad-phobic schoolboy star was the 'Fat Owl of the Remove', Billy Bunter of Greyfriars School.

The books were a smashing success, and no less than seven TV series followed, starring Gerald Campion, all written by Hamilton. There were theatrical versions and strip cartoons, parodies and catchphrases ('Yarooh!' was 'Hooray!' spelled backwards). Bunter, the obese, short-sighted, food-obsessed anti-hero, was supposed to weigh fourteen stone, which in the post-war years was considered vastly overweight. His slapstick exploits often ended with a caning. A few prim librarians came to regard him as politically incorrect, and for a brief spell he was banned from shelves. Others likened Hamilton's jaunty, fluid style to that of P. G. Wodehouse.

Once a household name, Billy Bunter never recovered from being deemed calorically challenged and utterly vanished – but not before he made his creator very rich indeed.

42

James Hanley

There's a lesson to be drawn from the Hamilton story: sometimes it seems that the more you produce (even if you manage to keep your writing up to scratch), the less you are likely to be remembered. Even authors whose output has exceeded a hundred books have often been entirely expunged from bookshelves.

Which brings us to James Hanley, hardly a household name but one of the major British writers of the twentieth century. What happened here?

The working-class Liverpudlian was born in 1897 and joined the navy at the age of seventeen, jumping ship in Canada to find manual labour. As he began writing, his life at sea became a strong influence on his work. Two years after his debut came the novel *Boy*, which really set the cat among the pigeons. The blistering tragedy tells of a ship's thirteen-year-old stowaway forced into a bleak and brutal work system, exploited by his parents and sexually abused by his crewmates. It delivers no cheering final-chapter joy either, as the now diseased-riddled 'Boy' is smothered by his captain in a Cairo brothel.

The book's raw, plain language led to it being charged with obscenity, but even the most careful reader would struggle to find anything overtly offensive in it. Far from being exploitative, it explores the idea of hardship *in extremis*. Despite this, at its notorious obscenity trial the publisher actually pleaded guilty.

Hanley's five-novel cycle 'The Furys' created his lasting reputation. He told his publisher, Faber & Faber: 'I want to show the downfall of a whole family excepting one, and that is the woman. That woman is heroic, powerful, exercises a tremendous influence over her family. I shall show her under every light. I cannot attempt to describe in detail the amazing lives of these people, sometimes fantastic, but never, never divorced from reality. Working-class lives are full of colour, of poetry, there is the stuff of drama in the most insignificant things.'

'The Furys' was compared to Conrad and Dostoyevsky, winning plaudits from E. M. Forster and William Faulkner. Hanley's novels were often downbeat, his heroes solitary and rootless, facing limited choices that would bring them death or madness, but there was much that accurately reflected the hopes and fears of ordinary working men and women.

In late life the modernist author embarked on another cycle of novels set in Wales, gaining further critical acclaim in his seventies.

Dark times produce fanciful reading, as today's sales of books about schoolboy wizards and super-powered teens testify, and Hanley's novels were perhaps too close to the bone for popular readership. Despite so much critical acclaim he never achieved major success, but is now being re-evaluated, with reprints, a biography, and questions being asked about how such a key novelist should suffer the fate of being forgotten.

43

Sven Hassel

When I was a child, my father guiltily read Sven Hassel's paperbacks, keeping them in his bedside table where the children wouldn't find them. Some hope. He thought I wouldn't find the key to the cocktail cabinet either.

Gruesomely illustrated with photographs of concentration-camp inmates and tanks rolling over corpses, Hassel's books were a sensation at a time when it was virtually impossible for the average reader to find this kind of material. Hassel seemed to represent the populist voice of war experience, but a question mark remains over his real identity.

Hassel maintained he was born Sven Pedersen in Denmark, taking his mother's maiden name and joining the merchant navy at fourteen. After this he became a naturalized German and served in the 2nd Panzer Division, later driving a tank into Poland during the invasion. He subsequently served with other tank divisions on every front except North Africa, was wounded several times, received the

Iron Cross, surrendered to Soviet troops in Berlin and spent time in various POW camps before retiring to Barcelona to write fourteen 'novels' in which he appears in the first person as a character. The books are graphically violent and portray soldiers as brutalized survivors who regard the Geneva Convention as a joke, killing without compunction or often any good reason.

However, there's another side to the story. Hassel's critics have been disputing his claims for years, saying that his identity was falsified for another purpose; he never served in the Panzer Division at all but was in fact a Danish Nazi who patched together his books from stories told to him by Danish Waffen-SS veterans after the war ended, having spent most of the Second World War in occupied Denmark.

Unfortunately, his biggest critic, the writer Erik Haaest, was discredited after denying that there were ever concentration camps. Haaest's version of Hassel's life, in which Hassel runs a porn empire and gets his wife to write his novels, is almost as hard to believe. But there's no denying that the series was a publishing phenomenon in fifty countries around the world, and apparently still sell well in Finland. It's also true that Hassel was encouraged to write by his wife, Dorthe.

Hassel's timing was good; young volunteers of Germany's new armed force, the *Bundeswehr*, took to his novels, but they were most popular in Britain with a new generation who was still trying to understand the war.

So what are the actual books like? Well, they're broadly anti-war exploits that rollick across Europe from the trenches to the brothels, with grotesque characters and lashings of graveyard humour. While the stupidity and horror of the Nazi regime is depicted in almost pornographic detail, the accounts are packed with 'Catch-22' absurdities, as well as some fundamental research errors that have prevented historians from ever taking the books seriously.

You would have thought it would be easy to fact-check Hassel, but that would be missing the point. Although his content was luridly visual and deliberately shocking, it was fundamentally correct in providing a much-needed sense of shock and outrage that was missing in drier accounts; one could perhaps say he was the Ken Russell of war books, true to the atmosphere of the time rather than the letter of history.

44

A. P. Herbert

I was once given an Alan Patrick Herbert book as a school prize (glance back at Lucille Fletcher's entry to see what American schools give *their* top pupils) but I'm glad I got it. Herbert is almost out of print, and should have more readers.

The author served in two world wars, and survived Gallipoli. This longstanding member of parliament was a social reformer who worked to end outdated divorce and obscenity laws, and was knighted by Churchill. He once highlighted the complexity of the British licensing laws by accusing the House of Commons of selling liquor without a licence. Inevitably, he also wrote the lyrics to popular songs and shows, including the hugely successful *Bless the Bride*, with its impossible-to-dislodge hit song 'Ma Belle Marguerite' (now rattling around in my head as I write this).

Mr Gay's London is Herbert's selection of crimes, court rulings and trials from the early eighteenth century, and is a lot more fun than it sounds. This interest in the absurdities of the legal system caused him to write *Misleading Cases in the Common Law* as a series of articles for *Punch* magazine.

The cases proved hugely popular and eventually turned into six published volumes that operate on a wonderfully simple premise: a judge, Mr Justice Swallow, and a defendant, one Albert Haddock, square off against each another in a series of litigious skirmishes designed to test the limits and limitations of the law.

Haddock is a tireless everyman who would stretch the patience of a saint; in 'The Negotiable Cow' he makes out a cheque on a cow and leads it to the office of the Collector of Taxes. 'Was the cow crossed?' 'No, Your Worship, it was an open cow.' The question is, did he break the law? Haddock also writes a cheque on an egg and puts a tax payment in a bottle, which he floats up the Thames. Haddock rows the wrong way up a flooded street, and is arrested. Haddock has his wineglass pinched by a waiter, and sues for damages. Haddock argues his way out of a charge of obstruction by referring to an obscure point in Magna Carta. The cases were fictional but were based on real legal points, and were sometimes reported in the press as fact.

Along the way, big issues were raised and serious political grievances were aired. How is free speech defined? What is the meaning of education? What exactly are politicians supposed to do? Do police officers provoke decent citizens? How much freedom do we really have? Herbert's tone is light, but the questions give one pause to think.

The *Misleading Cases* were so successful that they aired as a superb television series (disgracefully wiped by the BBC) that ran for three seasons in the 1960s, with Roy Dotrice as Haddock and the endearing Alastair Sim as the exhausted, eternally patient and fair-minded judge. Swallow is exasperated but clearly an admirer of Haddock's thorough knowledge of his rights. 'People must not do things for fun,' Herbert warns. 'There is no reference to fun in any act of parliament.' Read Herbert and bring back the fun.

45

Georgette Heyer

I'd vaguely heard of Georgette Heyer, and discovered that her books are readily available and regularly reprinted – but she has fallen into a strange and rather airless niche market, where once she was one of the most popular writers in the country.

In early photographs she appears as a glamorous flapper in a cloche hat and furs. Heyer was a literary phenomenon who wrote bestsellers throughout her career without ever giving an interview or making any kind of public appearance. A recluse in her private life, she was driven to communicate with her readers through a series of light Regency romances for which she had scant regard, saying only that 'I ought to be shot for writing such nonsense, but it's unquestionably good escapist literature and I think I should rather like it if I were sitting in an air-raid shelter, or recovering from the flu'. I can imagine that if they'd had audiobooks back then, hers would have been narrated by Jessie Matthews, whose clipped, rather stilted tones would have been perfectly suited to sentences like: 'Is it not unsupportable to be held down to a canter when you long to gallop for miles?'

Her novels received no critical acclaim whatsoever, but they sold so well that her name alone was enough to guarantee success. Fifty-one witty and occasionally erudite novels, short-story collections and mysteries were published, appearing at a rate of one or more a year throughout her life.

Heyer was born in London at the birth of the twentieth century, and continued writing until her death in 1974. Her narratives were peppered with wicked dukes, hearty knights, feisty ladies and headstrong rakes whose amorous escapades unfurled against colourful historical backdrops. Along the way horses rear, eyes flash, bosoms heave and ladies of quality exhibit a tendency to faint. Her pages are packed with arranged marriages, desperate elopements and abductions, crimes of passion and descriptions of the prevailing fashions. No wonder, then, that critics were sceptical and dismissed each arrival merely as 'the latest Georgette Heyer'. The gap between popularity and peer respect was created largely by Heyer's worldwide readers, who lapped up the romances while failing to notice their favourite author's meticulous attention to period detail.

Her books were a perfect combination of undemanding plot and colourful characterization, but to my jaded eye at least, they seem almost parodic in their earnest desire to entertain. It doesn't help that her prose is often like stumbling over bricks and her tasteful pastel covers look like boxes of Quality Street chocolates.

Most of the volumes stand alone, but four contain recurring characters. They're well-written, not very thought-provoking, but tremendously entertaining if you can cope with the awkward language. And her work improved; her late comedies of manners now best stand the test of time and exhibit a nicely cynical wit.

Heyer left behind the unfinished manuscript of a serious medieval book, since published, that revealed her real skill and love of research. Although she left no early drafts, dismissed her first four novels and kept only one fan letter, she was greatly concerned that her novels should provide historical accuracy. Why then was she so utterly self-deprecating about her work? Perhaps it was an English thing; her books were the kind my mother would have kept in the piano stool or the needlework table, because she didn't want anyone to think that she might find them enjoyable.

46

Eleanor Hibbert

Stay with me – this gets complicated. Eleanor Hibbert (née Burford) had a pseudonym, Victoria Holt, and was born in Canning Town in 1906 (she was very proud of her London roots). After signing books as Elbur Ford (a contraction of her birth-name), she used other pseudonyms including Jean Plaidy (a name taken from a Cornish beach), Philippa Carr, Kathleen Kellow and others, and wrote around 200 historical novels. By today's standards she shifted absolutely staggering amounts of books. Lately there have been some excellent reissues, so it's a good time to rediscover Britain's most popular historical novelist by far. She was feted for blending accurate period detail with strong plots and rich characterization, so what happened to 'The Queen of Romantic Suspense'?

Hibbert was first published in 1941 for an advance of £30. Soon she was writing about Catherine De Medici, Charles II, Katherine of Aragon, Marie Antoinette and Lucrezia Borgia. Her style had enough gusto to draw little more than polite applause from the critics, but her public adored her.

This wasn't enough; she chronicled criminal cases, then embarked upon great cycles of novels in chronological order, covering the Normans, Plantagenets, Tudors, Stuarts, Georgians and Victorians. It was as if she felt driven to recreate the whole of English history in a way that would make some progressive sense. She branched into gothic romance, mystery, non-fiction and children's books, and particularly enjoyed portraying feisty women of independence and integrity who fought for liberation. Her books written as Philippa Carr became known as the 'Daughters of England' series, and used a backdrop of social history that ran from the Reformation to the end of the Second World War.

The word that comes up time and again in conjunction with Hibbert's writing is 'solid', a term that would probably count as an insult now. 'Will you tell this author,' her first publisher said, 'that there are glittering prizes ahead for those who can write as she does?' The prizes came in the form of monetary success and reader loyalty, perhaps more rewarding than critical success.

But I like her good old-fashioned storytelling. Her viewpoints ring true: Hitler, she says in *The English Are Like That*, made the fatal mistake of frightening the English. Hamlet, she notes, is not incapable of action – he kills his man three times in the play. It's hard to find anyone with anything bad to say about her ideas, which makes her disappearance even stranger. It must be said, though, that her books had the kind of pastel covers no man would ever pick up.

Every year, Hibbert took a three-month cruise to avoid the English winter, and she died on one of them between Greece and

Egypt in her eighties. 'Never regret,' she once said. 'If it's good, it's wonderful. If it's bad, it's experience.' Not long before she died she recreated a pose for a photographer that she had adopted at the start of her career, chin resting on knuckles, kind eyes looking ahead, and the result was just as charming.

47

Harry Hodge

In the modern age of phone tapping and the super-injunction, one wonders what Harry Hodge would have said about the right to privacy. Fascinated by criminology all his life, Hodge felt that a trial should be at least twenty years old before it could prove notable enough for public discussion.

Hodge was the managing director of William Hodge & Co., publishers and shorthand writers. He followed his forebears into the shorthand business in Scotland, and became one of the nation's leading experts.

For half a century he was a well-known figure in the Scottish courts, and published many legal works. In 1905 he launched the 'Notable British Trials' series, which eventually extended to over eighty volumes. In 1941, Penguin started to repackage and sell the collected 'Famous Trials', commissioned, collated and edited by Harry, and later by his son, James Hozier Hodge.

As the Hodges were based in Scotland, it made sense to start this catalogue of criminality with the sensational trial of Madeleine Smith, accused in 1857 of poisoning her lover with arsenic tipped into a cup of cocoa. Although the case against her was not proven, it was largely accepted that the twenty-one-year-old beauty was a murderer, but Smith's lips remained sealed to the end of her life. The case was written up by F. Tennyson Jesse, and set the crisp literary tone for the cases that followed. In the same volume we have Oscar Slater, 'the right man convicted on the wrong clue', and the tragic, bizarre tale of Dr Crippen, whose crime and subsequent arrest play out like scenes from a pulp thriller.

These are reports written closer to the time of actual events, so they had yet to be overlaid with modern forensic research or ironic asides. In outlining Crippen's case, author Filson Young recognises the psychological clash between the delusional, spendthrift music-hall singer Belle ('she had nothing but vanity, no scrap of the ability or industry necessary for even her small purposes') and nondescript little Crippen, who maintained unswerving loyalty to his mistress, thus providing a certain mitigating sympathy for their impossible situation.

Best of all is the account concerning the superbly named Buck Ruxton, who killed his common-law wife because he was unreasonably convinced she was having an affair, then bumped off the maid who had witnessed his crime. From here things went from bad to worse. While he was trying to dump the dismembered bodies, he hit a cyclist, and before he could clean up the house, he had a steady succession of suspicious visitors, to whom he told a variety of lies. Finally he managed to wrap the corpses in unique editions of the local newspaper, thus tagging himself to a time and place for the murders.

Hodge clearly understood the universal appeal of these trials, and encouraged his writers to pick out the most salient details of the cases; there's a consistency of style over the entire run of books. Volume 4 of 'Famous Trials' was published at the end of the war, and topically included the traitorous 'Lord Haw-Haw', William Joyce, pointing out that radio listeners found his voice more irritating than his politics. These days, we're aware that the same propaganda tactics were being used by the British government at the time. Volume 7 is entirely dedicated to the trials of Oscar Wilde, and here we can watch as the tide turns in the course of the prosecution, as the great playwright's wit and overarching confidence start to fade in the face of careful, persistent questioning.

Throughout the series certain themes emerge – one is of continually repressed sexuality. Many of the cases hinge on frustrated desires that reach breaking point and culminate in murder. Another concerns the way in which the British legal system can be both fair-minded and remarkably shoddy, especially in cases where the charge is treason.

The series was later extended to cover war crimes, and the former barrister and novelist John Mortimer selected the best cases for a 1984 volume.

48

Sheila Hodgetts

She was one of my first failures: I couldn't discover anything about Sheila Hodgetts at all. It's as if she hid herself entirely. There was once a collectors' guide which had some biographical detail but it's now out of print, and when last I looked even her website had closed down. More worryingly, the site's owner offered his complete collection of Hodgetts books for sale, as if he had fallen out of love with her peculiar creations.

I have never been quite so stumped by an author, but I remembered her strange tales from childhood, and was eventually able to track down a much-scribbled-upon copy. Although it was dateless, the poor paper quality suggested that it was printed in the early 1950s, when decent stock was hard to come by and therefore expensive.

This would have been the era of magic painting books and rag books. It was the time of Babar the Elephant and Noddy in Toyland. Hodgetts's characters were similar to those in the adventures of Rupert the Bear. They lived in odd pastoral never-lands that existed somewhere between Narnia and the Home Counties, comforting safe havens for young imaginations. But whereas Rupert and Noddy's homelands were fairly well defined, Hodgetts's world was a little more slippery.

Her main character, Toby Twirl, was a partly human upright pig in baggy pants who was less Dr Dolittle, more Dr Moreau. His sidekick was Eli the Elephant, dressed in a smart jacket, grey trousers and shoes, and there was a penguin called Pete. Like Rupert, they spoke in rhyming couplets and lived in one of those attractive between-the-wars towns with an inn, signposts and a clocktower, surrounded by folk-creatures and Arcimboldo-like beings.

Perhaps every culture creates mythical beings for its children. Whether we remember them is often, alas, down to exploitability. Tove Jansson's Moomintroll books have arguably maintained their popularity throughout Europe in the same way that Hergé's Tintin has survived: via merchandising and licensing.

In Toby's world there were also witches, wizards, giants, elves, castles, mermen, gnomes and dragons – the full panoply of fairy-tale tropes. Some of the stories took place in Dillyland, a Lilliputian landscape reachable by a miniature train. Even though there were villains and obstacles to overcome, the Toby Twirl books exuded a powerful atmosphere of homeliness, security and warmth. Here, they said, nothing really bad can ever happen.

Defining these characters and their settings are many beautifully evocative drawings by Edward Jeffrey. He excelled in visits to enchanted isles, and in my copy there's a trip to Candytown which conjures up the strange pastel tones of cheap post-war confectionary.

Hodgetts's character proved immensely popular and her many volumes included regular annuals. Mine features a Toby Twirl theme song printed with the sheet music, which assumes we can all read music – and perhaps the well-mannered children at whom the books were aimed could do so. The adventures are all out of print, but I don't see why these rather charming volumes shouldn't become highly desired once more.

The Forgotten Queens of Suspense

Ignored, underrated, overlooked or taken for granted, the women who wrote popular fiction for a living were often simply grateful to be published at all.

Writing ghost stories was an acceptable pastime for a Victorian lady. They did it because their families needed the money, or simply to amuse themselves. Sometimes they hid their gender behind initials. Some were better known for other writing, like Edith Nesbit, whose book *The Railway Children* was largely saved from obscurity by a delightful film version. Nesbit's life was highly unconventional: she lived with the mistress of her priapic husband and adopted the children he fathered. Her hurt and disappointment surfaced in the creepy tales she wrote, but her publishers had pigeonholed her as a children's author, and powerful stories like 'Man-Size in Marble' were forgotten. In that tale, two stone knights come to life in a country church and abduct the hero's wife, and it's hard not to read it as a roman-à-clef.

Amelia B. Edwards is forgotten because her main career eclipsed her writing. She was one of the greatest women travellers of the Victorian age, 'the Queen of Egyptologists' who saved countless priceless relics from theft and destruction. Her natural flair for drama made her a superb lecturer, and while her travel books and achievements in Egyptology remain an enduring legacy, she also wrote wonderful murder mysteries and ghost stories. In her story 'The Four-Fifteen Express', a businessman shares a railway carriage with a ghost seeking to uncover the corporate scandal that led to his death.

Mrs H. D. Everett defined a true ghost story as one that never has a point, while a faked one dare not leave it out. Her atmospheric tales were filled with sinister parsons and revenants stalking snow-swept woodlands.

May Sinclair took the traditional ghost story and gave it a good shake-out, adding psychological underpinnings that suggested threats came from within rather than from some higher power.

Similarly, Charlotte Perkins Gilman's now syllabus-taught tale 'The Yellow Wallpaper' exposes the roots of feminism by suggesting that the heroine's psychosis is the result of repression at the hands of the husband who incarcerates her.

Single stories from writers like Edith Wharton, Marjorie Bowen and Ann Radcliffe, whose work influenced H. P. Lovecraft, tended to crop up in ghostly anthologies throughout the twentieth century, but gradually fell away. Many of these fine authors helped to inspire today's new generation of women writers.

If you look back at past anthologies you'll find many volumes without a single female voice, but not all editors were so male-centric. Herbert Van Thal's popular Pan Books of Horror proved that, when it came to provoking nightmares, women were every bit as devious as men. Lesser known were John Burke's 'Tales of Unease' volumes, which were published in 1966 and 1969. In the first of these, Virginia Ironside, journalist and agony aunt, penned the sardonic 'The Young Squire'.

Andrea Newman wrote the controversial novels *Three Into Two Won't Go* and *A Bouquet of Barbed Wire*, a frequent theme being the disintegration of the family unit, and her story 'Such a Good Idea' is one of the simplest revenge tales ever written. In it, Sarah, the protagonist, turns a key in a lock and changes her life forever. A lock of another kind sparked the plot of Penelope Mortimer's 'The Skylight', in which a mother and son find themselves shut out of a French summer home as it starts to grow dark. Ms Mortimer co-wrote the screenplay of Otto Preminger's *Bunny Lake Is Missing* and knew a thing or two about creating a disturbing atmosphere in the home.

The prolific Elizabeth Lemarchand, the mistress of misdirection, unfolded a terrific scenario in 'Time To Be Going', and never have drawers full of blankets appeared so ominous. In Christine Brooke-Rose's 'Red Rubber Gloves', household washing-up items become instruments of death viewed by a neighbour, and in Cressida Lindsay's 'Watch Your Step' a drunken night out tips one young couple's life out of balance when they discover their room the wrong way round.

These authors were able to locate unease in the most mundane domestic settings. Their fictions were set in ordinary houses, and resonated with many wives who found themselves back behind the ironing board after a war during which they performed tasks equal to men. Consequently the tales often have a claustrophobic, trapped atmosphere in which heroines are treated dismissively by husbands. The police rarely feature in such tales, and the dramas are contained inside the home.

A frequent theme in the late Victorian era was the fragility of the female constitution, in which poor, fluttering, pale birds quailed at the thought of acting independently and retired to their claustrophobic bedrooms to lie on plumped-up pillows and await the ministrations of their husbands. The 1950s found a similar role for wives in the kitchen. Heroines were frequently told not to worry their silly little heads and take a few pills. Family doctors seemed to be forever hovering in the background to handle constitution problems or patronizingly suggest that wives simply needed to get some rest.

American women writers had more confidence than their UK counterparts, and gradually branched out from the purely domestic. The photograph on Holly Roth's paperbacks shows a glamorous, attractive woman in the classic 1950s mould. Roth grew up in Chicago, Brooklyn and London, travelling the world because of her father's business. In the fifties and sixties there was plenty of fiction work to be found in weekly periodicals. She began writing tightly plotted suspense novels, which were serialized in *Collier's* and the *Saturday Evening Post*.

It seems likely that Roth considered herself a pulp novelist, but her books were well written and reflect the preoccupations of the times. Her thrillers were high-concept before the term had been created, and include *The Mask of Glass*, in which Jimmy Kennemore of the US Army's Counter-Intelligence Corps wakes up in hospital, injured and disfigured, his red hair turned white. Forced to piece together the events of the night that deprived him of identity, friends and a future, he discovers an international no-man's land where human life is the most expendable commodity.

Roth wrote twelve such novels, four under the pseudonym K. G. Ballard, an oddly coincidental choice of a name considering J. G. Ballard was a rising star at the time, but a bigger coincidence followed. In *Operation Doctors* a woman falls from a boat and loses her memory. Roth died after falling off a yacht in the Mediterranean, and her body was never recovered.

In the fifties, female suspense writers proved very popular, and Roth was compared to Mary Stewart, Charlotte Armstrong and Margaret Millar, frequently tackling the kind of Cold War-influenced subjects that were considered a strictly male province. Her books were critically overlooked at the time, and if the plots seem far-fetched, her ability to turn up the tension is unquestionable.

Now nicknamed 'The Lethal Sex', writers like Nedra Tyre were able to find a loyal readership. In her earliest photograph Tyre is elfin, angelic, fragile, with a beatific smile, yet there's a strange steeliness in her eyes. The soft-spoken Georgian wrote seven novels and over forty short stories, working as a librarian, clerk, advertising copywriter, sociologist and charity worker for very little reward.

She read avidly, stored books in her oven, would only eat in restaurants with linen napkins, lived austerely, took care of a sick mother, travelled alone, liked teddy bears – the only colour photograph I could find shows her and a bear in matching bowler hats and spectacles. She believed you should start by writing fifteen minutes every day, knowing that if you managed that you'd soon write longer.

In a time when female writers were patronizingly referred to as 'lady authors' she penned mystery-suspense tales that had an uncomfortable, even dangerous edge of truth. In a recently recovered short story, 'A Nice Place to Stay', the heroine, a saintly girl who always puts others first and asks for little in return, wants nothing more than somewhere nice to rest her head when her work is done. Treated with disdain and even hatred, she discovers that life can be crueller still when she finally gets the little room she always dreamed of – a jail cell.

Tyre's best novel is *Death of an Intruder*, an escalating battle of wills between two strong women that eventually leads to murder. The author abandoned writing after becoming completely deaf, and concentrated on charity work. She said: 'Almost everything defeats me and everything amazes me.' She was unable to write a dull sentence.

Ethel Lina White came from Monmouthshire. The daughter of an inventor, she seems to have been destined to write, starting young with essays and poems, quickly moving to short stories and novels.

She had a genius for sustained suspense, coupled with a slangy use of conversation that puts one in mind of the American author Mary Roberts Rinehart, creator of the phrase, 'The butler did it'. Both featured lonely heroines wandering in large darkened country houses, their journeys becoming metaphors for repressed states.

White wrote seventeen novels in all, and to my mind, her best work is *Some Must Watch*, a superbly eerie thriller in which a young carer, Helen, is taken on in a remote household at a time when a serial killer is targeting women in the locality. The novel is virtually little more than a description of a mental state, a brilliantly maintained exercise in escalating hysteria as the nine residents who protect Helen from the forces of chaos are stripped away one by one, not murdered but unable to help because of mundane problems: a brandy bottle, a broken door handle, sleeping pills or a distracting phone call. Finally Helen must survive alone. This is classic domestic suspense; the women are strong-willed but made vulnerable by the rigid hierarchical structure of the household.

The habit of classifying women into ages – the innocent maiden, the middle-aged spinster, the mad old harridan – was typified by W. S. Gilbert, with the creation of Mad Margaret in *Ruddigore*, but it was always lurking in the male psyche. The most senior archetype re-emerged after the Second World War to power her way through films like *What Ever Happened To Baby Jane?*, *Fanatic* and *Hush . . . Hush, Sweet Charlotte*, in which scenery-chewing crazy old women (played by actresses looking to revive flagging careers) took on their adversaries with cunning and, sometimes, an axe.

However, female authors had largely been responsible for this state of affairs. Naomi Hintze wrote *You'll Like My Mother*, in a genre that came to be known as 'Gynaecological Gothic'. In this the pregnant heroine is locked away and subjected to mental torture by her religious fanatic mother-in-law. Shelley Smith added to the sub-genre of crime fiction, also nicknamed 'Badass Biddies', with her novel *The Party At No. 5*, which featured the fabulously named Luna Rampage, a mean old bag who takes in a paid companion and wages a petty-minded war with her that soon turns murderous.

It was Yonkers-born Ursula Curtiss who really perfected this style guide for sinister seniors in a series of twenty-one crime novels written between 1948 and 1983, the peak being 1962's *The Forbidden Garden*, in which a destitute widow finds a way of supplementing her dwindling income by murdering housekeepers and burying them beneath trees in her garden, until one candidate grows suspicious and begins fighting back. It's darker than you'd expect, with a tasty twist at the end.

Elisabeth Sanxay Holding, Margaret Millar, Hilda Lawrence and Shirley Jackson were perhaps merely reflecting the conservative times in their fiction, when women we would now consider still young could be written off as neurotic lonely spinsters. Often their heroines had physical or mental fragilities, and their sell-by date appeared to be around thirty.

The idea of hysterical fantasies being a female weakness ('hysteria' comes from the Greek *hysterikos*, meaning 'of the womb') had been present from Victorian times, when fainting fits were blamed on everything from tight corsets to a reliance on laudanum. Consequently, many such stories have an obsessive, sexually repressive quality running through them, from the writings of Bram Stoker and Robert Bloch to Hammer's women-in-peril suspensers, which continued to suggest that women were irrational and prone to madness.

'You're highly strung!' warns a teacher to her charge, Janet, in Jimmy Sangster's Hammer film *Nightmare*. 'Hundreds of people are highly strung – it doesn't mean you're mad!' Pretty soon, though, Janet's convinced that she'll become as loopy as her mother who, says one sensitive relative, 'had to be locked away – in an INSANE ASYLUM!' Thankfully, a few decades of female empowerment brought an end to the idea of the crazy lady in fiction, along with the notion that an older woman was only interesting if she was deranged, but these paranoid paperbacks still make for fascinating reading.

Today women read more than men, and female authors have finally been accorded the prestige they always deserved.

49

Polly Hope

Seeking out lost authors requires two kinds of detective work; I track them down, but if readers become interested, they then have to locate their books. Throughout the process one author continued to block further investigation. I knew the Australian-born Maryann Forrest was someone to check out when I read a description of her in *Time Out* as 'a stunning writer, so superb and alive a talent'. Then Anthony Burgess picked up on her first novel, describing it as 'deeply disturbing' but 'a keen literary pleasure'.

Here (Away From It All), published in 1969, is an adult *Lord of the Flies* involving wealthy holidaymakers instead of schoolchildren. A Greek island has been ruined by opportunistic tourism; overrun with timeshares and package tours, its natives have been marginalized and employed as service personnel. One day an unspecified world event occurs which ends all ferry contact with the island, so that foreign currency is suddenly rendered worthless. Hotel guests find themselves paying their bills with watches, rings and necklaces. When the material goods run out, they need something else to barter with, and as the rules of civility become ever more strained, the islanders start to exact revenge.

In a post-Brexit world, the book reads more uncomfortably than ever. Its nameless protagonist, a young mother, watches in horror as the unidentified island – the world in microcosm – breaks down into rebellion and anarchy. The revengers have Greek names but there is no racism here, because a silver thread of humanity runs through the characters, refusing easy demonization, and the heroine remains upbeat and matter-of-fact even as all hope fades.

The tale is post-apocalyptic and descends inexorably to a horrifying climax, but is written from a deeply personal viewpoint. Cormac McCarthy's *The Road* is probably the only book that comes close in its bleak subject matter. *Here* remains in my head decades after I first read it.

However, when I tried to find out more about its author I drew a total blank.

One editor suggested that she had actually escaped the world by moving to the Greek island described in her novel, but this seemed unlikely as there were two more novels written within three years of her first. It appeared she was using a pseudonym, and although there were plenty of Maryann Forrests listed in the Australian electoral rolls, the trail ran cold after that. I decided to ask readers for help. Mentions of all three books could be (just about) found on the internet, but there were no reprints and I was relying on those with long memories and untouched bookshelves.

Some weeks later I received a letter which began: 'My first husband came across your piece about Maryann Forrest, asking if anyone knows where she is. I know, for I am she. Come to lunch.'

I visited Polly Hope, polymath artist, sculptor and opera librettist, in London's Spitalfields. Behind the door of a former brewery was what I first took to be a farm: a cobbled courtyard with a baroque opera-shaped hen-house, dogs, cats and sundry shrieking birds. Beyond stood a studio filled with sculptures and a chandelier that on closer inspection proved to be made of jam jars, bicycle wheels and kitchen utensils. Here, at the top of a ladder, was a tall, elderly lady who shouted, 'Quick, give me a hand with this, would you?'

On Midsummer's Eve (Polly's birthday), it appeared that a concert was to be held with a zodiac theme. As the bohemian guests gathered – a poker-thin lady who might be a modern Edith Sitwell, another dressed entirely in parrot feathers, a florid gentleman whose latest collection of ribald poetry, *Sodomy Is Not Enough*, was being tipped as a coming cult – I considered their hostess's remarkable career and found that she had adopted an alias – she'd had an Australian grandmother – to write the novel. Hope had been living in Greece during the period of the military junta, and would very likely have faced deportation upon publication of the book. This raised an idea I hadn't considered: perhaps other authors were also successful polymaths who simply sought to pursue varied careers. Polly covered her tracks so successfully that her books remained tough to find.

Hope was born into an aristocratic family. Her father, General Sir Hugh Stockwell, had commanded the Anglo-French forces during the Suez crisis. His daughter trained as a dancer, grew too tall and decamped to art school. Moving to Rhodes, she married, and bore a son. 'My husband and I lived by the week,' she explained. With a partner who felt that no gentleman should work, Hope started writing because she needed the money.

Here (Away From It All) garnered raves, and led to her second novel, *Us Lot*, which captures the thrill of being young, directionless and alive to the world's possibilities. It's a sexually precocious work, remarkably clear-eyed about the motives of men on the make.

She continued to a claustrophobic and mysterious third novel, *The Immaculate Misconception*, inspired by her own family, illustrating it herself, then switched to a bewildering array of media, including ceramics, murals, fountains, photography, jewellery, portraits, embroidery, bronzes, operas, even ecclesiastical vestments. She was as happy knocking up a wedding dress as she was designing a statue in Hyde Park.

Hope became something of a global phenomenon, her creations ranging from tapestries the height of a building to objects that could be placed in a matchbox. She married Theo Crosby, the architect of Shakespeare's Globe, and her designs grace that building. 'Whenever we signed into American hotels as Crosby and Hope,' she said, 'the desk clerks fell about laughing. I'm a Gemini, so everything came in pairs; two husbands, two countries, two careers.'

Polly's work was exhibited all over the world but she referred to herself as a 'jobbing artist'. Her home was filled with the kind of English eccentrics I assumed had vanished long ago. Accompanied by a three-legged dog, she directed entertainments for her guests and always gave sunflowers to the cast. She had finished a superb new novel about Byron's doctor, and I petitioned publishers to rediscover her. There were no takers.

Polly felt that her best work always lay ahead. 'After all, Verdi produced one of his great operas, *Falstaff*, at eighty,' she reminded me, lighting another cigarette. I encouraged her to republish her first book online, which she did herself at the age of eighty. Typically, having cracked the internet, she then made a new hardback version available, painting a fresh cover for it. Some while ago I planned to visit her for lunch, where she would serve a hot meal to any dissident composer, pornographic poet or misfit artist who was passing through the area, and discovered that after a very brief illness she had died.

I looked at the new version of the book she'd created. Inside was a dedication: 'To Chris, for finding me.' London became less colourful without her.

50

Richard Hughes

Hope was perhaps always something of an outsider. Hughes was very much on the inside. He first came to public attention at seventeen when his schoolmaster sent one of his essays to the *Spectator* (note to self: does this sort of thing still happen? Answer: I think not). Hughes wrote the world's first radio play, called *Danger*, broadcast in 1924. He became a journalist, travelled extensively, married the painter Frances Bazley, and spent a decade as a scriptwriter at Ealing Studios, but only managed to write four adult novels, two of which have ostensibly similar plots.

This is odd, because one of the quartet has such timeless power that it should probably be on every school curriculum. *A High Wind in Jamaica* was published to great acclaim in 1929, and is quite unique. It is an adventure about children, but is not aimed at them. The prose sweeps away a century of Victorian sentimentality and replaces it with something darker, more clear-eyed and modern.

What starts as merely masterful storytelling becomes something dreamlike and haunting; it's not a book you easily forget. The very first page sets the tone when it casually mentions that twin sisters were starved and fed ground glass until they died. Some British children living in Jamaica survive a hurricane and are sent back to England, but are captured by pirates. The description of the storm is filled with bizarre incident – a pack of wildcats is blown through the windows onto the dining table, and the shutters bulge 'as if tired elephants were leaning against them'.

It's a book about growing up and recognizing the natural cruelties that allow the young to survive. Nothing fazes the children, whose amoral attitude to their parents should be a warning that their captors are not psychologically matched to defeat them. The book's lack of sentimentality, its acceptance of sin and its black humour, raises its level of maturity to something far beyond a description of its pirate plot, the turning point of which is a casually shocking death that underlines the loss of innocence both sides suffer. Hughes is brilliant at pinning down the interior lives of children, and it would be interesting to know how today's kids would react to it.

Hughes's other seabound novel, *In Hazard*, feels like a spin-off, as it follows the crew of a British ship facing death in a hurricane. It's thrilling but much less memorable. Was *A High Wind in Jamaica* simply lightning in a bottle, a happy accident? Two further books outline a virtual history of the early twentieth century, but are patchy. Hughes was awarded the OBE, and died fifty pages into the last volume in the trilogy. Vintage Classics are to be commended for their editions of both *A High Wind in Jamaica* and *In Hazard*, but the others – and his excellent children's stories – are out of print at the time of writing.

51

Graham Joyce

We tend to think that books, like cockroaches, will survive the Four Horsemen of the Apocalypse, but they don't. They disappear, not just in the ravages of war like the Great Library of Alexandria, but through simple neglect, and it is our duty to keep fine novels alive.

Graham Joyce, born in Coventry in 1954, was a most unlikely author; unlikely because he had the bluff honesty of a Yorkshire miner's son but a writing style that was sensitive to the world's wonderment. Unlikely, too, because he frequently wrote from a female perspective, and his books were more concerned with moods and atmospheres than plots.

When asked why he hadn't attended one particularly fractious and territorial gathering of writers, he said, 'Well, it's all a load of bollocks, really, isn't it?' Nevertheless, Joyce became the multi-award-winning author of *The Tooth Fairy*, *The Limits of Enchantment*, *The Year of the Ladybird* and *Smoking Poppy*. There are touches of Jonathan Carroll and Christopher Priest in his work, but his prose was

52

Robert Klane

So far, many of our neglected writers have been sensitive souls whose dazzling prose has fallen from fashion. Robert Klane is the opposite: loud, lewd, offensive and hilarious, his books kicked black comedy back into style with a mix of taboo-busting farce and broad Jewish shtick. I remember being embarrassed to read one on the Tube.

Klane has been described as 'Max Shulman spiked heavily with the Marquis de Sade', but also incited comparisons to Joseph Heller and J. D. Salinger. His works are short sharp shocks of disgust.

In his first novel, *The Horse Is Dead*, published in 1968, the hero Nemiroff works as a counsellor at Camp Winituck, which looks 'like a poorly run concentration camp'. Nemiroff's bullied childhood leaves him with a hatred of all children, and he soon declares war on his charges. By the time Parents' Day and the titular dead horse arrive, most barriers of good taste have fallen. There's a ghastly set-piece in a swimming pool where Nemiroff is supposed to show off the kids' prowess, except that he hasn't taught them to swim. Jack Benny said it was the funniest book he had ever read.

Klane's prose is as fast and blunt as a chucked brick. He has no time for niceties (or even adjectives) and recognizes that the best dark comedy, like life, is painful, mean and brief. *Where's Poppa?* (1970) may be the ultimate Jewish mother novel. Trapped at home with an overbearing senile parent, Gordon Hocheiser, a dominated and sleep-deprived lawyer, continually loses his cases due to poor preparation, and can only stand by in despair as his girlfriends dump him the moment they realize they'll never separate him from the terminally confused Mrs Hocheiser. His attempts to frighten the old lady to death must be nightly defeated by his guilt-laden brother, who runs a gauntlet of Central Park muggers in order to prevent matricide and halt the receipt of said mother into his own chaotic home. The film version, made with George Segal and Ruth Gordon, suffered a failure of nerve in the final furlong and avoided the novel's brilliantly gruesome Oedipal outcome.

Klane's third novel was *Fire Sale*, in which the Jewish owner of a failing department store plans to have it torched for the insurance by hiring an arson-prone mental patient to do the job. Of course, the plan misfires spectacularly, resulting in death and madness. To describe the plot as merely non-PC is doing it a disservice. One character is missing a leg and has the stump set in a wheelbarrow full of earth, trying to grow it back. While Klane's brief novels have been surpassed now by much more tasteless fare, these three are oddly endearing because they capture the sheer unfairness of life, particularly as it was lived in the early 1970s. Like great farceurs before him, Klane tackled sex, family, madness and death, roughly in that order. It's easy to write in bad taste, but much harder to produce stories in which the bad decisions characters make result in unpreventable tastelessness.

Klane was, of course, loathed by highbrow and even lowbrow critics. His books are now all out of print but worth picking up if you stumble across them.

53

Thomas Nigel Kneale

Let's step slightly off the path for a breather here. Kneale didn't write novels, but he was an important writer worth remembering.

He became a legend in his own lifetime, a shining example of how to rigorously explore fantastical subjects without sacrificing believability. Kneale was raised in the Isle of Man, moved to London and joined RADA, but quickly abandoned acting to become a writer. His debut short-story collection, *Tomato Cain and Other Stories*, won the Somerset Maugham Award in 1950, but although his publisher pushed him to write a novel, he chose to write for television, something he did successfully for over forty years.

However, before he began working for the BBC he had never seen any TV at all. Kneale soon realized that British drama was everything he hated: polite, drawn-out and dull. Filmed live, it was trapped in a middle-class netherworld of drawing-room sets and cut-glass accents.

Kneale and his director wanted to open up stories and explore grander themes, but he was also keen to cut across the social classes. Although he wrote and adapted many other works, he is best remembered for his character Professor Bernard Quatermass.

For six weeks his TV serial *The Quatermass Experiment* gripped the nation. The story of a manned space flight that brings back a virus brilliantly exploited Britain's post-war insecurities, and was a massive hit for the BBC. The stumbling pilot, his arm swollen and bandaged as his infection spreads, is driven by the need to survive, and must have struck an uncomfortable chord with war veterans. A climactic sequence featuring the alien parasite invading Westminster Abbey was achieved with the aid of some gloves stuck through a photograph of the building, yet it worked.

Kneale subsequently adapted Orwell's *1984* in a production that was considered so shocking that questions were asked in Parliament about its suitability for television, even though the Queen apparently said she enjoyed it.

Kneale brought back his most famous character for *Quatermass II*, an even eerier exploration of government collusion and dishonesty. One of the key features of his writing was his ability to see the central story from a dozen different viewpoints, canvassing opinions from charladies and politicians. The next, *Quatermass and the Pit*, was the best yet. Inspired by the racial tensions Kneale had seen rising in Britain (the Notting Hill riots occurred during production), it suggested that the human race itself was racially 'impure'.

The Quatermass stories show a great mistrust of being instructed from above, as government yes-men inadequately try to convince a frightened populace that they know what they are doing (in *Quatermass II* they say they're creating artificial foodstuffs, when in fact the entire country is being flogged off to alien forces). It was science fiction, but Kneale, like so many great SF writers, created prescient plots and appeared to foresee the economic era of monetarism *in extremis*. Professor Quatermass remained a great English anti-icon, not just because he was a shabby, fair-minded boffin, but because he displayed a consistent suspicion of authority at a time when most heroes were themselves authoritarians.

Kneale tried scripting for US projects but the experience was always disastrous. Turning down James Bond adaptations, he instead wrote disturbing, perceptive British plays including *The Year of the Sex Olympics*, in which the British are kept stupefied with a diet of lowbrow entertainment (like that would ever happen). In his personal life Kneale was surrounded by writers: he was the husband of children's writer Judith Kerr, and the father of Matthew Kneale, the author of *English Passengers*. His concept for a Quatermass prequel set in pre-war Germany has yet to be realized, and it's a mystery as to why one of the great British heroes has never been accorded his proper status.

54

Ronald Knox

In popular fiction, priests and murder often go hand in hand. Ronald Arbuthnott Knox was a Catholic priest known for his theological scholarship; he single-handedly retranslated the Latin Vulgate Bible into English, often writing on religious themes. An editor, literary critic and humorist who wrote six decent mystery novels and three volumes of short stories, starting in the late 1920s, he also left behind a list of do's and don't's for crime writers. According to Evelyn Waugh, Knox saw his own mysteries as 'an intellectual exercise, a game between reader and writer, in which a problem was precisely stated and elaborately described'.

In January 1926, Knox broadcast a hoax radio programme on the BBC suggesting that a devastating revolution was sweeping across London. He intercut the report with live dramatic links, including one of a government minister being lynched. The broadcast went out on a snowy weekend, and the lack of newspapers getting through caused a minor panic as people assumed the revolutionaries had stopped them. It has often been suggested that the broadcast influenced Orson Welles in the making of his *War of the Worlds* hoax.

The mischievous Father Knox also drew up his 'Decalogue', a set of rules for fair play with the crime fiction reader of 1929. This is how the list ran:

1. The criminal must be someone mentioned in the early part of the story, but must not be anyone whose thoughts the reader has been allowed to follow.
2. All supernatural or preternatural agencies are ruled out as a matter of course.
3. Not more than one secret room or passage is allowable.
4. No hitherto undiscovered poisons may be used, nor any appliance which will need a long scientific explanation at the end.
5. No Chinaman must figure in the story.
6. No accident must ever help the detective, nor must he ever have an unaccountable intuition which proves to be right.
7. The detective must not himself commit the crime.
8. The detective must not light on any clues which are not instantly produced for the inspection of the reader.
9. The stupid friend of the detective, the Watson, must not conceal any thoughts which pass through his mind; his intelligence must be slightly, but very slightly, below that of the average reader.
10. Twin brothers, and doubles generally, must not appear unless we have been duly prepared for them.

Knox was partly joking, of course, but his rules have remained largely in place, or have been deliberately broken by authors seeking to prove him wrong. His novels recently started to reappear.

There's an American literary society dedicated to Monsignor Knox, which places as much weight on his Catholic writing as his crime novels. Knox apparently rejected the notion of performing a baptism in the vernacular, arguing that 'the baby doesn't understand English and the Devil knows Latin'. That kind of attitude wouldn't have washed in our house, where my mother, in between hiding her Georgette Heyers in the piano stool, would have voiced her low opinions of High Church.

55

Gavin Lambert

After a Hollywood orgy, a beautiful young girl emerges from a swimming pool in morning light. 'Is there anyone you should call?' asks the host. 'Anyone who'll be wondering where you are?' To which she replies, 'No, there's no one in the world.'

And as an ageing Hollywood star realizes he is losing the one commodity that makes others love him, his easy charisma is crushed in the panic for survival. 'When time's running out,' he notes, 'you get a touch of the fever.'

Welcome to the world of Gavin Lambert, a British scribe who left behind the editorship of *Sight & Sound* in order to head for Hollywood, where he became a close friend of Natalie Wood and Paul Bowles. There he lived with Mart Crowley, who wrote the groundbreaking and highly influential gay play, *The Boys in the Band*.

For this author of seven novels and half a dozen screen biographies, Hollywood's paradox never changed: how could so many men and women attempt to prove their individuality in a place that actively discourages independent thinking? It's an idea that raises the dramatic stakes between success and failure.

Lambert tracked these aimless lives across decades in a 'Hollywood Quartet' of novels. The best-known, *Inside Daisy Clover*, was written (and filmed with Natalie Wood) in the sixties, and *The Goodbye People* appeared at the start of the seventies, by which time the dream had truly soured, and the unscrupulous behaviour of studio bosses had paled into insignificance beside the waking nightmares of Charles Manson and Richard Nixon.

The Goodbye People throws a spotlight on the self-deluding characters who have become tainted by Southern California's dreamlike hedonism. It wafts temptingly around them like incense, imprisoning them in a glittering bubble, and prevents them from growing up. These are the so-called beautiful people, very rich and very poor, narcissistic, selfish, manipulative, forever moving apartments and changing phone numbers, unable to decide who or what they're running from.

Would a celebrity-obsessed youngster take these books as a dire warning? Probably not. After all, Lambert himself was drawn across the Atlantic to live with the damaged residents of La La Land, a self-perpetuating myth that continues to this day in a city that disfigures all with its luxurious blankness.

Like Nathanael West before him, whose 1939 classic *The Day of the Locust* skewered the emptiness of celebrity culture, Lambert's writing is wry and spare, which keeps his style modern. Only his 1959 classic *The Slide Area* (named after the land along Pacific Palisades that is 'likely to slip away without warning') remained in print; the rest slipped away, much like his lonely, disillusioned characters. Fiction was a sideline, after his star biographies and screenplays.

What disturbs most is the thought that his studies of lost lives are just as accurate today as they were when he wrote them. In *The Goodbye People*, the hero explains that he doesn't read books because the characters always get somewhere, and this frustrates him. 'Isn't that the trouble with most books?' he asks. 'They look so good on paper.'

56

George Langelaan

Although he was born in Paris eight years after the start of the century, Langelaan was an Edwardian Briton, and lived a life far stranger than almost any of his fictions.

By my reckoning he didn't get published until he was approaching fifty – so what was he doing in the intervening years? Well, he began as a newspaper writer until the start of the Second World War, then found himself working for British Army Intelligence. Rescued during Dunkirk after being stranded behind enemy lines, he was then employed by the Special Operations Executive, a secret unit involved in sabotage and spying. To aid the French resistance movement, he agreed to be parachuted back there in order to meet a key contact, but was worried about being recognized. His ears stuck out like taxi doors, so along with a new identity he was given some rather pioneering plastic surgery to make himself less recognizable. After being dropped, he was caught by the Nazis and condemned to death, but managed to escape from the Mauzac camp in 1942. He was awarded the Croix de Guerre, and wrote a memoir, *The Masks of War*, in 1959.

Two years before this, however, he penned another work about the power of transformation. 'The Fly' was a short story that appeared in *Playboy* magazine and was included in Langelaan's collection *Out of Time* in 1964. The tale concerned a scientist whose attempt to transmit himself across distances ended in disaster when his cells became mixed with those of a common housefly accidentally trapped in the machine. The tale was an instant hit with readers, and was reimagined as a rather oddly constructed murder mystery starring Vincent Price. The script was adapted by James Clavell, who wrote *King Rat* and *Tai-Pan*. The film version spawned two sequels and a remake that reimagined the story as an allegory for the AIDS crisis. After that came another sequel and finally an opera composed by Howard Shore, who had scored the soundtrack for the successful David Cronenberg version.

Langelaan also wrote war stories, tales in French and supernatural suspensers. He had a great feeling for high concepts. In 'Strange Miracle' the hero fakes paralysis in order to defraud his insurance company; in 'The Other Hand' a man loses control of his hand to someone or something else. Alfred Hitchcock (who pops up frequently in these pages) recognized his way with a good plot and co-opted him for television, but despite penning two volumes of richly detailed biography, plenty of other books and volumes of excellent short fiction, his protégé never again achieved the level of fame he'd received for 'The Fly'.

In the same way that W. W. Jacobs is now only remembered for his macabre story 'The Monkey's Paw', one short story had come to dominate Langelaan's life. Why had it proven so potent?

A tale of deception and disguise (his hero effectively gets a new head), it must have been a subject close to the writer's heart, and was perhaps more of a subconscious roman-à-clef than his memoirs. In Langelaan's story the physical alteration affects his nature. Did the author feel that his wartime change of identity also changed his personality? And how many writers unintentionally insert versions of themselves into their novels?

The Forgotten Nonsense Writers

Lewis Carroll will always be the great Victorian nonsense writer, but there were plenty of others who are now rather overlooked.

A talent for frivolously cruel humour is not something one expects from a man with the following heavyweight CV: Jocelyn Henry Clive Graham, nicknamed Harry, born in 1874, educated at Eton and Sandhurst. His elder brother became the British Ambassador to Italy. At the age of nineteen he joined the Coldstream Guards. He served in the Boer War, turned up at the Klondike Gold Rush in the Yukon, and finally became private secretary to the former Prime Minister, Lord Rosebery. Then he rejoined the Coldstream Guards and fought in the First World War.

Harry Graham had started writing fiction, light verse, journalism and history in his twenties. His memoir, *Across Canada To The Klondyke*, was published after his death and is mercifully lost, but in 1898 he published a volume under the pseudonym Col. D. Streamer called *Ruthless Rhymes*, which *The Times* compared to works by W. S. Gilbert and Lewis Carroll. It's a book that influenced many, including P. G. Wodehouse, W. H. Auden and George Orwell. In it were short, cruelly funny verses often involving death and loss. A classic example would be:

When Grandmamma fell off the boat
And couldn't swim (and wouldn't float)
Matilda just stood by and smiled.
I almost could have slapped the child.

Another runs thus:

'There's been an accident!' they said,
'Your servant's cut in half; he's dead!'
'Indeed!' said Mr Jones, 'and please,
Send me the half that's got my keys!'

His other callous and quotable verses include the tale of a father irritated by his crying infant who finds peace and quiet by sticking him in the fridge, and a man who despairs of ever being able to start the car again after his wife elopes with the chauffeur. Other Graham victims die from choking on fishbones, falling into fires, and being stung to death by bees.

When I suggested Edward Lear should be included in this section, a friend said, 'Why would you put in an artist?' For many it must seem inconceivable that Lear could be overlooked as an author, but I've mentioned his name to a number of younger colleagues and drawn blanks, although they can recall his sumptuous art, and 'The Owl and the Pussycat'.

Lear's written nonsense predates Lewis Carroll's *Alice in Wonderland* by nearly twenty years, but the difference was that he did not string his bizarre word-pictures into a complete narrative. Instead he concentrated on the five-line anapaest with an AABBA rhyme scheme, or limerick:

There was an Old Man of Thermopylae,
Who never did anything properly;
But they said, 'If you choose
To boil Eggs in your Shoes,
You shall never remain in Thermopylae.'

What drew him to this mystifyingly unamusing form is unclear (except in this case, which is clearly built around his determination to find a rhyme for 'Thermopylae'), but he popularized it, and in the process became famous for his fanciful neologisms, most obviously the 'runcible spoon'. There are many others, often used to describe animals.

Lear enjoyed surprising readers with odd words and rhythms, and seemed to possess such a nonsensical attitude that it was assumed he was the Earl of Derby writing under a pseudonym ('Earl' being an anagram of 'Lear'). Indeed, he was once called upon to prove that he wasn't. He sometimes introduced himself as Mr Abebika kratoponoko Prizzikalo Kattefello Ablegorabalus Ableborinto phashyph or Chakonoton the Cozovex Dossi Fossi Sini Tomentilla Coronilla Polentilla Battledore & Shuttlecock Derry Down Derry Dumps, a habit which must have grown old very quickly.

If his limericks lack the more familiar crudity of the form, they also lack any point, and don't encourage scholastic unravelling as *Alice* does. There was a time when it seemed every house had a volume of his nonsense verse, in which his spidery, angular drawings were complemented by his familiar handwriting. That time, clearly, has passed.

There was another nonsenseer who has worn better. Hilaire Belloc, the stern-looking Anglo-French historian and writer, was also a poet, satirist, soldier and political activist. Paradoxically kind and argumentative, in 1907 he penned *Cautionary Tales for Children*, squarely aimed at terrifying middle-class children into good behaviour with gruesome moralistic poems which included: 'Jim: Who ran away from his Nurse, and was eaten by a Lion'; 'Henry King: Who chewed bits of string, and was early cut off in Dreadful agonies'; 'Rebecca: Who Slammed Doors for Fun and Perished Miserably' (a marble bust fell on her); and of course the wonderful 'Matilda: Who told Lies, and was Burned to Death'. The tales have influenced everyone from Edward Gorey to Pink Floyd.

Perhaps these nonsense writers were a product of their conservative times. It rather makes one wish for modern-day versions: 'Darrell, Who Stared at his Phone and was Crushed by a Cement Mixer'.

The desire for something nonsensical never completely disappears. Every Christmas the shops are flooded with gift books based on TV shows, wartime hobbies and compendia of schoolboy knowledge played for ironic laughs. Who would have thought there was fun to be had by recovering children's hobbies from innocent volumes of 'Things To Make & Do' (see Arthur Mee's entry) or from retooling Ladybird books for adults?

Christmas wasn't always a cue to make money from out-of-copy-right old rope, though. In the past there had been some inspired comic volumes, and it's a pleasure to see that Luis Ricardo Carlos Fernand d'Antin y Zuloaga van Rooten's nonsense masterpiece is back in bookstores each December. His sophisticated humour books include *Van Rooten's Book of Improbable Saints*, but he should be remembered for creating a slim volume in 1967 that has become a perennial classic, the unique trick book *Mots d'Heures: Gousses, Râmes – The d'Antin Manuscript*.

To the untutored eye this appears to be a dry, annotated volume of obscure French poetry, complete with medieval woodcuts. The best way to give it to someone is not to tell them anything about it, and wait for the penny to drop. For this is a rare example of homophonic translation, a literary device that transforms a text in one language to its pronunciation into another with an entirely different meaning. Opening the pages to one poem we find:

Et qui rit des cures d'Oc?
De Meuse raines, houp! De cloques.
De quelles loques ce turque coin.
Et ne d'ânes ni rennes,
Écuries des cures d'Oc.

Because, of course, the book's phonetic title, '*Mots d'Heures: Gousses, Râmes*', is 'Mother Goose Rhymes', and those four lines introduce us to the mouse that ran up the clock. Luis then annotates each passage to explain the new meaning of the poem, thus rendering the translation into twisted, hilariously pseudo-philosophical gibberish. So here, the first line is translated back as 'a humble tribute to the monks of Languedoc.' Remember to take the wrap-around cover off the book if you buy it, as the most recent editions have stupidly given the game away on the front.

57

Noel Langley

I came to Mr Langley via a battered Penguin paperback of *Cage Me a Peacock*, a satirical version of the Rape of Lucretia that required the publisher to reassure readers with the rider: 'Written with such delicacy and cool assurance that I cannot imagine anyone taking offence.' But Langley could be a bitingly unsentimental writer. After growing up in Durban, South Africa, he moved to the USA, where he went on to become a novelist, playwright, screenwriter and director. *Cage Me a Peacock* was mysteriously banned in his place of birth (mind you, *The Belles of St Trinian's* was also banned in South Africa).

Langley attended his headmaster father's school, which severely tested their relationship. Langley Senior expected his son to be sporty and strong, but Langley Junior was barred from sports by his doctor and had a habit of drifting off to the library.

Noel was attracted to classical mythology, fairy tales and fables as well as theatre life. His novel *There's a Porpoise Close Behind Us* is a charming (and somewhat camp) backstage tale of two innocents,

Robin and Diana, and their attempts to survive in the poisonous London theatre world, written in 1936, but it was his children's book, *The Land of Green Ginger*, about the son of Aladdin, that made his name and became a perennial bestseller. It is also one of his only books that's still in print, and there's a very nice edition with sketchy illustrations by Edward Ardizzone, presumably dating from the 1960s, when Ardizzone's work was ubiquitous.

So far, Langley fits the 'forgotten author' bill quite nicely. He wrote jolly, negligible novels like his *Lysistrata* retelling, *Nymph in Clover*, and the pagan, *Candide*-like *The Rift in the Lute*, and he has largely vanished. But there's a specific reason for including him here, because his talents landed him a unique commission.

Langley went to Hollywood and began adapting films, where the success of *Green Ginger* got him the job of adapting *The Wizard of Oz* for the screen. However, his finished script was altered by two other scriptwriters. Edgar Allan Woolf and Florence Ryerson were hired to make sure that the film followed L. Frank Baum's book more closely. Langley hated the changes, feeling that the finished result was too sickly and sugar-coated. Altogether, fourteen writers worked on the adaptation, including Ogden Nash, songs were added ('Over the Rainbow' was almost removed because the studio thought it degrading for Garland to be singing in a barnyard), and still the film recorded a box office loss upon opening. Langley tried to write a sequel based on *The Marvelous Land of Oz*, using some of the concepts he had created for the original, but it never materialized.

Interestingly, some of the things we remember best about *The Wizard of Oz* were Langley's invention, like the ruby slippers and Toto revealing the wizard behind a curtain.

Langley went on to write the screenplay for *Ivanhoe*, and adapted *The Pickwick Papers*, *Svengali* and *The Search for Bridey Murphy*. He also worked on the screen adaptation of *A Christmas Carol*, *Scrooge*, with Alastair Sim.

Hollywood may have altered what Langley wrote, but the ruby slippers will always be his. And if you want to know what happened to the pair in the film, or their copies (seven pairs in all), read *The Ruby Slippers of Oz* by Rhys Thomas, which tells the astounding true story of the hunt for the shoes and the accidental creation of the movie memorabilia market. It would make a terrific movie thriller.

58

Marghanita Laski

Church halls are great friends of forgotten authors. A rootle about in the used-book stacks of St Giles brought me to this novelist, journalist and panellist, born to a family of prominent Jewish intellectuals in Manchester in 1915.

Rich early experience is often the key to wide-ranging interests, and so it proved with the beautiful Laski, who studied English at Oxford, worked in fashion and journalism, and married in Paris. I imagine it would have been easy to slip into a life of comfort and privilege, but her thirst for knowledge and natural curiosity led to excellence in a number of fields. A voracious reader, she was a compulsive contributor to the *Oxford English Dictionary*. She became the science-fiction critic for the *Observer*, an active campaigner for nuclear disarmament, a panellist on *What's My Line?*, *The Brains Trust* and *Any Questions?* and vice chairwoman of the Arts Council, as well as a biographer, novelist, playwright and short-story writer.

Although she wrote books about Jane Austen, Kipling and George Eliot, the volumes I found in a church jumble sale were her fictions. *The Village* is an evocative, unsentimental account of a couple separated by class in the Home Counties, and the shattering changes brought about by war and political change. *Little Boy Lost* tells the story of Hilary Wainwright, an English soldier, returning to a devastated France after the Second World War to trace the small boy who may be his son, lost five years before. Finding the child in a bleak orphanage, Hilary must consider the consequences of the reunion – what if the child is not his?

But it is her slender novel, *The Victorian Chaise-Longue*, that really got under my skin. Melanie, a young mother recovering from tuberculosis, is moved from her bed to a Victorian chaise-longue purchased in a junk shop. Falling asleep, she awakes in another sickened body in an earlier time, surrounded by solicitous strangers. The sights and smells of the Victorian era are seen through Melanie's modern senses as she tries to understand her plight.

The connecting bridge between the two eras of 1953 and the mid-1800s seems to be the chaise-longue itself, but Melanie cannot return because her earlier failing body keeps her trapped in the chair, and she is equally held in place by the repressive patrician attitude of the times. As her husband peers into her face looking for signs of life and seeing none, and others try to help but fail, we come to appreciate that she would have been trapped whether she'd been well or not.

The fable is eerie and disturbingly open to interpretation, and although two television versions were produced, the novel has largely been forgotten. Happily, Laski had a long and happy life. Appearing on Roy Plomley's *Desert Island Discs* in 1973, she chose a gold bracelet as her one luxury.

59

Michael McDowell

'I am a commercial writer and I'm proud of that,' said Alabama-born Michael McDowell. 'I think it is a mistake to try to write for the ages.'

McDowell's gothic deep-South novels appeared mainly as paperbacks in the golden age of the throwaway read, the early 1980s, but there's something about them that remains to inhabit the reader. McDowell earned high praise and good sales, producing some thirty volumes including mysteries, comedies, period adventures, psychological suspensers and family epics. He also adopted aliases for two sets of pastiche novels, one featuring a gay detective. Pointedly hailed by Stephen King as 'a writer for the ages', his prose was tight and his idiomatic dialogue was shorn of folksiness.

McDowell frequently returned to the idea of matriarchal revenge in his books, and his wonderfully conversational style made it feel as though he were imparting a terrible piece of gossip while describing all manner of disturbing events. It is generally accepted that his best book was *The Elementals*, in which two families fatefully clash during a summer holiday on a spit of land being slowly engulfed by tides and mournful spirits.

My guilty preference was for his six-volume 'Blackwater' serial, which chronicles a tragic fifty-year period in the lives of the Caskey family, whose women bear a strange affinity for water in all forms and whose vengeance knows no bounds. The baroque saga plays out like a gruesomely overheated Southern soap with fantastical overtones and outrageous cliffhangers, and is constructed for maximum page-turning efficiency. It also says something about the South's preoccupation with breaking levees and the omnipresent fear of inundation. The original paperbacks have sexy matching covers.

In *Gilded Needles*, McDowell creates a vivid historical tin-type of old New York that forms the backdrop to a nightmarish cascade of almost Jacobean retribution. In an extraordinary opening scene we fly over New York City, dipping down to observe lives lived in desperate circumstances. No one feels sorry for themselves; they accept their lot and make the best of what they have, but holding on to it is what spins the plot.

Once again we have two families, the aristocratic Stallworths and the lowly Shankses, one side taking revenge against the other. The slow build-up, shifting from Gramercy Park elegance to pawnshops, brothels, opium dens and beer houses, is designed to provide immense satisfaction when it delivers the goods. The drug-dipped needles of the title come into play as both families suffer losses, proving that revenge is a dish that satiates no one.

This time McDowell forgoes the opportunity to introduce any hint of the supernatural, instead concentrating on producing some of his most elegant and powerful prose. The author has an uncanny ability to deliver us into a world we can scarcely comprehend now; there's an early scene in which two children sing as they clear away a corpse in preparation for carting it off to medical students. It should appal, but simply feels right.

A late entry, *Cold Moon Over Babylon*, is set in the harvest season of a foggy Southern town, and has a marvellous feel for its location. McDowell frequently returns to the idea of being engulfed by natural forces, as man-made walls collapse and seas rise (in *The Elementals* sand pours in through the windows of an abandoned house), and he links these natural catastrophes to our own selfishness or blindness, flaws that leave dark stains on future generations. His characters are often powerless and insignificant in the face of time and nature.

McDowell was a creator of highly visual images, and wrote the classic comedy *Beetlejuice*, also collaborating on *The Nightmare Before Christmas*. Even when outlining horrific acts, there's a gentility and grace to McDowell's prose. He died shortly before his fiftieth birthday.

60

John McGlashan

Compared to other nations, the British reading public has a very odd attitude towards comics, cartoons and graphic novels. The *bande dessinée* art of France and Belgium is regarded as obscure and downright peculiar, Italy's *fumetti* are seen as excuses for sexist male fantasies, and Japan's *manga* comics, read by adults on every Tokyo subway, are dismissed as deranged fantasies. In the USA, Marvel has proven to be the saviour of Hollywood, yet various attempts to launch new illustrated narrative forms for adults in the UK invariably fail. We fear being considered childish because we still recall the *Beano*, the *Dandy* and *Viz*. As a result, we're missing out on an astonishingly rich area of literature.

Persepolis, by Iranian-born Marjane Satrapi, and *Logicomix*, about the foundational quest for mathematics, by a respected Greek novelist and a theoretical computer scientist, changed the playing field, and our ignorance about the power of the graphic narrative now seems churlish. Paul Gravett's indispensable guide, *1001 Comics*

You Must Read Before You Die, is an extraordinary work that carefully explains what we're missing and why. Thankfully he finds room for John Glashan, an Italian-Scottish artist who failed to make his name as a portrait painter.

One can't help feeling that Glashan chose the wrong subject matter, as he was rubbish at faces and brilliant with elaborate architectural detail. He dropped the 'Mc' from his name and became a cartoonist for *Lilliput* magazine, channelling his personal bitterness into his work but adding a level of joyful Scottish surrealism. Although his hand-lettered output often consisted of single panels, he had an epic eye and was drawn to grander, longer tales involving tiny bearded fools and insanely baroque, oppressive mansions. These stories juxtapose clever penniless tramps and greed-filled millionaire capitalists engaged in quests that lead to lunatic battles of wills.

Glashan delighted in placing inapposite words and phrases together, so that you're liable to find 'Mayfair' and 'fried bread', or 'chateau' and 'meths', in the same sentence. If surreal humour is an acquired taste, Glashan is the litmus test, and I've always been disappointed by those who fail it. The artist once stated that 'Being funny is not funny, humour is seriousness in disguise,' and the undertones of melancholic failure in his work make it all so much funnier. 'I have discovered the secret of the universe,' one of his characters tells another. 'If you give me all your money, I will tell it to you. If you go mad in the process, you don't get your money back.'

He published at least six collectable books, including *The Eye of the Needle*, *Speak Up You Tiny Fool*, *The Mental Health Workout Book* and *John Glashan's World* – but the wonderful 'Genius', featuring his hero Anode Enzyme, which appeared in the *Observer* magazine from

1978 to 1983, has never been collected. Enzyme discovered the meaning of the universe and listed its ingredients, which included 60 gallons of egg white, 25,000 feet of geranium wire and 40 lbs of thulium granules. Asked what form his genius takes, Enzyme replies, 'I can repair a chronometer whilst wearing motor-cycling gloves.'

Glashan also accepted peculiar commissions, including books about the lavatories of London and Paris, and illustrations for Helen Gurley Brown's *Sex and the Single Girl*, which ran to a 32-page supplement called '£ove $tory' and must have bemused the publishers.

He later happily settled to landscape painting, but it is a mystery that no complete compendium of his works has ever been published.

61

Julian Maclaren-Ross

I can't help thinking that decadence isn't all it's cracked up to be. From garrulous, gangrenous Jeffrey Bernard to stovepipe-hatted Sebastian Horsley, London's Soho dissolutes and dandies have proven an entertaining if somewhat trying tribe.

Maclaren-Ross fitted the classic profile of a brandy-breathed Soho *flâneur*. A handsome Scottish-Cuban Anglo-Indian educated in the South of France and the Bournemouth suburbs, he contributed to various literary magazines but never took one path for long, skiving and diving from one set of debts to the next, robbing Peter to pay Paul (sometimes literally), forever in need of a few bob, hastily following his suitcase out of windows and generally behaving like an utter cad.

But unlike many of his counterparts, Maclaren-Ross was the real deal. The story of his career is one of a spiralling descent, and his biographer Paul Willetts described him as 'the mediocre caretaker of his own immense talent'. In Anthony Powell's *A Dance to the Music of Time* he's fictionalized as the 'impecunious and thirsty bohemian' novelist X. Trapnel. Careless, feckless, cripplingly impractical, he squandered his grand ability, the talent to write like a dream. There are around twelve collections of his writings, but I haven't yet been able to track down any novels. One, *Until the Day She Dies*, begins, 'I am going to kill a girl called Francis Wilder, she has done me no harm, nor will I profit financially from her death, but I cannot rest in peace until the day she dies.'

Through the forties, fifties and sixties he remained one of the most colourful inhabitants of Soho and Fitzrovia (he could usually be found propping up the bar at the Fitzroy Tavern), and his collected memoirs are a scurrilous joy. He knew and wrote about Graham Greene, Cyril Connolly, Dylan Thomas, Nina Hamnett, Woodrow Wyatt and others, peppering his encounters with ever more fraught financial ploys involving delayed postal orders and postdated cheques. Always the dandy, with his waved hair, elegant overcoat and silver-topped malacca cane, and an effortlessly riveting raconteur, his shambolic life of short-leash rootlessness tacked around the fringes of the literary establishment, involving permanent insolvency and occasional bouts of homelessness.

He was also a dab hand at the long short story, and his novella about the smart set in Nice, *Bitten by the Tarantula*, is a cruel delight that acts as a reminder of the talent he tossed aside. His sharp comic timing and crisp, waspish dialogue owes so little to his own bibulous background that he must have become a different person when he sat down to write. His curse was to be born slightly out of time, too late for the Waugh set, too early for the Angry Young Men, but his biography is now back in print and his books have reappeared.

62

Richard Marsh

Here's an oddity, even by my standards.

The Beetle was a bizarre hybrid novel of supernatural romantic mystery published in 1897, the same year as *Dracula*, and initially it eclipsed the undead count's sales. Hysterical in tone, it concerned the worshipper of a secret Egyptian cult who possesses mesmeric shapeshifting powers, and his feverish pursuit of a British politician. Filled with swirling smoke, hypnotic commands and weird chemicals, it is told from four separate viewpoints and is really quite unique in the annals of Victorian literature.

But Richard Marsh didn't exist. In an act of prestidigitation worthy of the Beetle himself, he was one of the many aliases of Richard Bernard Heldmann, a high-living swindler who bilked innocent victims all over the country. When Heldmann was sent to jail for eighteen months, he killed his real name and reinvented himself as Marsh, then embarked upon a writing career.

Marsh managed seventy-six novels and collections of short stories, some of them very hurried and poorly written, but there was often an energetic fervour to his prose that has made his editions highly sought after. What's particularly interesting is how many times he wrote about characters with split personalities or false identities who end up in court. 'The Mask' features a lunatic female cross-dresser, and there's even a volume called *A Master of Deception*.

Another recurring theme in the novels is a fall from grace or a sudden massive reversal of fortunes. The author managed three novels a year, published through sixteen different houses, and was immensely popular, but *The Beetle* was his best book. Even in this, Marsh couldn't resist subterfuge, for the vampiric insect is actually an old man in a woman's body who can turn into a giant beetle 'with gluey feet'. The creature alters everyone it comes into contact with, smashing up the social order. In fact, almost everyone in the novel seems to shapeshift in some way, the most extreme being a smart young heroine who cuts her hair short and dresses as a tramp.

There's a possibly apocryphal story that Bram Stoker made a bet with him to see who could write the best supernatural novel that year. Why hasn't *The Beetle* survived as well as *Dracula*? It seems much more of a Victorian zeitgeist novel now, and is saturated with that decade's concerns, values and fears. At the last count, seventy-five of Marsh's books were out of print, but there's a very nice cheap edition of *The Beetle* available, and it's well worth reading in tandem with *Dracula*.

63

Arthur Mee

For readers of a certain age, this self-taught Victorian's name will ring a bell. Born near Nottingham in 1875, the second of ten children, Mee became a newspaper editor by the age of twenty and was soon the literary editor of the *Daily Mail*, where he expounded the patriotic, moral, temperance-driven views of his Baptist upbringing.

The editor of *The Harmsworth Self-Educator* ran a children's newspaper subtitled 'The most cheerful newspaper in the world' for forty-six years, but before we write him off as a bit of a pill, let's look at his masterwork, *The Children's Encyclopaedia*, which eventually ran to ten volumes. It's not an actual encyclopaedia but an 'encyclical', endlessly revolving around its data.

There's the usual jingoism that peppers books of this period, but also much to enjoy, even if Mee's contributors had a skewed grasp of world history. Each chapter ends with 'Things To Make & Do', including dolls made from clothes pegs, ice made without a freezer, how to fasten a door that has no lock, making cases for hankies and gloves, and the Chinese method of building railways (I found each of these by allowing a volume to fall open at a double page). Want to mark your name on fruit? Build an hour-glass? Keep a goat as a pet? Blow a brick over on a table? Here are some of the other burning issues of the day that Mee chose to tackle:

What to Make from an Elder Branch
How To Find Toadstools
The Story of Gas
Keeping Ants As Pets
Our Wonderful Glands
Crocheting a Pot-Holder for Empire Day
How to Cultivate a Monastery Garden
Flames That Would Shrivel Up The Earth
Things to Remember When Bathing
How George Eliot Lost Her Way in the World of Books

And . . .

What is wrong with this picture?
(Answer: 'The gentleman has buttoned his waistcoat incorrectly.')

The books are filled with the kind of questions asked by annoying children: Why do ship's masts taper to the top? Why don't fishes drown? How do fireworks get their colours? Unfortunately not all of the answers are entirely accurate. To the question, 'Why do some people lose their hair?' Mee answers, 'Because we do not trust our hair to do its natural work. Women do not get as bald as men because their hats do not interfere with the ventilation of the scalp'.

In an article on 'How to Build a British House', the final photograph showed a man standing on his roof behind actual crenellations, beneath a fluttering Union Jack, clenching a pipe stem between his teeth, staring pompously into the middle distance. Another article, entitled 'Things to See in London', included the Inigo Jones Watergate at the Adelphi (moved and forgotten), the Crystal Palace (moved and burned down) and, more obscurely, the W. T. Stead Memorial on the Embankment (Stead was a journalist and spiritualist who survived the sinking of the *Titanic*). The volumes were fascinating from an anthropological perspective, but also dusty, peculiar and vaguely offensive.

In the quiz, 'What is wrong with this room?', one answer reads: 'The maid is unable to use the coal scuttle without a handle.' There are also lovely magic tricks and puzzles that come from a time of Making One's Own Amusement, and an emphasis on encouraging children to do rather wonderful things, like making an orchard for a dining table and cutting up apples while leaving the skin intact. (To this day I can still perform a party trick that involves chopping a banana into slices without unpeeling it – it used to drive my mother mad.) There's poetry, art, biology, biography, history and literature – but also the alarming 'Must All Things End?' Indeed, many serious questions are asked, from why we should do good, to whether we should eat meat (surprisingly, vegetarianism receives a fair trial).

There are also sections exploring big ideas, like 'Instinct', 'Freedom', 'Immortality' and 'Liberalism'. Mee was keen on instilling enlightenment and adopted a similar approach for *London – Heart of the Empire and Wonder of the World*. He cheerfully admitted that he knew nothing about children, and has been the subject of much revisionist scorn, but he encouraged the young to think and create out of curiosity and pleasure, instead of passively idolizing celebrity.

64

Gustav Meyer

His photograph shows a fresh, innocent face above a tightly buttoned coat with the world's smallest lapels; he looks about twenty-one, which from my calculations would have placed him in Prague and made the year 1889.

He was the bastard son of Baron Karl von Varnbüler und zu Hemmingen, and at the age of twenty-four he decided to shoot himself in the head. He was interrupted in this endeavour by somebody slipping a pamphlet about the afterlife under his door, so he stopped to read it and started studying the occult, along with Eastern mysticism, various esoteric philosophies and yoga. And banking. He founded his own bank and became a member of the Golden Dawn – not, apparently, as mutually exclusive as you'd think.

In 1902 he was done for fraud; specifically, for using the dark arts in banking practices, clearly ahead of his time. Eleven years later he began his most enduring work, *The Golem*. He'd written satirical short stories, but this was something different. Although it was based on a traditional Talmudic story about a rabbi who makes a creature from clay (Adam being the first golem), that is not the plot of the novel. It was first published in serial form and remains the most accessible work by Meyer (now calling himself 'Meyrink'). Its final episode appeared just after the First World War had broken out, and the text is haunted by these gathering stormclouds. It is now barely possible to read without overlaying the subsequent tragedy of the ghettoes over it, as the innocent are manipulated by unseen individuals and organizations with shadowy powers.

Even so, the novel is hard to follow. It's ostensibly about a mentally unstable jeweller called Athanasius Pernath, his hallucinations and his continually altering identity. He seemingly becomes someone else after swapping hats with him, and the Golem appears as a coalescence of Jewish suffering, a physical manifestation of the ghetto. However, Meyer wasn't Jewish, and this is not, as is commonly assumed, a Jewish book; in Hebrew the word 'golem' simply means 'shapeless mass'. The book is a supernatural urban fantasy, the kind that might have vanished quickly after publication.

Instead, *The Golem* proved timely and touched a nerve. It became a huge success and was reprinted many times over. German nationalists were horrified and were quick to denounce the text. Meyer was a Buddhist who opposed the Church and the military, and the nationalists, fearing he would corrupt all who read him, sought a ban. Later his books were prohibited during the Nazi rise to power.

Other volumes of an even more esoteric mien followed. *The Angel of the West Window* is about the reincarnation of the

Elizabethan magus, Dr John Dee. It's exhausting, peculiar and confusing. Meyer's son Fortunat was crippled in a skiing accident and killed himself at the same age of Meyer's attempted suicide. The Golem, fully revived, lived on as the spirit of Jewish repression.

65

Margaret Millar

In the 1950s, there was a passion for psychoanalysis in US mystery novels. It underpinned several of Alfred Hitchcock's films – *Spellbound*, *Psycho*, *Vertigo* – and provided the motivation for many literary murderers.

Millar's twenty-seven novels were concise and short, very much the style back in the 1950s, but the ideas they contained were unusually complex. What elevated them was the rich psychology of her characters. She wrote with an unsentimental eye about the lonely, the failed, the insecure and the desperate, succinctly delineating their lives in just a few well-chosen phrases.

This is a hard trick to pull off; we're used to modern mysteries clocking in at over 400 pages with everything explained and examined, often to the detriment of the book. Millar offered you a small, clear window to a larger, murkier world. Like the better-known Shirley Jackson, she would show you the interior life of her fragile heroines, so that you could watch and empathize as they lost their grip on reality and slipped into madness. She was brilliant at revealing mental states, and her plots often hinged on the machinations of vulnerable people.

Adept at creating powerful visuals, it seems hardly surprising that Millar made a fan of Hitchcock and ended up working at Warner Bros. Her future fame would have been assured, but Bette Davis apparently turned down the lead role in Millar's brilliant suspenser *The Iron Gates* because she was off-screen for the last third of the book, so the film was never made. Thanks for that, Bette.

Millar was the true mistress of the surprise ending, carefully laying the groundwork that would lead to an entirely appropriate and organic reveal, especially in *Beast in View*. Helen Clarvoe, a wealthy 'old maid' (of thirty!) with low self-esteem, is harassed by a crazy woman and hires her lawyer to do something about it. Clarvoe is seemingly an example of what we now call a WIP (Woman In Peril). 'Behind her wall of money, behind her iron bars, Miss Clarvoe was the maiden in distress, crying out reluctantly and awkwardly for help.' Millar always plays fair with the reader, but by slowly revealing the psychological complexity of her characters she alters what we know or think we know.

To illustrate the point, I'm going to break a rule and reveal the ending of one of her short stories. In 'The Couple Next Door', a young mother is disappointed that the splendid isolation of her family's life will be ruined by new neighbours moving in. Their son makes friends with the other couple's son and spends more and more time at their house, but whenever his mother ventures over to welcome them to the neighbourhood she finds no one in. The boy explains that they're busy and successful, and, by implication, he finds this other family preferable to his own. The mother is gradually broken down by excited descriptions of her more glamorous rival, and after her son stays over there watching TV, her jealous anger boils over. Storming across the road to fetch him back, she finds the house derelict and her son sitting on the floor watching a dead TV screen. Her horror of having disappointed her child so much will never leave her.

Millar used three unconventional detectives, but her real interest lay in exploring the emotional lives of women of the 1940s and 1950s. Millar's marriage to the crime writer Ross MacDonald was feisty, but the arguments often resulted in the pair's best on-page dialogue. She never wrote with her husband, but it was said that their greatest collaboration was a mutual commitment to writing.

Her books fell from fashion partly because their psychology dated (one gay character kills himself after the shame of exposure) but now they can be read as period works. Intelligent populist fiction is partly about capturing the mindset of the times, something in which Millar excels. She once said, 'The real fear of the average adult must be what lies in the deepest shadows of his own mind.' Nearly all of her books have now returned to print.

The Forgotten Booker Authors

It's often pointed out that the purpose of publishing is to sell books, not to be the arbiters of taste. So who makes sure that good writers get public attention, and the whole industry doesn't disappear in a welter of *Top Gear* spin-offs?

We usually look to the agents, who can build a career on a single discovery. New York's Kirby McCauley rose to fame representing Stephen King, but also had George R. R. Martin, who attracted critical attention long before he started the 'Ice and Fire' book cycle that became the world-beating *Game of Thrones*. Deborah Rogers, who represented Ian McEwan, Peter Carey, Kazuo Ishiguro and Salman Rushdie, also worked for the thrill of discovering a new manuscript, placing excellence and innovation above market economics. The theatrical agent Peggy Ramsay became almost as famous as those writers she represented.

At this point it often takes another process to make a writer visible: a nomination for a major award. Nineteen sixty-nine saw the arrival of the Booker Prize for Fiction, and although in those first five years Muriel Spark, Iris Murdoch, Doris Lessing and Patrick White were all nominated, not only have many of the other nominees been forgotten, like Barry England, G. M. Williams and Terence Wheeler, but even some of the winners have disappeared from the collective memory.

Percy Howard Newby wrote some twenty-three novels, but was really only known for two things: increasing the amount of classical music on Radio 3 and winning the first Booker Prize with *Something to Answer For*, a dreamlike semi-thriller about a con man coming to accept the responsibility for his actions in a tumultuous Cairo.

Bernice Rubens wrote twenty-seven novels and won the next Booker in 1970 for a somewhat psychedelic tale of an amphetamine addict, *The Elected Member*. Several of her works were subsequently filmed, but most volumes have vanished. It's from writers like Rubens that we get the idea of the Booker trying too hard to represent zeitgeist works.

Around this time, J. G. Farrell won the Booker in spite of being dead (more on him later).

Stanley Middleton was a church organist, watercolour artist and reporter for *The Sunday Times* who won in 1974 for *Holiday*. This novel centres on a lecturer at a seaside resort, and (apart from its obvious quality) seems to have appealed to the judges because books which took place within the mind of the central character were very much in vogue. Middleton later refused an OBE because he felt he was just doing his job. In 2006 the opening chapter of his novel was resubmitted to publishers along with that of V. S. Naipaul's Booker winner *In A Free State*. Only one agent felt *Holiday* was publishable, while none wanted Naipaul's work.

Of course, hindsight is a wonderful thing. The only book that Margaret Mitchell ever published, *Gone With The Wind*, went on to win the Pulitzer Prize after being rejected by thirty-eight publishers.

Clearly, though, the Bookers were worried about their public image: too obscure, too fashionable, too impenetrable – the British press had a go at them whatever they did, so subsequent juries played it safe. For the next few years, tried and tested literary names won the prize – until the all-but-unknown Anita Brookner upset the apple cart by winning for *Hotel du Lac*. Readers turned into a living Bateman cartoon of shock and awe. It was readable, it was light and it wasn't a thousand pages long!

What's shocking now is to look at the nominees and winners and realize who lost: David Mitchell, Sarah Waters (twice), Beryl Bainbridge (five times), Ali Smith (three times). Another flirtation with readability saw Hilary Mantel win twice for a continuation of the same book. In 2016 it appeared that the Bookers might have returned to courting fashion by rewarding Paul Beatty's *The Sellout*, a coruscating, motor-mouthed satire about a black man who reintroduces slavery into his neighbourhood, described by the chair of the judges as 'a novel of our times'. Awards ceremonies are good for bringing prominence to literary BAME authors who might otherwise remain critically admired but under-read. However, in the history of popular writing in the UK they have been under-represented.

Roy A K Heath was born to a middle-class family in Guyana, and moved to the UK four years after the British Nationality Act of 1947 was passed. A committed Marxist, he studied modern languages and law in London, and became a schoolteacher before finding his voice on the page.

Heath's vivid stories had their roots in childhood memories, evoking a secretive society wherein families hid their damaging mistakes for generations. His Armstrong trilogy, *From the Heat of the Day*, *One Generation* and *Genetha*, powerfully evoked his homeland

and gained new admirers, although most of his praise came from literary circles. In 1991 he was Booker shortlisted for *The Shadow Bride*, overtly about a domineering mother's attempts to control her doctor son, but more broadly about the identity crisis created within a displaced community.

Although he only wrote about life in his childhood homeland, his work explores psychological landscapes as much as geographical ones. His greatest success came with the powerful, pessimistic psychological thriller *The Murderer,* about a man with destructive low self-esteem, also brought about by an authoritarian matriarch. Salman Rushdie considered Heath a beautiful writer and described the novel as 'unforgettable'. It went on to win the 1978 Guardian Fiction Prize. Heath's son became one of the founders of the Europop band Urban Cookie Collective.

Another Guyanese writer, Mike Phillips, became known for his excellent crime fiction (he has a secondary claim to fame; while working at Islington Library he met Joe Orton, who was busy defacing their books) but outside the Booker sphere, paperback fiction remains disproportionately unrepresentative.

What lessons can we draw from all of this? That agents concentrate on market forces while judging panels play a broader field? The picture is complex, but we can only judge the works for ourselves if we can track them down. In 2010 the Lost Man Booker Prize gave credit to twenty-two titles from an anomalous missing year. Nina Bawden said she had no recollection of writing her entry and Patrick White, who detested literary prizes so much he had asked to be struck off the list of nominees for the 1979 Booker prize, must have been spinning in his grave at being listed. Perhaps it's the reading public who ensure longevity, not judges.

66

Clifford Mills

Once upon a time, *Where the Rainbow Ends* was a book considered ideal for every young child's bedroom. In it, one illustration showed a girl being yanked into a shadowy forest by homunculi with razor-sharp claws, her pale English arms striped with crimson scars. It was captioned, 'Rosamund is Dragged into the Black Wood by Imps'. Even as a child, I had a bad feeling about what the author was suggesting.

The author was Clifford Mills, who wrote the piece as a Christmas entertainment with music for adults and children, and opened it at the Savoy in 1911 with Jack Hawkins and Noël Coward among the forty kids in the cast. The show was produced by Italia Conti. It was *Rainbow*'s phenomenal success that led to Conti setting up her children's acting school.

In fact, 'Clifford Mills' was a woman who had taken her husband's name to write the play, which concerns an 'ordinary' group of children, led by Rosamund and naval cadet Crispin (although in my edition they live in an incredibly grand house and own a lion cub permanently dressed in red, white and blue), who are visited by St George and travel to the titular land via a threadbare magic carpet called Faith.

The directions for how to reach the land where the rainbow ends are hidden in a library, and Crispin summons his best friend Blunders to help. Once they reach the far-off kingdom, the children must fight their evil aunt and uncle, and take on the Dragon King. Poor Rosamund is promptly tied to a tree and left to be eaten by hyenas. St George fights the Dragon King on a tower and all ends happily.

The play became a best-selling novel that delighted generations of children who failed to notice its racist tones. Much mention is made of the St George's flag and the rightness of being an Englishman, while the magic-carpet genie appears to be swarthy, hook-nosed and sinister. A magic-potion turns out to be labelled 'EMPIRE MIXTURE: Poison to Traitors' – it kills the evil uncle and aunt, and they're eaten by the hyenas. A frontispiece shows four blue-eyed, blond children staring adoringly at the red and white flag. There's also a character called Schnapps, who is 'German with Jewish blood'.

Rosamund asks protection of St George by telling him, 'I am an English maiden in danger and I seek your aid.' The stage play ended with St George coming to the footlights and crying out, 'Rise, Youth of England, let your voices ring, For God, for Britain, and for Britain's King,' at which point everyone jumped up and sang the National Anthem. Strewth.

For forty years, *Where the Rainbow Ends* was as big as *Peter Pan* – it had everything: goblins, elves, a magic carpet, a battle between good and evil, horrible foreigners, songs and a cuddly animal. Unfortunately it had something else in it: the roots of fascism.

And a personal footnote here. Remembering nothing of the book's disturbing undercurrents, I tried to buy the edition I'd owned as a child, and after much hunting found a copy for sale in Kent. I spoke to a very nice lady who said she would send it to me for the princely total of £7. When it arrived, it was indeed the version I'd owned. Opening the front cover I found my name written inside, aged seven.

67

Gladys Mitchell

Ah, the Mad Miss Mitchell! She was one of the 'Big Three' female mystery novelists, judged the equal of Dorothy L. Sayers and Agatha Christie, but that's not quite accurate – she's more like a mad combination of both, and she wrote for a very long time.

Philip Larkin adored Mitchell and many admired her mordant and morbid mysteries. Diana Rigg starred in some bland TV versions of her novels that turn her Mrs Bradley character into a glamorous flapper. (You can imagine TV executives discussing Miss Marple: 'Can't we make her thirty-five?') The exposure has resulted in new demand for her books, which is good because they're more interesting than Christie's, if more problematic. *The Rising of the Moon* and a few others have been republished, but there are some sixty-six volumes to choose from, some madder than others.

Mitchell's old lady detective has little of Miss Marple's cosiness. She certainly doesn't care much for other people. In *Hangman's Curfew* it's said that, 'Mrs Bradley herself kept out of the invalid's way for almost the whole of the fortnight. This was partly for the invalid's sake, but largely for her own.' She's physically repulsive, thrice married and witch-like, parchment-skinned and usually likened to a vulture or even a pterodactyl. 'If you're trying to be insulting . . .' rails one character in *Tom Brown's Body*. 'I'm not only trying, I'm succeeding,' replies Mrs Bradley. In *Dead Men's Morris* she's described as having 'the maternal anxiety of a boa-constrictor which watches its young attempting to devour their first donkey'.

Mitchell was a schoolteacher who believed in the idea of the professional, progressive, blunt-spoken and somewhat Sapphic woman. Her title character was controversial and emancipated, and even considered murder justifiable if the occasion demanded. With such an outspoken heroine, Mitchell naturally made enemies. The *Spectator* described her as 'a tiresome old trout' whose mannerisms were the most trying in detective fiction, but many (myself included) were delighted to discover her work. Her murder cases sometimes have ambiguous solutions, and an air of the supernatural is never entirely banished from them. Her characters have lunatic names and sometimes speak in hilariously cockney dialect. Her plots are on the farthest side of credulity and occasionally go overboard. But to worry about realism is to miss the fun of Mitchell's storytelling.

In *Merlin's Furlong* a necromantic don runs a coven of witches. In *The Mystery of a Butcher's Shop* the victim is minced into sausages and hung from hooks. Ultimately, Christie remained safer and more controlled, while the wild-eyed complexity of Mitchell's uber-eccentric mysteries eventually got the better of her. Mitchell tested the constraints of the murder genre by pushing them to breaking point, and by surprising too much, she sometimes disappointed – therein lies the clue to her canonical absence. But a flawed gem can still sparkle brightly; better an alluring failure than an underachieving success.

68

Brian Moore

There are too many Brian Moores. The less-discovered Moore is the Irish-Canadian novelist who wrote a number of haunting novels, often concerning life in Northern Ireland, exploring the Troubles and the Blitz. Born into a family of nine children in Belfast, 1921, he rejected Catholicism and explained his personal beliefs through the characters of torn priests and strong women.

Not that you'd know this from his early works; *Wreath for a Redhead*, *This Gun for Gloria* and *A Bullet for My Lady* aren't exactly masterpieces. Moore wrote thrillers under two pseudonyms while perfecting his craft, and yet there are signs of what was to follow.

Then came *Judith Hearne*, the story of an alcoholic piano teacher subsisting in rented rooms, which gains its heartbreaking power from the simplicity of clear prose. It was later filmed as *The Lonely Passion of Judith Hearne* with Maggie Smith and Bob Hoskins, but the movie is hard to find. Five of Moore's novels became films, and he scripted for both Alfred Hitchcock and Claude Chabrol, although he described the writing of *Torn Curtain* as 'awful, like washing floors'.

Financed by a grant from the Guggenheim, Moore moved to New York. He often returned to the subject of isolated outsiders facing the consequences of their actions, from the rabble-rousing missionary in *No Other Life* and the fascist officer awaiting discovery in *The Statement* to the conflicted priest living among Canada's Algonquin Indians in the harrowing *Black Robe*.

He was Graham Greene's favourite living novelist, mainly, one suspects, because he was able to explore the paradoxical dilemmas of faith, morality, redemption and loss within the structure of popular thriller writing. In *The Magician's Wife*, a Parisian prestidigitator is dispatched to Algeria by Emperor Napoleon III to trick the natives into believing that a Christian Frenchman can perform miracles, but his wife is not so easily hoodwinked. It's a typical *tour de force* from a truly international novelist who was thrice nominated for the Booker Prize (and should have won). To date he is the subject of three biographies.

Perhaps his least appreciated novel is *The Great Victorian Collection*, an exuberant fantasy in which a young assistant history professor dreams of an open-air market filled with a dazzling collection of priceless Victoriana, only to awake and find it standing outside his window. Now he must take care of it, and as we know, grand possessions come with a price.

Are Moore's novels popular fictions or literature? Of anyone in this book, he stands most on the dividing line. His books are effortless to read, pithy, unfashionably short, but thematically expansive. Today they would unquestionably be regarded as literary fiction, so that's where we'll put him. Moore died in 1999.

69

J. B. Morton

We revere Monty Python, so why don't we remember Morton? Britain does silly very well, and Morton was very silly indeed. G. K. Chesterton described him as a 'huge thunderous wind of elemental and essential laughter'. He was appropriately born in Tooting in 1893, the son of a serious journalist and theatre critic. Two years after his mother's death he was packed off to Harrow, which he detested and later recreated as the fictional Narkover School, seeing it as a sort of boys' St Trinian's.

Having decided to become a poet, he then realized that the pay was inadequate and started writing for a musical revue. The war put paid to that and he enlisted, heading off to the trenches with the Royal Fusiliers. Shellshocked in the Somme, he was switched to intelligence and wrote a novel about his experiences, *The Barber of Putney*.

Following in his father's footsteps didn't work out – he felt uncomfortable being an intrusive reporter – and he began a column,

'By the Way', on the leader page of the *Daily Express*. The column's title was changed to 'Beachcomber' and reflected his literary editor D. B. Wyndham Lewis's darkly surreal sense of humour (perhaps it was no coincidence that Wyndham Lewis was later involved in the development of the St Trinian's stories).

Morton made the anonymously penned column his own, filling it with rants about red tape, pretentious art, motor cars and public schools. It was hand-written (he never learned to type) and its gallery of grotesque characters, including twelve red-bearded dwarves and Mr Justice Cocklecarrot, were something of an acquired taste. A typical quote from the column reads: 'Not many of our old families can boast that a Savile Row tailor calls four times a year at their country estates to measure the scarecrows in the fields for new suits.' No, it didn't have me rolling on the floor either, but humour is a very personal thing, and Morton's small clique of ardent fans have proven loyal for a very long time.

Over at the *Daily Mirror*, meanwhile, William Connor wrote a regular humorous column under the name of 'Cassandra', which was suspended during the Second World War. After the war he recommenced his column with 'As I was saying before I was so rudely interrupted . . .'

Morton's first collection, *A London Farrago*, appeared in 1922, followed by another eighteen volumes over the next thirty years, whereas I could only find one collection by Cassandra. Despite being depicted as a young woman in the column's header, Morton's identity slipped out. It would have been hard to keep him down anyway; his roaring, bibulous, thick-set figure was known in all the Fleet Street pubs. He became a great friend of Hilaire Belloc and forever staged practical jokes, once littering Virginia Woolf's doorstep with dozens of empty brown ale bottles (now *that* I can appreciate).

Rediscovered by *Private Eye*'s Richard Ingrams, he found new fame and his popular radio show ran until 1994. Morton became lost and confused after the death of his wife, and entered a care home as his house was bulldozed and his papers were destroyed. He was a huge influence on Spike Milligan. Once, everyone knew Beachcomber; now he's largely forgotten.

70

Peter Nichols

While novels remain yellowing on shelves, most plays are ephemeral, vanishing after a brief trot around the theatre circuit. Nichols's plays proved more robust and cinematic – several were filmed – but he didn't go into the theatrical repertoire as much as his less demanding peers, and consequently disappeared in a theatreland glutted with jazz-hands musicals.

Nichols was born in Bristol in 1927, which threw him into the war in his teens. A contemporary of the equally brilliant Charles Wood, who wrote about the corrupting allure of war in a surreal, densely poetic style that demanded much of audiences, he began writing television plays (when there were such things), but where Wood frequently wrote about incompetence and survival, Nichols has always been harder to pin down in choice of subject matter. His work was often autobiographical. *A Day in the Death of Joe Egg* had been inspired by his own experiences of raising a child with cerebral palsy, and although a deeply compassionate piece, it's still profoundly shocking today. The play frequently breaks the fourth wall as Bri, the handicapped girl's father, talks to the audience with disturbing honesty about his child, thus providing himself and his wife with a coping mechanism.

Nichols clearly enjoyed making audiences uncomfortable. *The National Health* was a zeitgeist play presenting Britain as an ailing patient, as soap-opera medics fall in love while, in the real world, an imploding, cash-strapped, overworked NHS hospital proves unable to cope with the sick, who die in an atmosphere of indifference and exhaustion.

Privates on Parade rendered Nichols's ENSA experiences into dramatic form as the ditzy members of the Song and Dance Unit South East Asia, under the command of queeny Captain Terri Dennis, end up running guns on a hellish tour of Malaysia that sees most of them shot dead or wounded. Dennis is a glorious creation, screamingly camp and fiercely brave, with a penchant for the dressing-up box and a disrespectful range of one-liners: 'That Bernadette Shaw, nags away from arsehole to breakfast-time but never sees what's staring her in the face.'

In some ways Nichols's most subversive play was *Poppy*, which reimagined the Chinese opium wars in the form of a Christmas pantomime complete with panto cow, dame and cross-dressed principal boy. At one point the audience is encouraged to rise and join in a singalong about the appalling behaviour of British troops, while Dick Whittington's sister ends up a junkie. That this could be installed at the Adelphi Theatre in a spectacular Royal Shakespeare Company production says a lot about theatre's present low ambitions.

Nichols's rehabilitation into the theatrical pantheon always seems to be on the cards, but hasn't quite happened yet, although his clever study of marital infidelity, *Passion Play*, has been revived. The playwright-novelist Michael Frayn said about him: 'He doesn't have any of the techniques of self-censorship that other writers develop. Sometimes he says terrible things that no one else would say that absolutely strike home to one's heart, and sometimes he says things that are embarrassing. But that is part of being a dangerous writer.'

A terrific autobiography, *Feeling You're Behind*, began with this frank disclaimer about why Nichols wrote it: 'I needed the advance the publishers offered, which was far more generous than any given to me for a play; the theatre itself, once so alluring, now seemed past its best, the wrinkles showing . . . it would be a bitter pleasure to describe my disenchantment and blame the people who'd done me down; and if I didn't write a book about me, it was clear no one else would.' It was followed by an enlightening set of diaries covering Nichols's key years in the theatre.

There was another reason why Nichols stopped writing for the proscenium arch: budgetary restrictions kicked in, demanding that cuts be made to plays which had been written for richer, more expansive times.

It's a great shame. Clearly, theatre needs his angry, daring humanity more than ever.

71

Bill Naughton

Writers don't necessarily know what form their work will eventually take. While Peter Nichols was clearly drawn to plays at the outset, others, like Naughton, started in one format and found success in another.

Naughton came from relative poverty in County Mayo, Ireland, then moved to Bolton, where he worked as a lorry driver and a weaver. After the Second World War, the arts in Britain were pushing away from cut-crystal portrayals of upper-middle-class life and starting to take inspiration from the lives of ordinary working-class men and women. Naughton used his background to explore issues of family, religion and community in novels like *A Roof Over Your Head* and *One Small Boy*.

His radio play, *June Evening*, adapted and finally televised in 1960, was probably the one with the most lasting effect. At the time it caused a sensation as an early 'kitchen sink' TV play, nine months before *Coronation Street* began. Naughton had reason to be convinced that Granada appropriated his idea of setting a story around a single fictitious Lancashire Street with a corner shop. After all, it's what television networks do.

With the 'swinging' sixties approaching, Naughton found himself belatedly capturing the national zeitgeist and chronicling the changing times, especially in relation to sex. *Spring and Port Wine* revealed the stress-cracks in the traditional family, then there was *Alfie*, the adventures of a cockney Casanova who couldn't take his life or his women seriously. It began as a radio play and cemented Michael Caine's reputation in its film incarnation.

Naughton's play *All in Good Time* was also filmed, as *The Family Way*, with Hywel Bennett (and an elegant Paul McCartney score). The latter concerned a young couple's inability to consummate their marriage because of family pressures. Both were unnecessarily remade in recent years, while *Alfie* spawned a negligible sequel by Naughton himself, *Alfie Darling*, in 1970.

While he was producing plays, novels and memorable short stories like 'The Goalkeeper's Revenge', Naughton also kept a diary that he said would one day provide the key to all of his writing, to be entitled 'The Dream Mind'. To date, this has never been published.

If we place him beside Beckett, Pinter, Sillitoe, Orton and Osborne as one of the key literary figures of the post-war years, it's surprising how little of Naughton's work has remained in print. Certainly, many now consider Alfie's attitude towards women repellent by today's standards, but perhaps the answer lies within *Coronation Street*, which evolved from neo-realist roots to become a ludicrously camp parody of Northern life.

72

Emma Orczy

The Hungarian-born British novelist Baroness Emma Magdolna Rozália Mária Jozefa Borbála 'Emmuska' Orczy de Orci is not unknown but certainly unread in the UK nowadays. Her family left Budapest in fear of a peasant revolution and she fetched up in Great Portland Street, virtually penniless; there weren't too many occupations for a deposed baroness in late nineteenth-century London.

Her first novel, *The Emperor's Candlesticks*, published in 1899, was a failure, but she started producing pulpish mystery fiction, creating the first female detective with official status, the spirited feminist Lady Molly of Scotland Yard, a logic-minded armchair sleuth and a *Better Call Saul*-like dubious lawyer. Orczy also had some paintings hung in the Royal Academy. Although her literature is not to today's taste, the prose being overwrought and sentimental, it's certainly very pacy. Her characters tend to SHOUT! at each other in capitals and exclamations.

This style of gesticulatory melodrama went down a storm with

Edwardians. Emma proved hugely popular and is still collected today in historical and mystery anthologies of a more esoteric nature. She and her husband wrote a play about an English aristocrat named Sir Percy Blakeney, who rescued French royals during the revolution (an understandable choice, given her background). Much to their surprise it ran in London for four years, so Orczy novelized it.

The result was *The Scarlet Pimpernel*, a title so popular that it eventually entered the English language as a synonym for 'elusive', although in fact it's a small and rather pretty flower. More than a dozen sequels followed, and with the proceeds the Baroness was able to buy an estate in Monte Carlo. As you would.

Her style isn't the only thing working against her in terms of finding a modern audience. Being pro-aristocrat, she was profoundly in favour of British militarism and imperialism, and she was able to recruit many female volunteers during the First World War.

She wrote fifty-two novels and nine short-story collections, continuing until 1947, and found a nostalgic readership among those who faced the declining empire and the horrors of two global wars.

But why was the Pimpernel such a hit? He had a secret identity, switching from chinless fop to sword-swishing swashbuckler and escape artist; was shamelessly old-school in his politics, but found goodness in the solid yeoman stock of Britons; had his own catchphrase ('They seek him here, they seek him there . . .'); and, according to the Baroness, had been willed into existence by God. Amazingly, he's still in print. The Pimpernel has become an archetype, but it seems that nobody's seeking his creator.

73

Edward John Moreton Drax Plunkett

If that name doesn't ring a bell, try the 18th Baron Dunsany. He had an estranged brother, Admiral the Right Honourable Sir Reginald Aylmer Ranfurly Plunkett-Ernle-Erle-Drax, but let's not go there. Dunsany was an Anglo-Irish writer who lived in Ireland's longest-inhabited dwelling, Dunsany Castle, where he wrote novels, short stories, one-act plays, poems and essays. The dashing six-foot-four Baron was born in 1878, and was a huntsman, cricketer, chess and pistol-shooting champion of Ireland. After Eton, Sandhurst and the Coldstream Guards he married an Earl's daughter, Lady Beatrice Child-Villiers.

However, if you picture a bluff, no-nonsense aristo with little time for foolishness, you'd be wrong. Dunsany was an animal rights campaigner and a writer of the most extraordinarily detailed whimsical fantasies, which may sound like dabbling but was quite the opposite. His wonder-worlds are remarkably well realized, and populated by elves, fairies, trolls, gods and various immortals who, although clearly supernatural, possess the damaging characteristics of humans.

His tale 'How Nuth Would Have Practised his Art upon the Gnoles' features a thief who steals to order for people who have seen something covetable during their stays in country houses. Nuth and his sidekick Tonka are commissioned to swipe emeralds from the Gnoles, who are extremely sinister and do something awful to Tonka; his fate is not described, but still sends a chill down the reader's spine.

Strongly supported by his wife, Dunsany worked with a quill pen and supposedly never rewrote a word. He was a fashioner of worlds, and many images haunt, so that he fits rather peculiarly between Richard Dadd and the Moomins.

His most popular volumes were *The King of Elfland's Daughter* and *The Book of Wonder*, but I like the Jorkens stories, in which a portly, bibulous member of the Billiards Club unfolds fantastic tales to anyone who'll stump up for a drink. In writing these, Dunsany founded a literary archetype: the unreliable club raconteur.

In his own long lifetime Dunsany was better known for his successful plays and to some extent his poetry, as well as three volumes of memoirs, but his highly influential fantasies have stood the test of time well because they lack topicality.

There have been many film and TV adaptations over the years, rarely under their original titles and usually much altered, so that Dunsany's name has been unjustly forgotten. However, thanks to a dedicated fan base, his works are partially back in print. A second Edward Plunkett, the first's grandson, was an artist much feted for his portraiture and his beautiful abstract works.

74

Thomas Love Peacock

To say that Thomas Love Peacock is an acquired taste is something of an understatement. He's up there with Ronald Firbank in the oddity stakes, but in a very different way.

The English satirist was born in 1785 in a naval family. He moved to London in his teens, became a city clerk and taught himself poetry at the British Museum's Reading Room. Earning his crust as a private secretary to a naval fleet commander, he began to make a serious study of French, Italian and English literature. His minor poems (including one long one about the Thames, which he loved all his life) brought him to the attention of Shelley, who recognized his virtues as a romantic classicist. They remained close friends until the latter's death in 1822.

Peacock wrote a series of seven satirical novels which remain impossible to categorize and challenging to read; you need to know your classics to catch all of the allusions.

For a satirist Peacock is remarkably good-natured, but his

novels are rambling, vague and highly peculiar – so why should we remember him? Probably because the idea of the English aesthetic author has vanished, probably forever. *Nightmare Abbey* is what you might get if you removed the plot from *Gormenghast* and crossed the remains with Firbank's *The Flower Beneath the Foot*. It appeared in 1818, the same year as *Frankenstein*, with which it acts as a sort of bookend. The novel is so abstruse, and witty, and disconnected from everything, that it seems best to stumble from one page to the next and merely enjoy the juxtaposition of words. At one point a conversation about Dante turns into a complaint about readers, then writing and mermaids, and ends with a terrible song. There are discussions on ghosts and sea creatures, and the book doesn't so much end as stop. My paperback version is so old that some of the pages fell out, and it didn't feel entirely necessary to put them back in the right order.

Crotchet Castle, written thirteen years later, functions as a companion piece to *Nightmare Abbey*, and is longer but no more enlightening. Both lapse into theatrical dialogue packed with aphorisms when Peacock can't be bothered to scene-set anymore. His tales have no structure, wafer-thin characters, little human interest, and usually consist of people sitting around tables half-heartedly discussing the intellectual topics of the day, yet there's something here that can keep you reading. Peacock's books are a window to the past, and we feel we are eavesdropping on the kind of drunken, heady conversations English intellectuals must have had in pubs for centuries.

After the death of his mother, the inconsolable author stopped writing for a quarter-century, returning for a late finish before dying from injuries sustained in trying to save his library from a fire.

In a publishing world driven by hard commercial decisions, stumbling across such authors is like finding a secret garden filled with rare blooms.

Forgotten For Writing Too Little – and Too Much

There were authors who wrote just one novel and others who wrote a thousand, now all equally forgotten. Quantity has very little to do with quality (look at John Kennedy Toole and Harper Lee). Let's check out some authors who wrote too little, and some who wrote far too much.

Beware the novel that bears the legend 'Soon To Be A Major Film', for the film won't be made and the book is bound to vanish. Such was the fate of *The Auctioneer* by Joan Samson, a cautionary tale that took America by storm and became a bestseller. Hollywood came calling, and then – nothing. Samson only completed this one novel in her lifetime, although she was working on a second at the time of her death. *The Auctioneer* uses a popular trope in US literature: the sinister stranger who arrives in town and causes havoc. Perly Dunsmore is a charismatic auctioneer who arrives with a request for donations to support the police, and as his power grows the townspeople soon find themselves surrendering a lot more than their rusty tools and dusty furniture. The tale is a fable about the inexorably spiralling effect of power.

Charles Maclean's big novel was the astonishing metaphysical page-turner *The Watcher*. It was optioned in the early 1980s by, if memory serves, none other than Paul Newman, who bravely planned to star in a film version of it.

It seems likely that Mr Newman never managed to crack the on-screen presentation of the first scene, in which the nice, ordinary hero, Martin Gregory, takes an electric carving knife to his wife's dogs and presents them to her at breakfast. But here's the twist: Gregory has no idea why he should commit this bizarre atrocity, and psychiatric scrutiny reveals his action to be the outward result of a much greater ongoing war involving past lives. The trouble with the novel lies with its unlikeable protagonist, its over-complex plot and an inconclusive ending, although it's still a powerful, unique read. Apparently Stephen King was influenced by the book enough to write an homage, *Needful Things*.

A happier fate befell another one-off, *Burnt Offerings* by Robert Marasco, a classic haunted-house thriller in which the supernatural is used to explore materialism and the pressures of modern life. A seemingly perfect family comes apart at the seams after moving to a beautiful white clapboard house. Father attacks son, wife grows distrustful, mother ages from feistiness to senility, and as their misery compounds, the house flourishes. This one did make it to the screen, with the unlikely acting combination of hellraisers Bette Davis and Oliver Reed.

One-hit wonders are more trouble to publishers than they're worth: create a readership for the book and the readers may have nowhere else to go. The twisting psychological thriller *Blood Secrets*, by Craig Jones, played like a non-supernatural *Rosemary's Baby* and was championed by John Irving. Hollywood came calling. By now you know the rest.

Erich Segal was a competitive runner who wrote the screenplay for The Beatles's tiresomely twee film *Yellow Submarine*, and in 1970 there was one book everyone was talking about: *Love Story*, a mawkish boy-meets-soon-to-die-girl tale that was translated into thirty-three languages. Even the typeface on its cover became copied and is parodied to this day (indeed, some would argue that the novel owed its success to brilliant marketing). Seven years later a redundant sequel, *Oliver's Story*, appeared and flopped. But often one big hit is all it takes to change an author's life.

There's nothing wrong with only producing one measly book. Harper Lee once more became a discussion point all over the English-speaking world for producing a prequel to her only novel, the short but powerful *To Kill a Mockingbird*.

Interestingly, few readers recall the names of the most prolific authors in history.

At the top of the 'One Thousand Club' is Spanish writer Maria Lopez, born 1927, who hammered out more than 4,000 execrable novels. She's followed by Brazilian pulp writer and thoracic surgeon Ryoki Inoue, with 1,100 books. He worked under nearly forty identities and could knock off a chapter in the bathroom. In the time that it took the *Guinness Book of Records* to confirm his proficiency he had delivered a further fifteen titles, so it's safe to say that writer's block was never much of a problem. I imagine the one thing that unites these writers is RSI.

After him comes Kathleen Lindsay, born in 1903, who wrote 904 books under eleven pseudonyms. Her romances had titles that sounded like perfume brands: *Wind of Desire*; *Harvest of Deceit*.

There are other inexhaustible authors of passing interest; Kyokutei Bakin was an eighteenth-century Japanese author who wrote one of the longest books in the world, a 106-volume story called *Hakkenden* ('Chronicle of the Eight Dog Heroes'). It took twenty-eight years to complete and he went blind in the process, but it remains popular and has been adapted many times.

Also making the cut is Nigel Morland, real name Carl Van Biene, who became the secretary of the almost-as-prolific Edgar Wallace. He began as a ghostwriter, or what the French then charmingly called a 'literary negro', and set about creating his own detectives, including Mrs Palmyra Pym, who first appeared in *The Phantom Gunman* (1935). As was once the fashion, his heroine was employed by Scotland Yard, who were happy to have a busybody running around their crime scenes.

G. W. M. Reynolds was probably the busiest Victorian writer of them all, with at least thirty-seven fat novels to his name. He spoke *guernesiais*, so-called 'Channel Islands French', and became famous for his descriptions of grave-robbing, so realistically rendered that it was suggested he had insider information from his guardian.

It's hard to tell now where Reynolds the Penny Blood Writer ends and Reynolds the Teller of Whopping Fibs begins. Was he really a jewel thief? Did he really befriend the elderly Beau Brummel? We know he was repeatedly bankrupt and impoverished, an atheist and a political radical.

His work *The Mysteries of London* appeared in twelve volumes between 1844 and 1856, and are now hailed, somewhat dubiously, as the first steampunk novels. His books were designed to be read aloud to illiterate costermongers. Reynolds mixed the social realism of Dickens with melodrama, sex, violence and some very hasty writing, but it's hard to take against a man who once owned a bookshop called La Librairie des Étrangers. His tales of blackmailers, whores and resurrection men proved incredibly popular in India well into the twentieth century and, much like the resurrection men's contraband, have recently resurfaced.

Considering John Creasey is largely out of print, the facts about him are staggering. The English thriller writer was one of the most prolific authors of all time, producing 562 books under twenty-eight different pseudonyms. Even he had no recollection of some of his titles, and to date no comprehensive catalogue of his works has ever been completed. Although he received 743 rejection slips for his work, his sales totalled around 2.5 million copies a year, and he was awarded an MBE. He created eleven different series, writing longhand, and revised each volume half a dozen times before sending it out. He wrote with a special typewriter that was equipped with three extra keys (if you know what they were, let me know), and it took him around a week to finish a book. Creasey once said in an interview, 'Occasionally I find that a new plot is becoming a little vague because I am concentrating on too many at once.'

Finally, proving that you can write more than once about anything, Eden Philpotts turned out 127 novels with Dartmoor settings, not counting his short fiction, plays, non-fiction and poetry. But that's not all; he also wrote under a pseudonym. He was an agnostic in Victorian Britain so he presumably had Sundays free. Funnily enough, his work can still be found in the Dartmoor area.

Now we come to the all-time king of the sales figures. What's the most successful science-fiction story series ever written? How about one that has sold, with its various spin-offs, over *two billion* copies so far, and has influenced a generation of writers? *Perry Rhodan* was created in 1961 by K. H. Scheer and Clark Darlton, and was conceived as a thirty-volume epic with a single-story arc, back in the days when you could attempt such a thing.

When it reached the end of its run, such was the appetite for the series, whose main character was space explorer Rhodan, that it has continued to the present day, heading for nearly 3,000 instalments – so why have we never heard of it?

Well, despite being German, it was first published in English as far back as 1969, thanks to Forrest J. Ackerman, the editor of *Famous Monsters of Filmland*. His wife made the translations, and it continued in English with a variety of writers and translators. Perry was so popular in Brazil that Flash Gordon was renamed after him (Alex Raymond, the creator of Flash, had died in 1956).

Rhodan's exploits were inspired by the Russian–US space race, and rode the wave of euphoria that accompanied the moon landings, adding comic strips, collectables, encyclopaedias, audio plays and various pieces of music and art to the novels (the composer of TV's *Babylon 5* released an album inspired by Rhodan). The early books are juvenile and workmanlike, and while most of the dialogue is wretched, the plotlines became relatively complex.

Perry's subsequent authors stepped into one another's moonprints, utilizing an extremely adaptable prosaic style, but they did something few others had attempted, employing popular physics theories to create an immense cosmology of unified cycles, 'grand cycles' and themes, encompassing negaspheres and neuroverses, chronofossils and netrunners (no, me neither).

I have a low tolerance level for what Victoria Wood once christened the 'interplanetary ming-mongs' school of SF writing, but it's not hard to appreciate the youthful appeal of a fully formed alternative moral and physical interplanetary system.

George Lucas points out that many of the starships in *Star Wars* were influenced by Perry Rhodan, who even made it into space when a Dutch astronaut took one of the magazines with him, but while most English-speaking SF buffs claim to hate the series, they missed its development into a more complex and intelligent universe because by 1980 the stories were no longer being translated.

Perry's many authors created the grandest SF space opera ever written, but you'll mostly find only German copies available. Some American paperbacks exist sporting matching cover art by Gray Morrow, and are very collectable.

So the question remains: how many books make an author memorable? From the evidence we've seen so far, fewer are better than many. The reading public likes to tie a simple tag on a writer, and that's tougher to do when the writer has many faces.

75

Joyce Porter

What sort of writer numbers their books *One*, *Two* and *Three* instead of coming up with proper titles? And who would deliberately go against all the traditional tropes of the mystery genre? I have to admit I'd never heard of Porter until recently but I found her creation to be a winner, albeit a rather disgusting one.

Porter was born in Cheshire in 1924, and having studied Russian, worked in British intelligence. She didn't start writing until her forties, and produced ten intricately plotted mysteries featuring the obese, selfish, incompetent, misanthropic, lazy and frankly unhygienic Chief Inspector Wilfred Dover, and his long-suffering sidekick, Sergeant MacGregor. Dover is described as looking like a sweaty pastry man with thinning hair and 'a small black moustache that the late Adolph Hitler did so much to depopularize'. He's perhaps closer to Kyril Bonfigioli's criminal art dealer Mortdecai (although not the Johnny Depp travesty) rather than a traditional cop.

The books are comical because Dover is not the only grotesque;

the entire sphere he inhabits is an inversion of the mystery writer's usual cosy milieu, so the village where a maid goes missing in *Dover One* is a summation of everything townies find suspicious about the countryside. The village inn serves 'good plain English cooking at its best', consisting of 'tinned tomato soup, congealed shoulder of New Zealand lamb which might have been cooked and carved in that distant country, soggy potatoes and bright green cabbage'. The missing maid is no doe-eyed sylph but a gigantic frizzy-haired good-time gal, and her mother no tearful matriarch but a slattern who can blow the ash off her cigarette without removing it from her mouth. In this world even a posy of flowers purchased in Piccadilly is not sprayed with morning dew but with spit from the seller. We're a long way from Miss Marple, and all the better for it.

In *Dover Two* the Chief Inspector manages to accuse three different suspects of murder before stumbling on the right solution, but at least Porter's creation made it to a BBC radio series before vanishing.

There are also Porter's 'Eddie Brown' books, concerning a dim-witted reluctant spy who succeeds in his missions purely by accident. Given the preponderance of lesbian characters, Porter's mystery-shrouded private life and another series of novels featuring man-hating Constance Burke and her female companion, one might draw conclusions about the author that provide her with a refreshingly unrosy view of the male psyche.

76

David Pownall

From time to time this volume has had cause to mention writers who are or were very much alive and well at the time of writing. It's done with trepidation after, mortifyingly, I offended the cartoonist Bill Tidy, who was still producing his deliriously odd vignettes of Northern life. My aim was not to describe him as forgotten but to point out the lack of availability of his unreprinted work (Volume 11 of his epic Northern parody *The Fosdyke Saga* currently commands an asking price of over £200).

The case of Pownall is slightly different. Best known for his fascinating and wide-ranging plays, often built around the intersections of music, creativity, technology and politics, it's easy to overlook his superbly accomplished novels.

Liverpool-born Pownall started work at the Ford Motor Company and moved to Zambia for six years to work in mining the Copperbelt, where he also began writing plays for the mining-town theatres. The experience affected him enough to write two delicious

Waugh-influenced comic novels, *The Raining Tree War* and its sequel, *African Horse*. Set in the mythical state of Zonkendawon, Tarzan Cool Guy, Bwana Arse and the Bucket-Wheel Excavator Gang get mixed up in a comedy of errors described by *The Times* as 'a bawdy black fairy tale, a sort of Kaffirs and Boers in Wonderland'. In writing these, Pownall joined that odd class of English writers fascinated by the effects of colonialism in Africa. As enjoyable as these were, Pownall's first love was the theatre and he has always seemed to me rather dismissive of his considerable skills as a novelist.

Then came *White Cutter*, a remarkable novel about passion and duty, fathers and sons, set in the world of thirteenth-century stonemasonry. Unravelling the mysteries of masons and the architecture of cathedrals, it was a book that deserved at least as much fame as *The Name of the Rose*. Twelve years later, in 1999, he published a novel that married his passions for history and the theatre, *The Catalogue of Men*. Set in the last decades of Queen Elizabeth's reign and the first of King James's, it centres on Miguel, washed up on the south coast of England after the Armada and befriended by slick operator William Shakespeare, who enlists his help to write *Measure for Measure*.

Equally elegant is *The Ruling Passion*, a new version of a sensational episode in English history, the turbulent relationship between Edward II, then Prince of Wales, and his lover Piers Gaveston.

There are several other volumes, and each is a work of heartfelt originality, but they defy easy categorization. Pownall is a good example of an author who has chosen to remain as diverse as possible, writing about whatever intrigues him, and has therefore become the publisher's ultimate nightmare; a writer who perhaps finds novels less interesting to produce than other forms of communication. When last I looked, he had written over eighty radio plays and over forty stage plays. Such fecund diversity breeds a strange kind of invisibility. This most English of creative minds deserves to be recognized and honoured within his own country.

77

Philippa Pullar

So, perhaps like David Pownall, some writers never settle on a single style because their writings echo their own caprice. These are the ones who fail to fix themselves clearly in the public attention and eventually settle into the backdrop. A singularity (and it must be said, simplicity) of thought is far more likely to win a loyal readership. Philippa Pullar has been variously described as capricious, vivacious, riotous and tormented. She was raised conventionally in a solid middle-class West Country family, married a chicken farmer and came to realize that her perceived notions of rural life were overly romantic.

In the seventies a number of authors began to take up their pens against the horrors of factory farming. Pullar's belief in the sanctity of animal life informed her first and greatest book, the uncategorizable *Consuming Passions: A History of English Food and Appetite*, published in 1970.

Pullar had received a Cordon Bleu Certificate of Cookery and had been a restaurant manager, so she wrote of history of food like no other, incorporating such apparently unconnected subjects as phallic worship, cannibalism, agriculture, Roman mythology, wet nursing, prostitution, witchcraft, magic, aphrodisiacs and factory canning. Her chapters include 'Pudding, Pepys and Puritanism' and 'Culinary Erections'. Her style was scattergun and frequently hilarious, incorporating recipes, jokes, historical anecdotes and a persuasive explanation about why the English lost the art of cooking – an art still only in the early stages of revival.

She explains how medieval cuisine was really Roman, and how spices like 'galingale, mace, cubebs and cummin' were added after the Crusaders returned with Eastern influences. There are descriptions of dinner etiquette and the experience of table gatherings, the steaming trays of cranes and swans being served, the chamberpots being passed around, the men nodding off, the women stepping into the larder 'where the jars made a cold crack on the marble shelves as the potted meats, the confections and the pickles were taken up to admire and set down again'.

Consuming Passions is not quite a history nor a cookery book, but a treatise on the art of taste, and is unique. She followed it up with an exhaustively researched biography of Frank Harris, which was received with frosty politeness, although it is now highly regarded. Then came *Gilded Butterflies: The Rise and Fall of the London Season*, the autobiographical *The Shortest Journey* and a descent into various New Age lunacies. *Consuming Passions* has happily been recognized and republished.

Pullar set me off on a hunt for other authors who had written about gastronomy without merely delivering a list of recipes. Now I'm keen on having a crack at porpoise with wheat porridge, a rare recipe from culinary horror *The Curious Cookbook*, a collection culled from various anonymous authors in the British Library stacks by Peter Ross. He offers up mashed potato sandwich, roasted peacock, viper soup, parrot pie with beef and lemon peel, and curried kangaroo tails.

Likewise, *The Epicure's Almanack* is a never-before-reprinted 1815 good food guide to 650 eating establishments in London by Ralph Roylance, who visited tripe shops, coaching inns, tea gardens and London's first Indian restaurant in search of fine fare.

I return to Pullar's *Consuming Passions* regularly. It's one of the few books I can think of that discusses the historical *ideas* behind eating well. My copy was lent to me by the actor George Baker, who used to play Inspector Wexford and loved to cook for his daughters. I've had it for twenty years; I must give it back to his family.

78

Barbara Pym

Few careers are more easily destroyed than a sudden fall from fashion. Some writers return to popularity, but none in such a spectacular manner as Pym, a quintessentially English novelist whose twelve miniaturist novels can now be described as both popular and timeless.

Pym was born in Oswestry, Shropshire, one year before the Great War. She attempted her first book, *Young Men In Fancy Dress*, at sixteen and her second, *Some Tame Gazelle*, at twenty-two, periodically submitting it to publishers who always turned it down. She was writing about characters she knew and understood. Her mother was a church organist, so vicars and curates inevitably appeared in her books. She and her sister Hilary featured in the second, projected into the future as 'spinsters', and anthropologists tended to crop up because of her years spent working at London's International African Institute.

But by the time another world war broke out, she had still not been published. Later, she and Hilary moved to a flat in Pimlico, and she wrote stories for women's magazines without any real success.

Then, in 1950, Jonathan Cape published a revised version of *Some Tame Gazelle*, finally launching her career. The timing proved to be right, and Pym's first six books established her as a unique voice. Her plots left faint impressions but her style allowed her to explore the lives of unassuming, genteel characters with clarity and originality. She had found her voice and her audience.

In 1963, disaster struck. *An Unsuitable Attachment* was returned without a contract; in the era of The Beatles, she had suddenly fallen out of step with the times. Shattered by the rejection, she felt that no one would ever admire her style of writing again. Further books were rejected as publishers swept out their cupboards and chased new trends.

On 21 January 1977, after sixteen years of obscurity, Pym was named 'the most underrated novelist of the twentieth century' by both Lord David Cecil and Philip Larkin in the *Times Literary Supplement*. Overnight, her books were published (but not by Cape), she was shortlisted for the Booker Prize and discovered a huge, eager new audience in America, whose readers valued her traits of gentle English modesty.

Only two years after her rediscovery, she succumbed to a recurrence of breast cancer. She said: 'The small things of life were often so much bigger than the great things. The trivial pleasures, like cooking, one's home, little poems, especially sad ones, solitary walks, funny things seen and overheard.' She is buried beside her beloved sister.

79

Richard Quittenton

Victorian children's stories were often the stuff of nightmares. As a boy I inherited my grandfather's older books and was haunted by an illustration, 'Karik and Valya Trapped in the Lair of the Water-Spider', which showed two miniaturized Russian children being wrapped in slimy webbing by a gigantic eight-legged multi-eyed horror at the bottom of a pond, from *The Extraordinary Adventures of Karik and Valya*, by Yan Larry.

This volume paled to nothing compared with 'Uncle Two-Heads Sinking into the Quicksand', an illustration that cursed my nights for years. I tried searching it out, and finally received the edition my family would have inherited in the 1930s, entitled *Giant-Land*. Created under the pen-name of Roland Quiz, it's one of four Tim Pippin novels first published in 1874 that continued to be reprinted until the end of the Second World War, after which they vanished.

Probably with good reason; the horrors of the war are never far from these pages. Swords are constantly brandished, battle armour is donned and brutal threats are pronounced on every page as Pippin enters different realms. Often a bystander as a gallery of grotesques duke it out for supremacy of the kingdom, he stands by as Giant Blackbeard attacks a dragon and Redbeard fights King Gobble-All. The stories are clearly spun from old English fairy tales, and in one illustration a naked and sensual Queen Mab (first mentioned in *Romeo and Juliet*) poses astride a grotesquely severed head. J. M. Barrie also featured Mab, and it is to Barrie (and Lupino Lane, the vaudevillian who popularized the Lambeth Walk) that this book is dedicated.

Quittenton (1833–1914) wrote the Tim Pippin stories for *Our Young Folks' Weekly Budget*, which began publication in 1870 and changed its title to *Young Folks*. He became the joint editor, writing humorous sketches, rhymes and stories for children, as well as 'blood and thunder' adventures for older readers. The deeply unsettling illustrations were by 'Puck', the pseudonym of John Proctor, and helped to raise the paper's circulation dramatically. Proctor later wrote the 'Jack the Valiant' tales for the same paper.

As always in such volumes, the villains are the most colourful and memorable characters. Foreigners are inevitably portrayed as swarthy, untrustworthy and coarse of features, but it's the hook-nosed, money-grabbing Hassidic Giant Greed whose description disturbs most, appearing in drawings which are sinister and clearly anti-Semitic. These once-beloved books are now extremely rare and collectable, but they are certainly no longer the tales to read to your children. To this day I'm amazed that my grandparents thought these volumes perfectly acceptable to thrust at a nervous and somewhat fearful child.

80

T. Lobsang Rampa

W. H. Auden was wrong: there are some books which are best forgotten. Erich von Däniken built a cash-cow career on the idea of alien contact, most notably with *Chariots of the Gods*, a book which suggested that constructions on the plains of Nazca in Peru are actually rocket launch sites. It turns out the world's sacred books really describe gods zooming down from the heavens in fiery chariots with promises to return and Sanskrit texts can be translated to reveal journeys in spaceships. His bestseller appeared just as art students were going through a particularly wibbly-wobbly phase of quasi-mysticism. But it wasn't the first piece of post-war dipsy-doodleism to catch on.

By the time the memoir of a Tibetan monk entitled *The Third Eye* turned up on the desk of Secker & Warburg, it had been turned down by most leading houses. S&W took a punt and published it in 1956, and the book shot into the bestseller lists, with the esteemed *Times Literary Supplement* suggesting it was close to being a work of art. Doubts were quickly raised by Tibetan scholars; after all, the book included trepanation as a standard procedure for induction into priesthood, neophyte monks zipping about on giant kites and Rampa's meetings with both his mummified former incarnation and an abominable snowman (I'm surprised Doctor Strange didn't put in an appearance as well).

The press scented a story and exposed Rampa as a Devon plumber called Cyril Hoskin, who had never been near Tibet. This Blavatskyan revelation did not appear to bother his readers, who were happy to purchase another *eighteen* volumes of his Tibetan memoirs. Hoskin held back a late chapter involving his visit to the planet Venus, and said he had been possessed by the spirit of the monk after falling out of a tree while trying to photograph an owl. He further stated that his book *Living with the Lama* had been dictated by his Siamese cat, Mrs Fifi Greywhiskers. Naturally this was enough to convince his credulous New Age followers.

With an entire industry springing up around him, as well as his family turning out books to capitalize on his success, Rampa grew weary of being described as a con man and decamped to Canada, where he remained until his death in 1981. By now he had many new Canadian fans who accepted the books as proof of Buddhist principles, and were happy to endorse his unpublished chapters on flying saucers. They still maintain his fan site, should you wish to purchase the latest Lobsang Rampa calendar. It's a bit like those people who make crop circles with a rope and a plank, then debunk them with photographic evidence, only to find that believers now accuse them of being conspirators in an alien cover-up.

For non-believers the books are problematic, especially when

Hoskin explains auras or soul transference in terms that would make any scientist fall off a chair laughing. Still, the books give an alarming insight into the naivety of ideas about exoticism in the post-war spiritual vacuum of the 1950s, and will always be tracked down by intellectually inert seekers of easy enlightenment.

81

Simon Raven

Simon Raven was often described as a cad, but sounds like a horrible human being. After his death at seventy-three it was said that by rights he should have died of shame at thirty and of drink at fifty. He had a passion for privilege, no sense of obligation, a love of classical literature (which he supposedly kept by his bed and read in the original versions every day), a cheerfully filthy mind, a fondness for beans on toast and too much guilt about tipping waiters to be regarded a gentleman. Nor was he upper class – his family had made their fortune from socks.

It appears that from an early age Raven set out to live a hedonistic life, in which he succeeded all too well. In 1945 he was expelled from Charterhouse for homosexual activities. One contemporary said 'he trailed an odour of brimstone'. Intelligent and charming, he had a tendency to strike eighteenth-century attitudes, marrying 'for duty' and sending the notorious telegram to his penniless wife: 'Sorry no money, suggest eat baby.'

Despite just avoiding a court martial for conduct unbecoming, he enjoyed his army years and followed their instruction to be 'brief, neat and plain' in his writing. He was employed by the publisher Anthony Blond on the condition that he left London at once, as it was getting him into debt, and set about producing chronicles of upper-class life, including *The Feathers of Death* and the eerie *Doctors Wear Scarlet*, which is now regarded as something of a classic.

A pair of rancorous, scathing novel cycles, *Alms for Oblivion* and *The First-Born of Egypt*, eventually ran (somewhat loosely) to some seventeen volumes, and take on a mystical edge, although supernatural occurrences always held a fascination for him. Raven said of his writing, 'I arrange words into pleasing patterns to make money,' and although he never found a huge readership, he did grow more industrious. He's a lot more fun than Anthony Powell, and has often been described as 'a cult waiting to be discovered'. At least, that's what I think they said.

One must never confuse decadence with a lack of discipline. Raven worked hard. The public became familiar with his TV adaptations of *The Pallisers* and *Edward and Mrs Simpson*, but he also wrote dialogue for *On Her Majesty's Secret Service*. His memoir *Shadows on the Grass* was described as 'the filthiest cricket book ever written', and Prion Humour Classics recently published a selection of his non-fiction writings, which include a treatise on recognizing rent boys.

A gambler, cricketer, controversialist, imbiber and fine host, he revelled in pushing his restaurant bills to astonishing levels. He once ordered (knowing that he would not be paying for it) two half-bottles of the same wine simply because they were more expensive that way.

He was at his best when writing about himself or sex, or other people talking about him and sex. His prose manages to be flabbergastingly frank and erudite, although rather obsessed with his schooldays and cricket, like most of his class.

Of gambling, he cheerfully described 'the almost sexual satisfaction which comes from an evening of steady and disastrous losses'. Passionate yet aloof, dissipated yet energetic, he lost his looks, most of his friends and all of his money. Raven represents the perfect paradox of a certain type of Englishness. After obeying his publisher's restraining order to live at least fifty miles away from London, he did so for thirty-four years but eventually returned and died in an almshouse for the impoverished, regretting nothing. He wrote his own epitaph: 'He shared his bottle, and when still young and appetizing, his bed.' Beware the man who boasts he was a friend.

A vague suspicion besets me, though. What if all of this was a grand game, and Raven was bigging up his own reputation as an incorrigible reprobate? He was immensely industrious. Could there also have been a part of him that was kind and decent and caring? If so, what better way to hide it than to brag about your own shortcomings?

82

Maurice Richardson

Here's a forgotten author with a single remembered book to his name, but what a book! I found very few hard facts about Maurice Richardson. I know he was born into a wealthy family in 1907, and was a manic-depressive Communist ex-amateur boxer/journalist who hung out with a pretty low-life crowd in the drinking dens of Soho, where the talents of many a fine writer were poured into the gutter.

Richardson reviewed books throughout his life and was a classic example of a talented man with too many under-developed interests. Most of his writings and books left no trace. *Little Victims* concerned his hated prep school education, *Fits and Starts* was a fine collection of journalism including a superb essay on the Moors murders, and *The Fascination of Reptiles* was a study of snakes and lizards.

His first novel, *A Strong Man Needed*, was about a female boxer and failed to knock anyone out. His great success was entirely unexpected: a compendium of linked pieces that has remained in print through the decades. These stories were illustrated by several idiosyncratic artists including Ronald Searle and Gerard Hoffnung. *The Exploits of Engelbrecht*, as it became known, was loved by J. G. Ballard, and is certainly one of the most unusual books ever published.

Engelbrecht is a dwarf surrealist boxer who goes ten rounds with a grandfather clock (needless to say, his opponent gets punched in the dial) but he's an all-round sportsman who'll tackle any game or match, no matter how peculiar it gets. We first meet him taking part in a witch hunt that unfolds like the Glorious Twelfth, then at a golf game which takes him around the world in one course. When he battles a demon bowler, the bowler is, naturally, a real demon – the innings closes at 333,333 for 9. The surrealist sporting calendar is filled with alarming events like the Interplanetary Challenge Cup, where Engelbrecht and team-mate Salvador Dali thrash the Martians on the Moon.

Engelbrecht may take all night to wrestle the Kraken and get involved in an angling competition that shares the druggy, nightmarish quality of a Hieronymus Bosch painting, but he is also a man of culture; he attends the Plant Theatre and the Dogs' Opera (the contralto is a Great Dane and the libretto is in dog Latin) before eloping with a cuckoo clock. The book is packed with quotable one-liners, and I once read a chapter aloud to a roomful of kids who fell around laughing.

The Exploits of Engelbrecht is available in an illustrated edition supplemented with Richardson's wedding report involving Holmes, Moriarty, Dracula, Frankenstein and Poirot, as you would expect it to. The question remains: why would a manic-depressive Communist ex-amateur boxer write such an effervescently silly book? It would be nice to think that there's a little bit of foolishness in everyone.

The Rediscovered Forgotten Authors

One reader's favourite author is often unknown to others, and the works of Rudolf Ditzen were shamefully unfamiliar to me; not anymore, for they haunt my sleep. In the time of this book's gestation he has gone from being barely recalled outside his homeland to newly discovered international popularity. His real life, which involved murder, theft, madness, suicide, alcoholism, drugs and Nazis, is as disturbing as anything he wrote. Ditzen's pen-name, Hans Fallada, was supposedly drawn from the Grimms' fairy tales, but his novels had little in common with the moralistic fantasies of *mittel*-Europe. If they can be considered as fables, they're remarkably detailed ones.

Ditzen was the son of a German magistrate, raised in Berlin and immersed in Dickens, Flaubert and Dostoyevsky. At sixteen he suffered a terrible road accident in which he was kicked in the face by a horse. A year later he contracted typhoid. His adolescence actually worsened: forming a suicide pact with his best friend, the pair staged a duel to cover their intentions and Ditzen shot his friend dead. In order to keep him from prison, he was declared insane. In the sanatorium he struggled with painkillers, but started writing.

What saved him from becoming just another casualty in the coming German tragedy was his literary ability. *Peasants, Bosses and Bombs* established him as a fresh talent. Never in good health, Ditzen found himself on the receiving end of a string of escalating calamities, including morphine addiction, imprisonment for embezzlement and repeated nervous collapse in the face of escalating fascism. Tortured by the wartime death of his brother, he committed a string of alcohol- and drug-related thefts, but finally emerged from hospital cured.

He married and his books started to sell, despite being critical of German politics. The smashing success in 1932 of *Little Man, What Now?*, the story of a young couple trying to stay afloat during the rise of National Socialism, was a poisoned chalice. It became a hit Hollywood film, which brought him to the attention of the Nazis. It didn't help that Hollywood was felt to be a hotbed of Jewish sympathies.

Fallada now fell under the scrutiny of the rising party, who trumped up a charge of 'anti-Nazi activities' and jailed him for a week. The book was removed from public libraries. Persecution led to falling sales and another nervous breakdown. Having been banned in Germany (Ditzen was a nationalist who loved his homeland too much to leave), his sales dropped and further mental instability followed.

After being declared an undesirable author, he switched from social realism to writing harmless children's stories. He soon grew tired of this, and in 1937 his adult novel, the immense *Wolf Among*

Wolves, had the misfortune to be approved by Joseph Goebbels, who saw it as an indictment of the Weimar Republic. Goebbels now enthusiastically suggested that Fallada should write the great anti-Semitic novel, leading the author into a trap from which he could not escape. Fallada needed to conform but at the same time be true to his beliefs. Intimidated into starting a carefully ambiguous work about a real-life fraud case involving two Jewish financiers, he decided to emigrate, but changed his mind at the front door.

Staying behind meant undergoing Nazi predations (including a lack of paper). When he finally found himself back in an insane asylum, suffering from further drink and drug problems, he wrote an extraordinarily bleak novel, *The Drinker*, a roman-à-clef about his alcoholism, which was critical of life under the Nazis. It escaped attention partly because his handwriting was deliberately indecipherable, and because by 1944 the Nazis had bigger problems on their hands.

Every Man Dies Alone and *Alone in Berlin* (were there ever more downbeat titles?) were his great late books. The latter is tension-drenched and gruellingly depicts fascism as experienced by the residents of a single house. It's based on an extraordinary true story, and some editions contain photographs of the protagonists. The question must have haunted Ditzen: was it better to stay and compromise, or flee (like Thomas Mann and others) and be true? With the book's surprise rediscovery and appearance as a movie, many more may now ask themselves that question.

In the years ahead we may look back and find it hard to believe that such a major writer of the twentieth century was erased for decades. I found my first Fallada in a second-hand bookshop under 'War

& Military'. I'm convinced we'll also see the mainstream acceptance of James Farrell, too. J. G. Farrell is a classic example of the novelist cut short in his prime. Had he lived, 'There is no question that he would today be one of the really major novelists of the English language,' said Salman Rushdie.

The handsome Irishman came from Liverpool, but his father had been an accountant in Bengal, and James spent time teaching in Dublin and France, which informed his developing interests. A bout of polio left him debilitated, and he settled to writing.

The 1960s were a golden time for finding publishers willing to take chances with new voices; Farrell's first novel, *A Man from Elsewhere*, was published in 1963 and centred on grand themes: Catholicism, Communism and existentialism, in particular the conflicting positions of Sartre and Camus over the idea of 'noble sacrifice'. Critics admired its ambition but, unsurprisingly, found it too cerebral. Another two novels failed to quite lock Farrell into his own tone of voice, although they were respectfully received.

The big change came with his 'Empire Trilogy'. The first, the excellent *Troubles*, was set in a faded hotel from which vantage point the hero could observe the Irish struggle for independence. The third, *The Singapore Grip*, concerned the capture of the British colony by the Japanese in 1942. But it was the second, *The Siege of Krishnapur*, that caught the attention of critics and public alike, winning the Booker Prize. This inventive novel amalgamates several colonial sieges into one grand fictional clash, and is by turns angry, shocking and hilarious.

In his Booker acceptance speech, Farrell attacked his sponsors over their international business interests. This might be seen as typical behaviour from a man who described the hypocrisies of colonialism and religion in such sharp-eyed prose. Farrell was fascinated by the decline of Empire, which he said was the most interesting thing to have happened in his lifetime.

Before he could finish his fourth volume in the colonial series, *The Hill Station*, Farrell was swept from some rocks while he was fishing and died at the age of forty-four. Various conspiracy theories (MI5, IRA, suicide) sprang up around his death, but an eyewitness later emerged to describe how he fell, polio having robbed him of his balance. Farrell was far from suicidal, having just signed up with the legendary Hollywood agent Irving 'Swifty' Lazar.

In 2010 Farrell was posthumously given a second Booker Prize for *Troubles*, and like Fallada, the rediscovery led to renewed interest in his work. It seems to me that both authors wrote about ordinary people tested in extraordinary times, which is why their work feels even more essential now.

Lionel Davidson is another of those authors who used to turn up a lot on the racks of second-hand bookshops, usually in a colourful, frayed paperback edition sporting a review that calls it 'a real page-turner!' Davidson was a Yorkshireman who spent years as a freelance reporter, and his versatile, pacy novels propelled him into the forefront of thriller writing. Although they're now back in print, mentioning his name to younger readers produces blank looks. Let's put that right; he's a terrific writer. His first novel, *The Night of Wenceslas*, concerns a young spendthrift forced into a spying trip to Prague during the Cold War in order to retain his beloved car (used as a stake in his debts). Our anti-hero manages to get beaten up before flushing the information down the toilet, and falls deep into a trap of his own making. It's a typical Davidson ploy, to graft a sympathetic character into an increasingly elaborate plot.

His second novel, *The Rose of Tibet*, had something of Henry Rider Haggard about it, and was a grand old-school adventure that won the admiration of Graham Greene and Daphne Du Maurier. This tale of a quest for treasure from India to Tibet should, by rights, have been a Harrison Ford film.

I first discovered Davidson in *Smith's Gazelle*, and being of an impressionable age, was moved to tears. It's a fable concerning a small Jewish boy and a wizened old Arab who join forces during the Six Day War to save the titular gazelle (the last of its species) from extinction. The story has a wonderful timelessness and a compelling message of unity.

The Chelsea Murders won Davidson the Gold Dagger Award for best thriller. It presents a chillingly disguised murderer and a raft of memorably louche Chelsea characters, although the plot favours method over motive a little too much. It also poses a common problem with books from the 1970s: a lack of political correctness that simply reflected the attitudes of the time, which is no direct fault of the author's.

It would seem that at this point Davidson was firing on all cylinders, and then he simply vanished from view. No new adult novel appeared from him for sixteen years, although he did write a children's novel called *Under Plum Lake*, described as a 'genuine one-off'.

Davidson's absence made his late-arriving thriller, *Kolymsky Heights* (1994), all the more of a shock. It had a terrific premise, which it delivered on brilliantly. The hero is a Canadian-Indian with a linguistic talent that allows him to infiltrate one of the most forbidding places on earth, a secret laboratory buried deep in the permafrost of Siberia. The question is not just whether he'll succeed in his mission, but how he'll ever get back out.

The style and pacing was so slick that it felt as if Davidson had never been away. When it was rereleased without fanfare, *Kolymsky Heights* became a bestseller driven by public appreciation, and his other books returned. It made me think there's another reason why writers are forgotten – they stop producing because they're busy doing something else.

83

Arnold Ridley

This is a very sweet story. Ridley was a one-time elementary school teacher from Bath, technically a Victorian (he was born at the end of the nineteenth century), who fought in the First World War and longed to be on the stage. Unfortunately he suffered injuries at the Somme – his left arm was badly damaged, he was bayoneted in the groin, and he was later prone to blackouts from a fractured skull.

It seemed his injuries might end his dreams of a career treading the boards, but his passion for the theatre and its memorabilia remained, and he joined Birmingham Rep in 1918, taking a wide variety of roles before retiring when the physical wounds and mental trauma began troubling him again. One evening he was stranded at Mangotsfield railway station, and was inspired to write a play about a mysterious train that appears at night on a branch line, only to subsequently vanish.

In *The Ghost Train*, the station through which it passes is considered to be haunted, and a group of stranded passengers have to solve its riddle. The comedy-drama was a massive hit in London and was filmed as a vehicle for Arthur Askey, who is so annoying in this that it was a wonder the rest of the cast didn't make him vanish too. Encouraged by his success, Ridley became the prolific author of over thirty plays between the wars, including *Keepers of Youth*, *The Flying Fool* and *The Wrecker*, which concerned a train driver who comes to believe that his engine is possessed by a malevolent sentience.

After failing to establish a new British film company, Ridley rejoined the army in time for the Second World War and saw active service in France, where he suffered flashbacks and shell shock all over again. Afterwards, he adapted an Agatha Christie novel, *Peril at End House*, for the West End, and later returned to acting, appearing in *The Archers* as Doughy Hood in the 1960s.

We remember Ridley now, not for his writing successes, but for his role in *Dad's Army* as the easily confused, mild-mannered Private Godfrey. It's ironic to think that an officer in the two biggest wars of the twentieth century should find his equilibrium playing a committed pacifist. He continued to appear in the show into his eighties – he even appeared in the stage version, which coincided with his eightieth birthday – and was awarded an OBE. He married three times and died in 1984 at the age of eighty-eight. Captain Mainwaring would no doubt have been pleased by the longevity of his recruit.

84

Tom Robbins

For publishers, timing is crucial, and if they're lucky they can catch the zeitgeist or refashion a long-dead genre. *Fifty Shades of Grey* was a brilliant piece of marketing that modernized unfashionable romantic fiction, but the idea of palpitating young ladies legally contracted to patrician millionaires dates back to the mid-nineteenth century. In the 1970s publishers spotted a rich new market: befuddled dopehead students who could be persuaded to stuff their backpacks with *Jonathan Livingston Seagull*, *If on a Winter's Night a Traveller*, and *Zen and the Art of Motorcycle Maintenance*, so Tom Robbins must have seemed like a gift from heaven.

Robbins was born to be hip. The grandchild of Baptist preachers, he described his youthful self as 'hillbilly'. After working in the Special Weather Intelligence Unit, he read Beat poetry in a Richmond, Virginia coffee house, became an art critic for the *Seattle Times* and hosted an alternative radio show. So rarely photographed without his Ray-Bans that I started wondering if he was blind, he was building the hipster student credentials that would ultimately give him a dedicated fan base.

For an avowedly private man he gave an awful lot of interviews, but what he said was contradictory. He felt readers should focus on the work, not the author, but shamelessly courted publicity. Robbins was fond of making beard-stroking pronouncements, few of which showed much deep thinking, such as: 'We're our own dragons as well as our own heroes, and we have to rescue ourselves from ourselves.' He was considered a wild, dangerous writer, but carefully honed his prose, producing less than two pages a day.

One of his novels was described thus: '*Still Life with Woodpecker* is a love story that takes place inside a pack of Camel cigarettes. It reveals the purpose of the moon, explains the difference between criminals and outlaws, examines the conflict between social activism and romantic individualism, and paints a portrait of contemporary society that includes powerful Arabs, exiled royalty, and pregnant cheerleaders.' *Jitterbug Perfume* concerns a janitor and the god Pan. *Fierce Invalids Home from Hot Climates* is about parrots, *Finnegans Wake*, a South American shaman's pyramid-shaped head, a Matisse painting, stilt-walking, government intelligence policies and rogue nuns.

The tangled plots are messy mosaics informed by the fallout from 1960s counter-culture. Robbins's biggest student hit was *Even Cowgirls Get the Blues*, about a beautiful hitcher with enlarged thumbs, but a literal film version rendered his idiosyncratic imagery into stoner drivel. Robbins's novels were not about random oddities, of course, but about the freedom of freefalling through ideas and making connections. His style was very much in vogue in the mid-seventies, but he soon tried the patience of fans who were starting to get the munchies and wonder how they were going to make a living after college. They put away foolish things, and Robbins went with them.

However, the wheel keeps turning; the rising conservatism of the twenty-first century may yet propel us back into the magical world of a writer who could start a book with the sentence: 'Amoebae leave no fossils.'

85

Cynthia Propper Seton

It was typical of Cynthia Seton to go and see *The Graduate* only to come out identifying with Dustin Hoffman's mother, for having to put up with such a trying son. The reason for this becomes clear when you check her dates; she was born in 1926 in New York, in her teens when war broke out, in her thirties during Eisenhower's years of plenty, then coping with the radicalism of a generation marked by Nixon and the Vietnam war.

Are all women who write from a woman's point of view automatically feminists? Of course not, no more than men are chauvinists for writing about male experience, but Seton's stance was complex; she was certainly a feminist who wrote traditional comedies of manners in exacting language, featuring a gallery of middle-class wives and mothers who for one reason or another had become dissatisfied with their lot, but she didn't entirely blame men. 'I want to write about husbands who may be obtuse,' she said, 'but who are not brutes, and remind their wives that there is a great deal to hang in there for.'

She married a psychiatrist and had five children, worked as a journalist and wrote a column about modern motherhood, but the roots of her literary passion lay in the past. She learned to write the kind of prose that George Eliot and Proust employed, having taught herself French just so that she could read Proust in the original, but most of all, her graceful style was compared to that of Jane Austen. Her women tried to understand what they wanted and/or deserved, but beneath their calm exteriors were deeper channels. She wrote six novels, many essays, and died too young of leukaemia.

These are books in which manners are minded. Her heroines are noble and move in domestic spheres that limit their actions, but they somehow find room to glitter. Seton identifies strongly with her leading characters. The amount of change that women went through, from the old moral code to the new era of Free Love, made her more of a feminist. About her college years she had this to say: 'I matured in a manner appropriate to my time, manoeuvring through a mating game unconfidently, fearing that my new politics, my finer ethics, were they ventured, would be lost.'

Her third novel, *A Fine Romance*, was nominated for the National Book Award in 1976 and should have won. Although her books are now available again, at the time of writing not one has warranted a reader review on Amazon; read one and make a difference.

86

Idries Shah

Blame it on the 1970s, a time when paperback authors began to delve into magic, astrology, mysticism, Eastern religions, spiritual healing and a panoply of alternative self-help explorations. Unfortunately, many of the books were spurious and shallow, yoking together everything from dowsing to yoga. It was a time when *Man, Myth & Magic*, a rather dubious part-work written by more than 200 specialists and published in 112 sections, became one of the most successful magazines in Britain.

Shah was born in Simla, India, in 1924. Of Afghan descent but raised in London, he first wrote about the occult but became a teacher of Sufi philosophy, translating Sufi classics and titles of his own. He redefined Sufi writings as a timeless, adaptive set of stories with multiple meanings designed to trigger insight and reflection, framing them in comprehensible Western terms.

In 1964 he published *The Sufis*, with an introduction by his friend Robert Graves, to critical acclaim. Not all academics were convinced. Some found his work slovenly, muddled, smug, filled with pseudo-mystical mumbo-jumbo.

In 1967 Shah published a new translation of *The Rubaiyat of Omar Khayyam*, supposedly based on a manuscript his family had held for 800 years. Orientalists were convinced the story was false. Shah's father was supposed to show Graves the manuscript but died in a car crash in Tangier, and as Idries prevaricated over providing proof of the document's existence, Graves's reputation suffered.

The modern consensus is that Graves fell prey to a hoax. Although Shah was overtaken by showmanship, he still popularized Sufi philosophy in the West, using humour, emotion and psychological insight to create a new audience of admirers, including Doris Lessing, who was deeply influenced by his writings.

And he used the immortal Mullah Nasrudin, a Persian Sufi folk character, as his hero. The brilliant Canadian animator Richard Williams spent almost thirty years working on a widescreen feature version of Shah's 'Nasrudin' stories entitled *The Thief and the Cobbler*. Shah produced tie-in books that reached a new readership, but Williams lost control of the film after completing only forty-nine minutes of footage. It fell into the hands of a producer who fatally vulgarized the final version.

The lost work subsequently became 'the greatest animated film never made'. Shah's 'Nasrudin' books are filled with wonderful brain-teasers and are back in print, although sadly the editions that were filled with Williams's beautiful drawings have vanished. Shah only came to my attention because I once met Williams, who introduced me to the script of his animated masterpiece, then voiced by

Vincent Price, Eartha Kitt and Kenneth Williams. Shah's greatest work now seems to have been lost forever but was reassembled in a fan edit by the devastated animators and can be found online in a blurred labour of love.

87

Richard Shaver

There are authors like Tom Robbins whose imaginations run away with them, and in the process some writers lose their wits; it's virtually an occupational hazard. Their writing might become increasingly erratic, peculiar and unreadably dense, until finally they shed even their most avid fans. Occasionally, though, the author is matched by someone who is determined to bring his words to the attention of the reading public.

Richard Sharpe Shaver was one such writer, born in Pennsylvania in 1910. When he was seven an accident damaged his spine and stunted his growth. He became an avid reader of science fiction, then a welder. Unfortunately he was also a paranoid schizophrenic who believed his welding guns allowed him to hear the thoughts of his fellow workers 'by some freak of its coil's field attunements'. He also picked up telepathic torture sessions conducted by malevolent aliens deep inside the Earth.

Shaver left his job, became a tramp and was hospitalized. For the next eight years he was in a mental institution and not, as he insisted, 'in the Cavern World'. This was the secret prehistoric landscape within our planet, whose inhabitants, the Deros, sometimes popped out to kidnap surface-dwellers to sado-masochistically torture and devour them. Shaver's world was very contradictory; although the Deros lived inside the Earth, they seemed to have space rockets . . .

Wait, come back! From here the story gets stranger. In 1943 Shaver wrote a letter to *Amazing Stories* magazine, explaining that he had learned 'Mantong', the Deros' language. The magazine's editor, Ray Palmer, tried translating phrases. He was no fool; he had bought Isaac Asimov's first stories and knew a good thing when he saw it. Palmer replied with a request: 'What else have you got?' Shaver sent back the whole story of his capture and torture, which Palmer tidied up and published in 1945 as 'I Remember Lemuria!'

The resulting publication caught both of them by surprise. Sales of the magazine went through the roof, and thousands wrote in wanting more (probably T. Lobsang Rampa's Canadian fans); Shaver was more than happy to supply them. The Hollow Earth theory took off around the world; in other countries readers claimed to be able to access the caves from secret tunnels and basements. 'Shaver Mystery Clubs' were formed. *Amazing Stories* became devoted almost exclusively to Shaver tales. Inevitably, the stories were mixed with UFO sightings and various other bits of bonkers phenomena. Readers started blaming the Deros for everything from plane crashes to getting stuck in a lift.

By 1948 the craze had burned itself out and *Amazing Stories* stopped publishing Shaver's work. Naturally, the author announced that this was the result of a conspiracy.

Shaver stayed in the limelight with accounts of 'rock books', stones that contained alien recordings. He even mailed readers slices of agate from his alien rock lending library, although we have no record of anyone who read them. His influence was enormous and long-lasting, from Nigel Kneale's *The Stone Tape* to concert posters, toy lines and stunning artwork produced for *Amazing Stories*. The question remains: was Shaver exploited or simply allowed to flourish?

As a footnote, I wondered if I had gone a step too far in including Shaver here until I mentioned him to a friend who cried, 'Maybe now the Deros will be taken seriously!'

88

Matthew Phipps Shiel

H. G. Wells and M. P. Shiel were exact contemporaries, entering and leaving the world within a year of each other, but Wells's reputation as the father of science fiction has continued to grow, while Shiel has disappeared from bookshelves.

Both were socialists with an interest in future fiction and scientific romances, and there is evidence that Wells was influenced by Shiel, but Shiel was a West Indies-born author writing in the flamboyant style of the Decadent movement.

Around the turn of the century he created the first future history series in science fiction with a trilogy that began with *The Last Miracle* (although, more fairly, the books offer three unconnected alternative futures). This was followed by *The Lord of the Sea*, based on a critique of the private ownership of land. Dashiell Hammett was a big fan, describing it as a book full of 'plots and counterplots, kidnappings, murders, prison-breakings, forgeries and burglaries, diamonds large as hats and floating forts'. But Shiel's reputation rests mainly on the third part of the sequence, *The Purple Cloud*. It's an apocalyptic novel that brushes off casual readers with a series of false starts, but settles down to become a truly extraordinary work of fiction.

The book was produced at a time when there was great interest in the unexplored Arctic, and tells the tale of a man named Adam Jeffson who travels there, only to return and find the Earth decimated by a vast purple cyanide cloud. Without the constrictions of a moral society, crushed by the burden of terrible isolation, Adam wields a power that tips him from eccentricity into megalomania. Dressed as a sultan, he takes explosives from the Woolwich Arsenal and burns London down. Laying waste to cities becomes a habit, a cry of rage for his imprisonment on earth, and he destroys nations before meeting another survivor, a woman in Istanbul, who may have the key to his endurance.

Shiel wrote twenty-five novels, but many are bland romances produced more for profit than the passion of language on show in *The Purple Cloud*. Shiel's private life was, it seems, as decadent as his early writing. He served sixteen months' hard labour in prison for molesting his twelve-year-old stepdaughter, and showed a penchant for underage girls throughout his life and his fiction. He also reckoned himself the King of Redonda, a small inhospitable isle in the West Indies, but this may have been concocted as a joke at the expense of critics.

His trilogy was published out of sequence, having first been serialized, and when I last looked, *The Purple Cloud* was available in a beautiful new edition.

89

Peter Tinniswood

In my doomed quest to rehabilitate popular writers whose fame has been diminished by time and fashion, no one is more deserving than Peter Tinniswood. There's a strong tradition of Northern comic writers who can hold tragedy and comedy in harmonious balance. Alan Sillitoe and David Nobbs both excelled in this area. Comic writing requires a finely attuned attitude, mainly because comedy is thought to mitigate believability. Northern writers are particularly well placed to blend resigned amusement with discussions about death, illness and general misfortune.

Nobbs and Tinniswood were scripting partners, but went separate ways in their literary styles. Nobbs wrote the charming 'Reginald Perrin' books, while Tinniswood commenced the long-running saga of the Brandon family with *A Touch of Daniel*, which was popular enough to be serialized by the BBC. He's a lovely scene-setter: 'It was the time of year when bus conductors first appear in linen jackets.' The sequence of novels ran to seven volumes, over which Tinniswood's style changed from deadpan to a staccato Northern comic version of James Ellroy. Here he is on the journeys made by house martins: 'Desert. Ocean. Stab of lighthouse, swoop of falcon. Lime trap. Storm. Draught. Pellets of shot gun. And here they are. Back home.'

He wrote the surreal and much-loved cricketing series *Tales from a Long Room* and created a series of tales told by cricketing raconteur 'The Brigadier', but he was capable of far stranger stories. When an author is made more popular by television adaptation, the success seems to remove longevity from his unadapted work. I can think of no other reason why his comic masterpiece has disappeared from the public radar.

The Stirk of Stirk is a highly peculiar prose poem that drops the reader into Robin Hood's darkest winter as, with rumbling stomach and perishing soul, the bandit faces his greatest enemy. Hood knows that creeping age and his inability to live up to his own legend will finish him off, yet simply refuses to die. The book is suffused with Northern chill and melancholy, but even in the blackest moments Tinniswood lights candles of hope. Here, a laugh is described as 'a sound that would curdle the eggs in a goldcrest's womb', and 'saliva makes bitter fountains in the mouth' as the starving Hood staggers on into history – and out of the bestsellers' list.

This kind of heightened stylization has fallen from popularity. Reading Tinniswood is like skimming any recent book on fast-forward, such is his ability to drag the reader through a colourful story. At his best, he's capable of reminding you that reading should always be a pleasure, never a chore. *A Touch of Daniel* was reissued in 2001, two years before he died, killed by his pipe, which is how he would probably have reported his throat cancer.

Lost In Translation: The Forgotten World Authors

Why do so many terrific novels and collections of short stories remain untranslated, their authors barely known outside their own countries?

Two examples: a baroque, fantastical vampire tale reminiscent of Borges or Calvino, *Natural History* is set in Barcelona during the 1830s. In 1990 it became the first of Catalan author Joan Perucho's works to be published outside Spain, and remains his only fiction to appear in the English language. Catalan voices were suppressed for decades; in Franco's Spain the language was forbidden, causing the collapse of a unique literary style. Today, Catalan writing is flourishing. On St Jordi Day, Catalans present each other with a book and a rose, and authors stroll the city signing volumes.

A friend from the Netherlands once told me: 'If you want to understand who we are as a nation, you must read *Character*, written in 1938 by Ferdinand Bordewijk.' This Dutch classic concerns a bailiff who tyrannically rules over the slums of Rotterdam, and the ambitious son who becomes a lawyer in order to destroy him. A keystone of twentieth-century literature in its own country, it's impossible to find in an English translation. A film version won the Oscar for Best Foreign Film in 1998, but the book is still unavailable.

The list of missing world authors is huge and seemingly obscure, yet Wes Anderson's film *The Grand Budapest Hotel* was inspired by the writings of Stefan Zweig, an Austrian novelist who wrote through most of the twentieth century and had once been one of the most popular authors in the world.

The diaries of Theodor Koch-Grünberg, the only explorer ever to record the lives of the lost Amazon tribes, remain untranslated at the time of writing, yet the Cannes-winning film *Embrace of the Serpent* was based on his works. Perhaps a film director should rescue a masterwork about the Latin temperament, *Idearium Español*, which is lost to readers in English. Its author, Ángel Ganivet, was greatly admired by Lorca but died at thirty-three, surely making him a candidate for cultdom.

It's hard to uncover these books yourself unless you're recommended them by someone who grew up with them on their shelves. India has a fine record of postmodernist literature, and Manzoor Ahtesham's *The Tale of a Missing Person* could apparently educate us further. The Argentinian Marcelo Cohen's *The End of the Same* is, I'm told, a brilliant Kafkaesque novel. I know what you're thinking: there aren't enough hours in the day. But as someone who handles occasional bits of jury duty on world cinema, I've forced friends to watch amazing movies that will never be found in cinemas. Unfortunately, you can't do that with a book. We take what we're given.

English readers rarely even tackle novels from the other countries in their union. Irish has been used as a literary language for over 1,500 years, and Gaelic has been intelligible to modern speakers for more than 400 years. Yet *Cré na Cille*, a comic masterpiece about the talking dead by Máirtín Ó Cadhain, has not even been able to settle on the same English title, being either 'Churchyard Clay' or 'The Dirty Dust', depending on which translation you go with. A similar situation exists with Welsh novels, but we tend to choose stories that directly reflect our lives. Even so, if we're to truly learn about our world, international novels with universal themes deserve wider distribution.

All of which brings us to the French. You know the French: frightfully awkward people, committed to the preservation of their language yet curiously in thrall to American noir thrillers and anglophone fantasies. No less than 16 per cent of the UK speaks French while 39 per cent of the French speak English (not including the driver of your Paris taxi, obviously). As a result, a great many popular French authors have appeared in translation.

France gained its ingrained love of noir and the *fantastique* from a huge number of authors who disappeared. The political upheavals of nineteenth-century France saw the creation of the first superheroes and the sudden arrival of *romans noirs*, French gothic novels. Melodramatic serials became all the rage, peaking with the arrival of the elegantly attired Rocambole, by Ponson du Terrail, in 1857. Before Raffles and Sexton Blake, this former villain turned into a hero and began fighting crime.

Five years later came the sinister Jean Diable, the menace of Scotland Yard, from author Paul Féval; then Gaboriau's exciting Monsieur Lecoq, inspired by the real-life exploits of criminal-turned-Prefect of Police, Vidocq (who had inspired Edgar Allan Poe). Féval's *The Black Coats* ran to a seven-novel saga about a criminal empire, and led to the creation of other mysterious heroes, including Kriminal, Fantômas and Judex, in his hat and cloak, brandishing powers of hypnosis. Pretty soon the country was awash with disguised crimefighters having death-defying adventures, from Doctor Omega to Belphegor, the phantom of the Louvre, to Arsène Lupin, the charming gentleman burglar. All of which was strange, because with the exception of Jules Verne French literature had hitherto largely shunned science fiction or anything too fantastical.

Many of the creations have parallels in English literature: Lupin has much in common with Raffles, Fascinax, the investigator of the occult, seems a counterpart to Dennis Wheatley's Duc de Richleau, while Rocambole shares elements of The Saint. These top-hatted heroes, masked villains and glamorous countesses who dashed across the rooftops of night-time Paris on missions to catch master criminals enjoyed thousands of adventures, forming an immense library of French Victoriana that continued until the start of the Second World War, when vicarious tales of heroism in the face of plans to subjugate the nation were replaced by horrors which were all too real.

Very few of these wonderful exploits have been translated into English, but lately some heroes, like Vidocq, Belphegor and the dashing Arsène Lupin, started reappearing in French films.

Pierre Boileau was born in Paris in 1906. Pierre Ayraud, aka

Thomas Narcejac, arrived two years later in Rochefort-sur-Mer. They were both winners of the prestigious Prix du Roman d'Aventures, awarded each year to the best crime novel. They both loved locked-room mysteries, both came from seafaring families and both admired the classic French adventures of Arsène Lupin and Fantômas.

Growing bored with the mechanics of traditional mysteries, they wanted to explore tension and character, so two years later they started writing together. They set out to create a new style, separate from English puzzle-mysteries and American violence, by building ironic, suspenseful situations where victims, often possible murderers themselves, were more interesting than the detectives.

Hitchcock adapted the duo's novel *The Living and the Dead* for his masterpiece, *Vertigo*, although the film is markedly different from the book. Boileau and Narcejac's stories flirted with the fantastic and the macabre, erupting full-blown into the novel *Les Diaboliques*, with its much-imitated twist ending. Again, the film version veered far from the story on the page. The pair's style was eerier for being so filled with realistic detail, as protagonists sit drinking in empty station bars, waiting for the rain to stop.

Narcejac continued after his writing partner's death in 1990, and died eight years later. Their collection *Forty Years of Suspense* has never been published in English. Very few of their seventy-six works have been translated. It's staggering to think that nearly all of these award-winning, seminal volumes still remain beyond reach.

Sébastien Japrisot came from Marseilles, arguably the home of French noir. He created an anagrammatic pseudonym from his real name, Jean-Baptiste Rossi (writers love doing that sort of thing), and became an author at the tender age of seventeen with *Les Mal Partis*.

International success beckoned with the first of his crime novels, *The 10:30 from Marseilles*, in 1950. My favourite is *The Lady in the Car with Glasses and a Gun* – was there ever a better title to sum up the world of the noir thriller? The narrative delivers all the key genre elements in a plot of audacious simplicity. A beautiful young woman impulsively drives off in her boss's white Thunderbird, heading for the South of France, but locals react as if she had made the same journey the night before. Then she finds a dead body in the boot . . .

Translated works are notoriously hard to find, vanishing and reappearing with irritating randomness. Six elegant Panther paperbacks of Japrisot's work turned up in 1999, when I first came across them, but a first edition of *Rider on the Rain* will set you back more than £500. So, of all the out-of-print noir authors, why should we particularly seek this one out? Well, there's something about Japrisot that just gets everything right. His plots are complex but easy to follow, and they have clever, simple hooks. He's a master of building tension, and resolves everything organically and elegantly. He writes rounded, intelligent, sexy female characters you care about, and his language is precise and clear, with minimal description and hardly a wasted word. Best of all, he writes the kind of thrillers you want to recommend to others.

Finally and most obscurely, Louis Pergaud is virtually unknown in the UK and his greatest book is currently unavailable in translation. In 1912 he wrote *The War of the Buttons*, about a play-war conducted by two gangs of boys from neighbouring villages. Anyone who is captured suffers the indignity of having their buttons cut from their clothes. As the tale progresses, the tone darkens from one of playful good humour to something crueller and more violent.

Although the story is specifically tied to a time and place in French history, there's a primal sense of allegory about it. Certainly the novel touched a national nerve. It has been endlessly reprinted and often filmed – at least six times by my count. Each reinvention of the story has changed the time and location to suit the message that its director was keen to convey.

The War of the Buttons still appears on the French high school curriculum. A recent film remake moved the action to German-occupied France during the Second World War.

To my mind the French language has never had quite the same level of unregulated pliancy you find in many English novels. A great number of fine books have never reached us in any form of translation, but it would be in the interests of the French cultural imperative to share their writers with the world.

90

Thomas Tryon

Tryon had it all: charm, intelligence, style, popularity, success, and he was ridiculously handsome. Did I mention he was also dating a (male) porn legend? Tryon was in *The Cardinal* and played the lead in the cult hit *I Married a Monster from Outer Space*. He almost starred opposite Marilyn Monroe in *Something's Got to Give*, until she was fired from the film. Bored with acting (and humiliated by Otto Preminger) he thought he'd write, and was damned good at that too. His novels included civil-war sagas, and were popular successes. Three became movies.

Tryon's style was American Expansive: grand themes and resonant plots, set in Connecticut or New England. His first novel, *The Other*, about a Russian grandmother teaching a dangerous game to two brothers, one gifted, one harmful, was reissued in 2012 in a new edition complete with a contextualizing essay. The narrative contains a blindsiding mid-tale twist, and was subsequently filmed.

The next, *Harvest Home*, occupied *Wicker Man* territory. A family relocates to a perfect New England town, but the idyllic setting proves deceptive. The Constantines flee the rat race and come here to enjoy the nation's old ways. To that end they at least get exactly what they wished for – but it comes at a price. Their dilemma is presented so appealingly that the reader cannot help but empathize, and is lured into the same nightmarish trap. The novel is filled with lyrical passages extolling the virtues of the land and nature, its fertility and bounty – and its cruelty. Once the screw is turned, Tryon increases the tension until it is well-nigh unbearable. A faithful but flat television version appeared with Bette Davis, who took the part of the novel's best character, Widow Fortune, a village elder with the ability to heal using traditional remedies.

Tryon specialized in strong female characters, never more so than in *Lady*, a sweeping novel about a *grande dame* who lightly rules her town between the wars, and who hides a lifelong secret that pinpoints America's damaging attitude towards miscegenation. Two portmanteau novels, interlinked tales concerning Hollywood players and their efforts to survive public taste and changing times, display insider knowledge. One section of the first, the tragedy of an ageless star called Fedora, became the basis for a late Billy Wilder film.

By this time, though, something odd was happening to Tryon's writing. It had started to become twee and sugary in a way that seems to afflict certain types of popular American writing. By the time he introduced his hero as a white-faced mime in *Night Magic*, the books had become filled with purple prose and were a trial to read. Tryon died tragically young, and his final works were published posthumously. He remains virtually unknown in the UK.

91

Arthur Upfield

Golden Age crime-writing was not the exclusive province of the British and the Americans. The forgotten author Arthur Upfield is an interesting case because of his involvement in a very disturbing murder investigation.

He was born in 1890 in Hampshire, but after faring poorly in his exams (he was planning to become an estate agent), Arthur's father shipped him off to Australia in 1910, where he eventually settled – if you can call it settling, for he led an itinerant life. He fought at Gallipoli and in France, and married an Australian nurse in Egypt. Down under, he became particularly interested in the Aboriginal culture, and for the next twenty years travelled extensively through the outback, taking all sorts of short-term jobs. He soon began writing, using the unusual characters and atmospheric locations he encountered.

During his travels, Upfield met an Aboriginal man known as

Tracker Leon, whose character he utilized as the basis for a fictional investigator. 'Boney' (misprinted by the publisher as 'Bony'), the first Aboriginal detective, was short for Detective Inspector Napoleon Bonaparte. Employed as a tracker by the Queensland Police, Boney's investigations took him to some remote sites, from mountain ranges, lighthouses and sheep stations to reefs and deserts, and along the rabbit-proof fence in the wheat belt of Western Australia.

Upfield's novels were highly regarded, and H. R. F. Keating included *The Sands of Windee* (1931) in his Top 100 list of the best crime and mystery novels ever written. Was a man overwhelmed in a dust storm or was he murdered? When the thoughtful Boney sees something odd in the background of a police photograph, he begins to piece together the secrets of the sands.

During the book's writing, Upfield needed to devise a method of getting rid of a body, and asked a friend for help. The friend suggested a disposal method: burn the victim along with a large animal, sift out any metal fragments, dissolve them in acid, grind any surviving bones and throw the remains to the wind. But the method was so efficient that, after Upfield discussed it with a stockman called Snowy Rowles, Rowles used the method to commit three real-life murders. Rowles followed Upfield's instructions, leaving no physical evidence that could be used in a court, but in one murder he had omitted an important step: the wrong kind of solder in the remains of a melted wedding ring identified him. Rowles was arrested and hanged.

Upfield's books became very popular in the USA after servicemen were stationed in Australia and took the books home with them. A hit TV series was made featuring his detective tracker, and as a record of Australian outback life between 1930 and 1950, the thirty-seven books are invaluable.

92

Edgar Wallace

He's a name that exists on the tip of the tongue, but it's now hard for anyone but aficionados to recall a Wallace book. Happily, you can have a drink with him to refresh your memory, because he was eventually paid the greatest British accolade. There's a splendid London pub named after him, just off Fleet Street, and it's filled with copies of his paperbacks. He even has a literary society with members in over twenty countries. Although he has hardly ever been out of print, how many people have actually read Edgar Wallace?

Conceived out of wedlock in a cupboard, born in Greenwich in 1875, and raised through a complex set of circumstances in a theatrical troupe by his mother, Wallace ended up selling newspapers in Ludgate Circus at the age of eleven. But he was to become one of the most ubiquitous authors of the early twentieth century.

He became a newspaper editor and decided to write 'crime and blood and three murders to the chapter; such is the insanity of the age that I do not doubt for one moment the success of my venture'.

His first novel, *The Four Just Men* (1905), was a prototype of the modern thriller, and concerned four handsome young vigilantes who kill in the name of justice. Ambitious and attuned to the power of marketing, the often childishly naive writer launched a 'Guess the Murder Method' competition that went horribly wrong after dozens submitted the correct answer, expecting to be paid in full.

After causing two further expensive lawsuits to befall the *Daily Mail*, he was fired from his job and started the *Sanders of the River* stories, which are steeped in the colonial attitudes of the times and are rarely reprinted. They were, however, made into a film starring the excellent Paul Robeson.

No one could have accused Wallace of being a slacker. He was banging out eighteen novels a year, fortified by between thirty and forty cups of tea and eighty to a hundred fags a day.

Only months after his beloved wife died, Wallace became rich and famous. The success of a crime novel called *The Ringer* led to an extraordinary deal. He gave the film company British Lion a first option on all his future output. Despite suffering from undiagnosed diabetes, his energy was prodigious. He ventured into politics, then headed for Hollywood.

In 1931 he began the five-week writing stint that resulted in *King Kong* (he died still working on it). In this draft it was established that the ape was thirty feet tall, and was killed by a bolt of lightning hitting the Empire State Building. Sadly, Wallace never saw the completed film, but you can't help feeling that he would have loved it.

A famously fast writer, it was a standing joke that if someone telephoned Wallace and was told he was writing a book, they'd reply, 'I'll wait.' He produced around 175 novels, twenty-four plays, hundreds of articles and short stories, and about 160 films have been made from his work, including *The Edgar Wallace Mysteries*. There were apparently thirty-four novels written in 1929 alone, although I couldn't verify all the titles and wonder if perhaps this figure was another example of Wallace's famously fanciful memory.

Popularity does not always translate to longevity, and Wallace's slam-bang tales are often regarded unsubtle and improbable. Critics were sniffy about him, but there was an element of snobbery in their reviews, for Wallace was one of the first truly working-class crime writers.

It was said that the King of Thrillers' soul was left behind in London. There is now a plaque on the Ludgate Circus end of Fleet Street that reads: 'He knew wealth & poverty, yet had walked with kings & kept his bearing. Of his talents he gave lavishly to authorship – but to Fleet Street he gave his heart.' Newsprint was in his blood, but for many he will always be the man behind the giant ape.

93

James Redding Ware

Some while ago the venerable British Library started championing a number of forgotten authors. The jewel in their crown was the republication of the world's first detective novel, *The Notting Hill Mystery* by Charles Warren Adams, which had been serialized in the magazine *Once a Week* between 1862 and 1863. Until crime expert Julian Symons mentioned it in 1972, the number one slot had always been taken by Wilkie Collins with *The Moonstone*, although Gaboriau's *L'Affaire Lerouge* had been published in France three years after Adams's work.

The British Library's collection evolved over 250 years, with more than 150 million items including books, journals, manuscripts, music, photographs, patents, newspapers and sound recordings, so there's plenty of scope for rediscovery and repackaging rarities. Their unearthing of lost crime novels led to a huge resurgence of interest, and the discovery of James Redding Ware.

He published under a pseudonym, but nobody knew who he

was, or cared. There was no particular subterfuge in this; at the time (1863) many part-work 'sensation' stories appeared without their origins attached, such was the lowly status of those who wrote for money. However, when one of Ware's stories was rediscovered in the form of a pamphlet, more were traced through the periodicals in which they first appeared, and they revealed their creator.

This son of a Southwark grocer became a jobbing writer, producing stories for the *Boy's Own Paper* and *Bow Bells Magazine* (someone should restart the latter – I'd buy it). He also turned out books on chess, photography, mistaken identity, 'The Life and Speeches of His Royal Highness Prince Leopold' and some essays on police court life. He wrote a non-fiction book called *The Road Murder*, about the Constance Kent case, which Kate Summerscale investigated for *The Suspicions of Mr Whicher*, and after his death he became famous for his dictionary of Victorian slang, still a useful tool for researching authors and inventive swearers.

But Ware had another claim to fame, although he didn't recognize his achievement. He invented the world's first female detective. Others were working on similar projects; Edward Ellis created *Ruth the Betrayer, or The Female Spy*, a character he described as 'a female detective – a sort of spy we use in the hanky panky way when a man would be too clumsy'. His was a fifty-one-part Penny Dreadful that doesn't really give us a fully formed female detective. William Stephens Hayward's racy *Revelations of a Lady Detective* features a distaff dick who daringly smokes and carries a Colt revolver, but Hayward missed the deadline by just six months. You could argue that Marian Halcombe in Wilkie Collins's *The Woman in White* acts as a detective, but James Ware got *The Experiences of a Lady Detective*, a collection of seven cases, out ahead of the competition under the name of Andrew Forrester. His heroine Mrs Gladden solves mysteries in the way we have come to expect: by visiting crime scenes, talking to witnesses and adopting subterfuge to hunt down murderers. It's likely that Ware drew on the real-life murder cases that captured the imaginations of Victorian readers, so the novel has the stamp of veracity.

Only a few copies survived in world libraries, and the book had effectively become lost when the British Library rediscovered it. They reprinted it with a new foreword by Alexander McCall Smith. This and the other books in the series have all been repackaged with artwork reminiscent of those holiday posters you used to find in old railway carriages, adding a lush nostalgic feel.

94

Keith Waterhouse

'A novel from the author of several previous books,' said the Amazon logline about *Jubb*, one of Waterhouse's astonishing black comedies, and for years that description remained. Was there ever a less appealing sentence?

I'm not sure I want to live in a world where Keith Spencer Waterhouse is out of print, but being forgotten he surely is. Soon after his demise I found that many of his novels were now only available from second-hand shelves. It was said that he passed through the stages of being a survivor, an anachronism, a dinosaur and a monument. Now he should be honoured.

Many readers are familiar with Waterhouse's greatest hit, but I've argued for his inclusion here because there was much more to him than the story of one mendacious teenager. My focus group of well-read readers were unable to name any of his other novels.

In some ways Waterhouse ties up the themes of this book in one career trajectory. He was born to a working-class family in Leeds, and came to London at the age of twenty-one to be interviewed for a job on the *News Chronicle*. He'd automatically assumed he would get it, but they sent him home. On the way back to the station, he dejectedly stopped in Ludgate Circus before the plaque commemorating Edgar Wallace, and felt that he had failed. Within five years he would be offered the editor's job.

After a stint in the RAF he came back to London, and this time he was hired. He became a campaigning journalist, arguing against the colour bar, human rights abuses and arms sales. A powerful sense of moral outrage and an irrepressible sense of humour led him into the new satire scene, where he wrote for zeitgeist TV shows like *That Was The Week That Was* and *The Frost Report*. He penned a screenplay for *Whistle Down the Wind* and rewrites for Hitchcock's *Torn Curtain*, taking over from another writer in these pages, Brian Moore. He also penned the books for a number of doomed musicals, including *Andy Capp* – I recall they released racing pigeons in the theatre auditorium that crapped on everyone – but by this time his 1959 novel *Billy Liar* had truly put him on the map.

Playing like a bleak Northern English version of *Catcher in the Rye*, it's the tragi-comic tale of an imaginative nineteen-year-old who sees his dreams being crushed and must decide whether to risk all on a career in London or remain at home, a constrained fish in a very small pond. Lying to his girlfriends, his bickering family and his funeral-director boss, commitment-phobic fantasist Billy's dark night of the soul takes on a resonance that remains pertinent today. A stash of unposted Christmas calendars hidden in his bedroom becomes the albatross around his neck, but everyone seeks to tie him down and clip his wings. The stay-or-go ending memorably soars into tragedy, making Billy one of the great British literary characters. Waterhouse transformed the novel into an award-winning film directed by John Schlesinger, with a debut by the radiantly youthful Julie Christie. It was followed by a hit TV series and a musical version starring Michael Crawford, with songs from John Barry.

Sixteen years later he would write a negligible sequel called *Billy Liar on the Moon*, which saw the now older anti-hero trapped in suburbia, but between the two there were other joyous novels, including the workplace satire *Office Life*, in which a handful of befuddled employees set off to discover what their company actually does for a living, and *Maggie Muggins*, the melancholy story of a down-at-heel, hungover London lady reaching the end of her tether over the course of a single hellish day. In this respect it plays out like an earthier reversal of Woolf's *Mrs Dalloway*.

Although Waterhouse never lost his Yorkshire sensibilities, he was also an old-school Fleet Street journalist who believed in good grammar and correct spelling, and created the definitive manual about clear writing, called *On Newspaper Style*. Originally written as an in-house style guide for the *Daily Mirror*'s journalists, it remains just as relevant and funny today, and stayed on my desk until I had memorized it. Within were laid out all of the journalist's cheap tricks for grabbing readers by the throat, from hitting interviewees with fixed questions to rewriting dull stories into tabloidese, using short, tough action verbs like 'rap', 'probe', 'bid', 'swoop' and 'axe'. Waterhouse didn't live long enough to see his beloved profession wrecked by the press release, which allowed hacks to churn predigested copy onto the page with barely a rewrite.

Waterhouse's admiration for other hard-drinking journalists

extended to mythologizing Soho and its denizens, with whom he could often be found, especially the alcoholic columnist Jeffrey Bernard, whom he immortalized in the play *Jeffrey Bernard is Unwell.* It featured a stellar performance by Peter O'Toole as the acerbic scribe who is forced to examine his life while locked in the Coach and Horses pub overnight.

In later years Waterhouse became ubiquitous as a TV pundit, writing two melancholy volumes about his childhood, and in the process was incorrectly dismissed as a nostalgist by critics who had failed to see the astringency in his books; this ultimately damaged his standing, together with his impatience for political correctness and his reliance on old habits (only working on a manual Adler typewriter, having champagne at lunch). His sparkling, evocative novels deserve a far better fate.

He felt he was lazy, which, if true, made him the hardest-working lazy writer around. In bars he performed his egg trick, with a biscuit-tin lid, a pint-glass of water, a matchbox and an egg balanced on top of each other. It involved hitting the lid with a shoe to drop the egg in the water, and sometimes it left egg over everyone. I think this was his approach to writing: he took chances that didn't always work, but when they did, the result was extremely satisfying. He lived a long and happy life.

95

Winifred Watson

When it comes to literary success, timing is everything. Before J. K. Rowling's ubiquitous boy wizard there had been a virtual industry of magic-schoolboy tales from other authors, some very good indeed, but Harry Potter was the one who clicked. Winifred Watson's literary career was curtailed by three major events: the Depression, the attack on Pearl Harbor and the Blitz.

Watson was born in Newcastle upon Tyne, and remained there all her life. Due to follow her sisters into higher education, she found the way blocked when her father's shoe shops failed in the Depression of 1929. She wrote her first book, the Northumbrian historical drama *Fell Top*, in dull days stuck behind a secretarial desk, after her boss suggested bringing in knitting to keep herself amused. Finishing the novel in just six weeks, she stuck it in a drawer and forgot about it until she spotted an advertisement from publisher Methuen, looking for new writers.

The book was critically well-received and became a radio play.

Watson was young and pretty and smart, and got good local coverage, so the publishers asked her for more. The result was *Odd Shoes*, produced in a different style that benefited from proper research.

Her third book horrified Methuen. Instead of being serious it was light-hearted and fun to read. More criminally, she was writing on subjects she knew nothing about. The book was *Miss Pettigrew Lives for a Day*, about a frumpy governess who is accidentally sent by her agency to work for a louche actress and nightclub singer running a complicated love life. 'I didn't know anyone like Miss Pettigrew,' Watson said. 'I just made it all up. I haven't the faintest idea what governesses really do. I've never been to a nightclub and I certainly didn't know anyone who took cocaine.'

The book was an immediate hit with the public, and a big-budget Hollywood musical was planned starring Billie Burke, the good witch from *The Wizard of Oz*. The bombing of Pearl Harbor put paid to that. 'I wish the Japanese had waited six months,' Watson said later.

She married and continued to write every day, but when the house next door was blown up in the war, her family was forced to move into one room with her parents, making further writing impossible.

Persephone Books persevered with the republication of *Miss Pettigrew Lives for a Day*, and the book found its way onto Hollywood desks once more. A rather charming film version starring Amy Adams finally appeared six years after Watson's death.

This kind of serendipity once happened all the time. I have had film versions of my novels derailed by everything from the star's messy divorce to the director suffering a near-fatal skiing accident. In an attempt to circumvent unforeseen problems, the new Hollywood requires 'pre-recognition', a state of fan service wherein the film's story is already known, i.e. *Star Wars*, *Star Trek*, *Batman* or *Sherlock Holmes*. Few producers search the backlists of forgotten authors anymore.

The Justly Forgotten Authors

Having made it my mission to restore lustre to unfairly misplaced popular writers, let's pause to ask a question: are there some who don't deserve resuscitation?

The archetypal rubbish poet is of course William Topaz McGonagall, whose epic doggerel 'The Tay Bridge Disaster' offers a masterclass in crap writing:

Beautiful Railway Bridge of the Silv'ry Tay!
Alas! I am very sorry to say
That ninety lives have been taken away
On the last Sabbath day of 1879
Which will be remember'd for a very long time.

There's something about those who, brushing against others of genius, assume they can do it too, and they're often drawn to verse. The awkwardly spelled Vyvyan Holland, second son of Oscar Wilde, turned to limericks of such dreary vacuity that I actually binned my copy (you can still pick them up for about a fiver). Then there's hopelessly wet Lord Alfred Douglas, usually described as 'The Tragic and Litigious', although after reading *The Duke of Berwick and Other Rhymes* it's hard to avoid adding 'And Astonishingly Stupid'. How about:

I wish you may have better luck
Than to be bitten by the Duck
And though he looks so small and weak
He has a very powerful beak.

Even when he tackled the story of his own life, *Oscar Wilde and Myself*, he had to have it ghostwritten, but in such cases the name makes the sale. Lord Alfred 'Bosie' Douglas became a rabid Wilde-hating anti-Semite and is buried in Sussex, where he puts the creepy into Crawley.

When considering duff prose let's not leave out the master, Edward Bulwer-Lytton, the Victorian baron who wrote incredibly popular bestsellers, who coined the phrases 'The pen is mightier than the sword', 'the great unwashed', and the immortal 'It was a dark and stormy night'. He influenced Bram Stoker's *Dracula*, popularized the Hollow Earth theory and died rich, to be buried in Westminster Abbey. But much of his prose stinks. His name is given to the annual Bulwer-Lytton Fiction Contest, in which entrants have to write a single opening sentence of such awfulness that it would be impossible to go on reading.

So perhaps some authors should remain forgotten. There are

certain books that only college students have the patience to read. And back in 1970, students were prepared to read a book exploring the life philosophy of a seagull.

Richard Bach's *Jonathan Livingston Seagull* smashed the bestseller records. The slender square tome was to be found poking out of backpacks the world over. It concerns an anthropomorphic seagull that yearns to fly higher instead of just worrying about where its next whiting is coming from. Millions swallowed the inspirational Christian parable which, at 120 pages (heavily illustrated), took about twelve minutes to digest. It was so successful that it became a film consisting of shots of seagulls floating about to whiffly Neil Diamond songs, the overall effect of which was like lapsing into a coma caused by getting a paper-cut from a Hallmark card.

Bach followed this with *Illusions* and *One*, the message being that we transcend the gravity of our bodies and believe in ourselves, or something. Bach described *The Bridge Across Forever* as 'a story about a knight who was dying, and the princess who saved his life', which, as it concerned the second lady in his life, must have felt like a smack in the face to his first and third partners.

Claiming to be a direct descendant of Johann Sebastian Bach, the former-pilot-turned-novelist loved to explore the metaphysical aspects of flying. Bach's books are fictional versions of moments in his life that illustrate his philosophy. Call me a curmudgeon, but I like to think that his books fell from popularity because students became too sophisticated not to see through this kind of tendentious artery-hardening New Age sputum.

The Bards of Bad include William McGonagall, Georgina Weldon (a sort of reverse muse whose incoherent and self-deluding volumes of memoirs inspired Brian Thompson to pen a hilarious biography, *A Monkey Among Crocodiles*) and the spectacularly verbose Amanda McKittrick Ros, regarded by many critics to be the worst writer of all time.

Ros married a stationmaster who financed her novel *Irene Iddesleigh* in 1897. In the self-delusion ranks she beats Weldon, imagining 'the million and one who thirst for aught that drops from my pen', and predicting she would 'be talked about at the end of a thousand years'. In her last novel all the characters are named after fruit, so long-term recall is entirely possible; just not in a good way.

She had many camp-followers, including Siegfried Sassoon, Mark Twain and Aldous Huxley, who felt that she'd written the best unintentionally humorous novel ever. At Oxford, J. R. R. Tolkien and C. S. Lewis supposedly held a competition to see who could read the largest amount of her work aloud without laughing. Here's a good sample sentence, from the opening of her novel *Delina Delaney*: 'Have you ever visited that portion of Erin's plot that offers its sympathetic soil for the minute survey and scrutinous examination of those in political power, whose decision has wisely been the means before now of converting the stern and prejudiced, and reaching the hand of slight aid to share its strength in augmenting its agricultural richness?'

Er, no.

Her overripe prose is liberally scattered with abused adjectives in a style once described as 'literary diabetes'. She also bashed out volumes of poetry, one entitled *Fumes of Formation*, which contains her poem 'Visiting Westminster Abbey' and begins: 'Holy Moses! Take a look! / Flesh decayed in every nook! / Some rare bits of brain lie here, / Mortal loads of beef and beer!'

Although humorist Barry Pain had a running feud with her, Ros had her revenge. She garnered quite a fan club in the 1930s, championed by Huxley, who regarded her works as genuine folk art. There was even a biography, *O Rare Amanda!,* and a collection of her best worst prose. Uniquely dreadful, Ros believed that her work 'disturbed the bowels of millions' and that critics were too stupid to recognize her talent. They weren't.

The loss of the Titanic inspired reams of doggerel from would-be poets. One called Arthur Holmes wrote a poem with rhymes that included 'Britannic', 'mechanic' and 'panic'. I'll let you guess how the last line ended.

To understand the continued appeal of bad writing we should look to the present, and the renowned writer of big novels, Mr Dan Brown. The problem, of course, is that he's entirely beyond parody, as demonstrated by numerous club-footed reviews mimicking his style. His chases around the world's libraries and churches to uncover secret manuscripts have been parsed for their historical inaccuracy and his prose has been eviscerated for its poverty, but this is to miss the point.

Brown does have a style, which frankly is more than many authors have. He makes readers turn pages, and he's fun to read, albeit in the same way that you'd watch a viral video of a drunk Russian falling over a railing. More to the point, there have always been writers like him. The real sin of bad writing is being boring, and Mr Brown is certainly never that. There are intellectual writers whose prose is so clumsy that the act of reading them is like repeatedly stubbing your toe. What's more, any writer who can trick the Vatican into responding to a piece of fiction does not deserve the level of critical opprobrium Brown has endured.

There has always been an air of snobbery around writers, evinced by the dismissive attitude of a tiny handful of critics and booksellers. Some things are implicitly understood: you don't eat crisps at the opera and you never admit that an author beloved by the intelligentsia leaves you cold. For millions of readers, tales of adventure and romance were once the only way of escaping a grimmer reality. Is that so wrong? Dan Brown wrote a pulp novel that encouraged argument about the veracity of religion, just as Michael Crichton got readers believing that mosquitos could provide the key to reconstructing dinosaurs. We may laugh now, but at the time we bought in – which is how that Devonshire plumber persuaded the world that he was a Tibetan monk.

96

Dennis Wheatley

'Really?' said a friend. '*Wheatley*, out of print, now? Are you sure?' And indeed, a little checking proved the case. One of the world's bestselling authors (he shifted over fifty million copies from the 1930s to the 1960s) is fading away. It's not hard to see why; in our dark modern world Satanists seem rather quaint and ridiculous, and certainly not worthy of the hilariously puritanical warning Wheatley always placed at the front of his supernatural novels about the 'very real dangers' of witchcraft.

Dennis Yates Wheatley (1897–1977) was an inventive, prolific author who conjured forbidden thrills by selling the virtually non-existent 'reality' of black magic to aghast British readers. His best novel is generally agreed to be *The Haunting of Toby Jugg*, in which a monstrous, malevolent spider-thing taps at Toby's bedroom window trying to get in, and is there night after night, glimpsed beneath the curtains. Toby is a wounded Battle of Britain pilot and thinks he's hallucinating, but there are devilish forces at work and he's powerless to stop them. The novel was written three years after the Second World War and still harbours an oppressive fear of Nazi invasion. This is Wheatley's most atmospheric work, filled with the dread of the sickroom at night and the unnameable terrors that lurk in the shadows. It's also one of the few Wheatley novels into which you can read a psychological subtext – the unwholesome spider feels like the manifestation of illness and death drawing near, Toby is the paralysed, helpless victim, and there's a strangely ambiguous patrician carer called Helmuth who seems to represent the state. The more prosaic climactic good-versus-evil battle feels less real than the ominous spider.

Gregarious and clubbable, Wheatley hailed from an upper-middle-class family who owned a wine business. His adventure stories were packed with bigotry, sex, Satanism and the kind of institutionalized snobbery one so often finds in books of this era. His stories were linked with shared-world characters and teeming with ludicrous incident, which gave him the kind of instant popular appeal Ian Fleming enjoyed. He was drawn to creating titled heroes in the grand traditional vein, like Gregory Sallust ('The man the Nazis couldn't kill!'), but his fantastical novels were less stiff-necked and offered more disreputable hijinks.

The author of *They Found Atlantis* also invented board games and created several interactive murder dossiers containing physical pieces of evidence (a lock of human hair! A fag end!), with a sealed last section revealing the killer.

Wheatley's wife found him a job coordinating secret military deceptions for Winston Churchill, who asked him to suggest what the Germans were up to. It was typical of Churchill's lateral thinking that he would approach a fantasy writer to get predictions about the future of the war – after all, this was the man who had asked Royal Academy artists, rather than the army, to improve military camouflage. Surprisingly Wheatley's ideas about what the Germans were up to were often near the mark, although his fears that the enemy would invent a death ray proved unfounded.

'The Dennis Wheatley Library of the Occult' appeared in mass-market paperbacks that brought new audiences, and Hammer Films adapted his work, their sharpest being *The Devil Rides Out*, in which the Duc de Richleau defeats the forces of evil, although Hammer's budget did not stretch to a chase across Europe and instead culminated in Buckinghamshire. Phil Baker's definitive biography, *The Devil is a Gentleman*, fills in the details and catches Wheatley's breathless appeal.

97

T. H. White

Sadly, good book sales often have little to do with good writing, and some of the finest authors featured here have struggled throughout their careers. T. H. White took a long time to find the right readership, and I feel he would be far better remembered had he been born a little later, rather than in 1906.

His policeman father was an alcoholic, and when his parents' marriage ended badly, fearful Terence was moved from Bombay to Gloucester. At college he wrote a thesis on *Le Morte d'Arthur*, then started teaching. The desire to write grew, and one of his earlier volumes included a memoir, *England Have My Bones*. A countryman absorbed in rural pursuits, he loved falconry and fishing, describing his occupation as 'keeping out of London and wondering why nobody cares about the country labourer'.

Earth Stopped and *Gone to Ground* were science-fiction novels about the end of the world, and he should have been punished for writing a novel called *Burke's Steerage*, but it wasn't until his twelfth book that White decided to tackle a preface to Malory's Arthurian legend.

The result was *The Sword in the Stone*, published in 1938, featuring the time-travelling, body-swapping wizard Merlin tutoring young Arthur ('the Wart'), a situation reflected in White's own mentoring by the Cambridge scholar L. J. Potts. The book is a dazzling *tour de force* of imagination that puts contemporary language in the mouths of its protagonists for the first time. Merlin is living his life backwards, and is capable of transplanting Wart's mind into forest creatures. This was to be the first volume in the increasingly powerful and moving tragedy of King Arthur.

Arthur's childhood is lightly magical, but as he grows to maturity the tone of the books matures with him. Lancelot is revealed to be a physically ugly, self-hating sadist, determined to overcome his natural inclinations, and Sir Galahad is so perfect that everyone hates him.

Over the next two decades, further parts appeared, and the revised, more tragic whole was published in 1958 as *The Once and Future King*. This definitive tetralogy was altered partly to incorporate events and pacifist themes that White had originally intended to cover in the fifth volume, but many critics and readers preferred the separate originals, which are *The Sword in the Stone*, *The Witch in the Wood*, *The Ill-Made Knight*, *The Candle in the Wind* and *The Book of Merlyn*. I can think of only a handful of novels which have undergone major revisions after publication (John Fowles's *The Magus* being one). White was clearly in need of a good, decisive editor and his novels are inconsistent – the tone of the first jars somewhat with the others – but together they still constitute one of the most powerful works of twentieth-century fantastic literature. Yet, tracking down the individual volumes is now as difficult as withdrawing the sword itself.

White moved to the Channel Islands, uncomfortable with his seemingly undeveloped sexuality, never forming close relationships, and continued to write. My other favourite novel of his is *Farewell Victoria*, which covers the changing century of its hero Mundy's life in just 128 exquisitely detailed pages, starting in 1858. Of the adolescent Mundy he tellingly notes: 'The forward maturity of the others had confused his secret manhood; he had been frightened of the freemasonry and difference which they possessed.' Of his beloved rural countrymen, he says: 'Manners, etiquette, regulation; these were a recognition of the pleasures of life, which they respected enough to order it.' This moving history of an examined life has utterly disappeared, along with much of White's work.

However, White's delightful novel, *Mistress Masham's Repose*, about an orphan girl who discovers the Lilliputians from *Gulliver's Travels* and sets out to protect them, has finally come to be regarded as one of the most magical children's books ever written.

98

Kathleen Winsor

Authors are prone to accidental notoriety. Any printed display of opinion is bound to raise questions, and can result in feuds, curtailed careers and, in the case of the deliberately provocative Salman Rushdie, a fatwah, but a censored novel is often its ticket to popularity. Here we have a case of censorship in America that went badly wrong – something Kathleen Winsor (1919–2003) discovered the hard way.

Winsor was a smart, energetic sports columnist who subsequently became fascinated by the Restoration period. After years of research she produced a sprawling fifth draft of her first novel that topped out at around 2,500 pages. Her publishers hacked it down to a more manageable size, just under a thousand pages, and it appeared in 1944 as *Forever Amber*.

The novel was a *billet-doux* to a city she had read about but never visited, a bodice-ripping romp through London in times of plague and fire, taking in the society chatter and politics of the times. There were a few mildly titillating passages, and the book was generally well received by critics who saw parallels between the enduring Restoration wives and their wartime counterparts. It didn't hurt that the attractive author, then twenty-four, was seductively photographed for her press releases.

No one had foreseen that Winsor's glamorous looks would count against her, or that the book would actually be banned. When the Massachusetts Attorney General cast a magnifying glass over the text, he found more than seventy veiled references to sexual intercourse, thirty-nine out-of-wedlock pregnancies, seven abortions and ten scenes in which women undressed in front of men.

Critics grimly accused the novelist of glorifying the superficial, immoral life of a courtesan. State after state followed suit, blocking the blockbuster and pronouncing it pornography, and soon Winsor found she had created a national scandal with the mildest of all bonkbusters. Naturally, *Forever Amber* became the bestselling novel of the 1940s.

Winsor's own sin was to write something that was a tiny bit sexy and fun in a time of deeply entrenched conservatism. Instead of wartime austerity, her heroine offered something more appealing, notoriously announcing that 'Adultery is not a crime, it's an amusement'. The end of the Second World War was not a time to be sexually frivolous, even when discussing the past. Men were coming home, women had been independent for long enough, and it was time to corral them back into the home.

Scandal and success combined to destroy Winsor's marriage. She wedded handsome band leader Artie Shaw (his sixth wife after Lana Turner and Ava Gardner), and when that relationship failed she married her own divorce attorney. In her next novel, *Star Money*, she wrote a thinly disguised biography about becoming a bestselling author, but despite being billed as the new fiction from the author of *Forever Amber*, it was received with indifference.

The moment had passed. When Winsor married into Washington society she turned her back on her notorious past. She continued to write until 1986, but none of her fiction made any impact. It can fairly be said that the success of her first novel upset the balance of her life.

99

Cornell Woolrich

I hate to end the book on a dark note, but perhaps it says a lot about the authors we've looked at: no matter how hard they tried to disguise who they were, something of their nature could always be glimpsed through their work – for better or worse. And in the case of Woolrich, what made him bitter and miserable in his personal life also made him brilliant on the page.

For a long time the big three names of American crime writing were considered to be Dashiell Hammett, Raymond Chandler and Erle Stanley Gardner (the bestselling American author of the twentieth century at the time of his death). But just behind them was the name we've now almost completely forgotten.

It's been a theme of this book that a writer's longevity has been improved by translation into another medium, and Cornell Woolrich's so-called 'paranoid noir' novels lent themselves to visual versions so well that he had a profound effect on popular cinema.

Woolrich had begun his career writing light jazz-age novels in the style of F. Scott Fitzgerald, but found his feet in a series of bleak, superbly plotted detective pulps, writing pseudonymously to skip around his publisher's ownership of his name. His 1942 story 'It Had to Be Murder' was later filmed by Alfred Hitchcock as *Rear Window* (Woolrich having based it on an old H. G. Wells tale), and François Truffaut directed both *The Bride Wore Black* and *Waltz into Darkness*. *Phantom Lady*, *Night Has a Thousand Eyes* and *I Married a Dead Man* were also successfully filmed.

Woolrich's tales were page-turning races against time to prove innocence or take revenge, but the stories were rooted in character. In *The Bride Wore Black*, a groom gunned down on his wedding day is fabulously avenged by his wife, while in *Phantom Lady*, a convicted wife-strangler must find the only woman who can provide him with an alibi.

Woolrich also wrote 'All at Once, No Alice', a spin on a nineteenth-century urban legend in which a man briefly leaves his bride in their hotel room on their wedding night. When he returns, the room no longer exists, his bride can't be found, and everyone with whom they came into contact denies having seen them before. Woolrich recognized a good story archetype when he saw one, and could always retool it for a new market.

Woolrich's heroes were persecuted victims frequently beset by obsessive fears as the options left open to them vanished one by one, although they could come over as cold and remote. He was known as an ideas man, and had trouble producing characters that connected with readers. The author's bitter pessimism was perfectly suited to the noir genre, but his worldview extended from his private life; after a brief, disastrous marriage he returned to live with his saintly mother while cruising the docks for sailors, and was by all accounts uncomfortable and unpleasant in company. He usually wrote with his mother looking over his shoulder.

Bouts of alcoholism exacerbated his diabetes, and his remaining friends were finally driven away. Although wealthy, he spent the last decade of his life entirely alone and angry, his gangrenous leg amputated, as if a noir character had sprung from his own pages. It's hard for authors to prevent their own natures from bleeding through to the page, and looking back over the lives of these authors it seems to me that the bitterest books have the lowest survival rate. Woolrich left behind 250 stories and nearly twenty novels.

In 2016 I found a couple of his books holding up a three-legged chair in the Yum Yum Thai takeaway in King's Cross, London. The owner was happy to donate them to me for the price of a *mee goreng*. Like Woolrich, the Yum Yum has also vanished.

I don't feel too sorry for Woolrich. Even a soured life could leave behind books that continue to give pleasure. If you only rediscover one author from this selection of ninety-nine, you will have conferred upon them a kind of immortality.

The Last Word

LADY: You're always reading, aren't you?

HANCOCK: Yes.

LADY: You'll hurt your eyes, you will.

HANCOCK: I'll hurt yours in a minute.

Second-hand bookshops are best visited alone and in the rain. Last year I was mooching along Charing Cross Road, visiting the last remaining bookshops to survive, looking to buy a book as a gift, and stumbled across a cheap volume from 1954 called *Hurrah for St Trinian's!* by Ronald Searle and D. B. Wyndham Lewis. When I opened the flyleaf at home, some letters from Ronald Searle to his agent fell out. This is another reason for showing an interest in this esoteric branch of reading. Life is not a box of chocolates, it's a weathered old paperback, and you never know what you're going to find in it.

The love of books is an obsessive and sometimes dangerous passion. A mate of mine loved books so much that he went to jail.

He'd go into libraries, see which rare copies hadn't been taken out in five years, and liberate them – usually under his raincoat. He figured that if fine literature was going to waste it should come to live with someone who worshipped it. For him it was like smuggling the least-visited concubines out of a seraglio.

I came to adult reading via the kind of comics most mothers would have taken away and burned – horror comics with no redeeming social value whatsoever, about killer scorpions and attacking jelly-people and talking shrunken heads. Somewhere in each story was a screaming blonde in corsetry that looked like it could only be removed with a chainsaw, and there was a weird use of slang that was dated long before it appeared in comics. When one character had an eye operation, his barman said, 'I'm glad the sawbones fixed you up with new peepers.'

These tales had no authors. Nobody ever expected to be name-checked. They were probably just glad to find work indoors. And so I read about killer moths and skeleton cowboys, men chasing after their own weight in gold and hotter women than their nagging wives. Women were there to be tied up, drowned, fed to beasts, sold to the Devil or slowly stripped by mad doctors and killer apes. And somehow these nameless writers caught the sense of grave-yard-reeking insanity that the great gothic Victorian writers sought.

Next came anthologies, which are not collections. (Anthologies are compilations from a variety of authors under the aegis of an editor who draws out a common theme; the latter stem from a single writer.) In 1937 *Fifty Strangest Stories Ever Told* was published and became an instant classic that stayed on the nation's household shelves for decades. The 700-page volume introduced readers to perfectly respectable authors they had never heard of. My parents kept a copy, but it was not placed on shelves within my reach. Obviously I managed to reach it. Perhaps that's what parents should always do with books they want children to read.

At one of my very first publishing parties, I found myself among a group of bright young things discussing new books. I felt a little out of my depth because the Bright Young Things all worked for literary publications and were littering the floor with titles of philosophical novels I hadn't read. I had no real reason to be lacking in confidence; I'd studied the classics and was a voracious reader, but I was cripplingly shy and they were an intimidating pack. I felt like an outsider guiltily listening in at the keyhole while a private conversation took place on the other side of an elaborately locked door.

Being excluded from groups is a sensation familiar to everyone at some time or other, and thinking back to that first party, it was hard not to notice that it was almost exclusively male. Fiction has now undergone a revolution. Powered by a largely female readership, it has rubbed out the dividing line between so-called 'important' novels and 'popular fiction'.

Social media has helped to kick the locks off previously closed doors, but there's still one golden key that opens all of them: the ability to write well and engage readers. Of course there are pinnacles of fine writing for readers to scale, but popular fiction can be just as revelatory. Books have the power to calm, enlighten and energize, but it seems to me that of all the arts they are at the most risk. The easiest way to make reading effortless is to make books a habit, so that they become a retreat, a sanctuary, a call to arms.

The works of even the most obscure authors are still out there somewhere, and thanks to the dedication of publishers, collectors, sellers and readers, they are once more being found and enjoyed again.

Acknowledgements

This book began in a very different form as 'Invisible Ink' for the *Independent on Sunday*, so I'd like to thank Suzi Feay, its terrifyingly well-read former literary editor, and Katy Guest, the tranquil-tempered editor who subsequently brought her own unique style to its pages. It's also for the many people who contacted me over the years with their own stories and reminiscences, the husbands, wives, agents and friends of authors who expanded my knowledge. Special thanks to Chris Ade, who sent me the names of further authors throughout the life of 'Invisible Ink'.

Publishing houses like Persephone Books, Pushkin Press, Rue Morgue Press, Tartarus Books and Mark Pilkington's oddly brilliant Strange Attractor Press are uncovering authors now considered to be esoteric. They deserve the support of book-lovers everywhere. Any factual errors are the result of having to rely on limited and often contradictory research materials, much of which only became available with the authors' returning popularity. Following a fine tradition set by the *Independent* newspaper, I'm happy to incorporate any changes you uncover in future editions.

It's clear from looking over the lives of these authors that many would have had a better survival rate with a decent editor. I was lucky enough to get Rich Arcus, who showed me the difference a great editor can make to a book.

Index

Aberson, Helen 34
Adams, Charles Warren
The Notting Hill Mystery 327
Ahtesham, Manzoor
The Tale of a Missing Person 313
Aldridge, Alan 20
Allingham, Margery 5–7, 8
Coroner's Pidgin 6
Look to the Lady 7
The Tiger in the Smoke 6–7
Amazing Stories magazine 305
Andersen, Hans Christian
'The Snow Queen' 36
Andrews, Virginia 8–10, 11
Flowers in the Attic 9–10
My Sweet Audrina 10
The Obsessed 9
Anstey, F. *see* Guthrie, Thomas
anthologies 356
Antrobus, John 25
Ardizzone, Edward 207
Armstrong, Charlotte 11–14, 15, 170
The Chocolate Cobweb 13
Mischief 12
Night Call 13
The Other Shoe 13
Askey, Arthur 295
Atkinson, Kate 92
Auden, W.H. 101–2, 278
Avengers, The 7
Ayraud, Pierre *see* Narcejac, Thomas
Bach, Richard 339
The Bridge Across Forever 339
Illusions 339
Jonathan Livingston Seagull 339
One 339
Bainbridge, Beryl 234
Baker, Frank 15–17
The Birds 15, 17
Lease of Life 17
Miss Hargreaves 16–17
Mr Allenby Loses the Way 16
The Twisted Tree 16
Baker, George 273
Baking, Kilo-katal
Hakkenden 262
Ballantyne, R.M. 18–20, 21
The Butterfly's Ball and the Grasshopper's Feast 20
The Coral Island 18, 19–20
The Gorilla Hunters 18
Ballard, K.G. *see* Roth, Holly
Bambi (film) 34
Barber, Francis 375
Barnes, Peter 24–6
Laughter! 26
Red Noses 26
The Ruling Class 25–6
Baron, Alexander 21–3
From the City, from the Plough 22
The Human Kind 22
Kind Dido 22
The Lowlife 22
Strip Jack Naked 22
There's No Home 22
Barrie, J.M. 277
Bawden, Nina 235
Beaton, Cecil 28
Beatty, Paul
The Sellout 234
Belloc, Hilaire 203
Cautionary Tales for Children 203
Bennett, Alan 25, 90
Bernard, Jeffrey 333
Billy Bunter (character) 144
Billy Liar (film) 332
Birds, The (film) 15–16
Blanch, Lesley 27–9
Round the World in Eighty Dishes 29
The Sabres of Paradise 29
The Wilder Shores of Love 28–9
Blochman, Lawrence G. 104
Body Snatchers, The (film) 114
Boileau, Pierre 315–16
Les Diaboliques 316
The Living and the Dead 316
Bond, James 105–6

Bonfiglioli, Kyril 30–2
After You with the Pistol 31
All the Tea in China 31
Don't Point That Thing At Me 30–1
The Great Mortdecai Moustache Mystery 31
Something Nasty in the Woodshed 31
Booker Prize 232–5, 243, 275, 290, 291
Bordewijk, Ferdinand
Character 312–13
Bornemann, Ernest 38–40
Bang! You're Dead 39
The Face on the Cutting-Room Floor 39–40
Tremolo 39
Boulle, Pierre 41–3
The Bridge over the River Kwai 41–2
Monkey Planet (Plant of the Apes) 42
Planet of the Men 42
Bowen, Marjorie 167
Bowman, W.E.
The Ascent of Rum Doodle 128
Braddon, Mary Elizabeth 44–6
Lady Audley's Secret 45, 46
Brahms, Caryl 47–8
A Bullet in the Ballet 47–8
Casino for Sale 48
Don't, Mr Disraeli 48
Envoy on Excursion 48
Lost Clouds and Discords 48
No Bed for Bacon 48
Six Curtains for Stroganova 48
Branch, Pamela 49–51
Lion in the Cellar 50
The Wooden Overcoat 49–50
Braun, Lilian Jackson 104–5
Bridge over the River Kwai, The (film) 41–2
British Library 327, 329
Broken Blossoms (film) 56
Brooke-Rose, Christine
'Red Rubber Gloves' 168
Brookner, Anita
Hotel du Lac 234
Brophy, Brigid 52–4, 118
Baroque 'n' Roll 54
Fifty Works of English Literature We Could Do Without 54
Hackenfeller's Ape 52
In Transit 53
The King of a Rainy Country 52
Prancing Novelist 53–4
The Snow Ball 52–3
Brown, Craig 31
Brown, Dan 341–2
Brown, Fredric 65–6
What Mad Universe 66
Brynner, Yul 39
Bulwer-Lytton, Edward 338
Burgess, Anthony 175
Burke, John
'Tales of Unease' 168
Burke, Thomas 55–6, 137
'The Chink and the Child' 56
'The Hands of Mr Ottermole' 55
Limehouse Nights 55–6
Nights in Town 55
Burnt Offerings (film) 260
Burton, Isabel 28
Burton, Richard 131
Buzzati, Dino 57–9, 60
'The Elevator' 58
Il Colombre 59
'Just the Very Thing They Wanted' 58
'Seven Floors' 58
The Tartar Steppe 57, 59

Caesar, Sid 94
Carlon, Patricia 60–1
Circle of Fear 60
Hush, It's a Game 61
The Whispering Wall 60–1
Carr, Barbara Comyns 62–3
Our Spoons Came from Woolworths 63
Out of the Red and into the Blue 63
Sisters by a River 63
The Vet's Daughter 63
Carr, John Dickson 68–70, 98
The Hollow Man 69
The Judas Window 69
Carr, Philippa *see* Hibbert, Eleanor
Carroll, Jonathan 183
Carroll, Lewis 200
Catalan writing 312
Chabrol, Claude 13
Chandler, Raymond 352
Charteris, Leslie 71–3
Meet - The Tiger! 71
Chaze, Lewis Elliott
Black Wings Has My Angel 64–5
Chesterton, G.K. 244
Christie, Agatha 43, 89, 101–2
Christopher, John 74–6
The Death of Grass 75
Empty World 76
The Little People 75
'Tripods' books 75–6
The Winter Swan 74–5
The World in Winter 76
A Wrinkle in the Skin 76
The Year of the Comet 75
Churchill, Winston 344–5

Clayton, Richard *see* Haggard, William
Clemens, Brian 7
Coe, Jonathan 39
Cohen, Marcelo
The End of the Same 313
Collier, John 77–9
Defy the Foul Fiend 78
'The Devil, George and Rosie' 78
'Evening Primrose' 78
Fancies And Goodnights 78
'Green Thoughts' 78
His Monkey Wife 63, 77–8
Tom's A-Cold: A Tale 78
Collins, Norman 80–3
The Bat That Flits 82
Bond Street Story 82
The Facts of Fiction 81
Flames Coming Out of the Top 82
The Governor's Lady 82
London Belongs to Me 81–2
'London from a Bus Stop' 80
Collins, Wilkie 135
comics 215–16
Conan Doyle, Adrian 98
Conan Doyle, Sir Arthur 98–101, 103, 126, 133
Condon, Richard 84–6
An Infinity of Mirrors 85
The Manchurian Candidate 84–5
Mile High 85
Prizzi's Honor 85
Connor, William 245
Conti, Italia 236
Cooper, Basil 101
Creasey, John 263
Crichton, Michael 342
Crippen, Dr 161
Crispin, Edmund 87–9
Gervase Fen books 87–9
Crowley, Mart
The Boys in the Band 194
Curious Cookbook, The 273
Curtiss, Ursula 172–3
The Forbidden Garden 173

Dad's Army 295
Daly, Elizabeth 102–3
Däniken, Erich von
Chariots of the Gods 278
d'Antin y Zuloaga, Luis Ricardo Carlos Fernand 204–5
Mots d'Heures 204–5
Darlton, Clark
Perry Rhodan 264–5
Davidson, Lionel 291–3
The Chelsea Murders 292
Kolymsky Heights 292–3
The Night of Wenceslas 291–2
The Rose of Tibet 292
Smith's Gazelle 292
Davis, Bette 230, 320
Deep Purple 20
Defoe, Daniel
Robinson Crusoe 19, 33
Delafield, E.M. 3, 90–2
The Diary of a Provincial Lady 90–1
The Provincial Lady in Wartime 91
'They Don't Wear Labels' 92
Dennis, Patrick 93–4
Auntie Mame 93–4
First Lady 94
Little Me 94
Depp, Johnny 32
Derleth, August 100–1
detective stories 98–105
Devil Rides Out, The (film) 345
Diaboliques, Les (film) 316
Dickens, Charles 133–6
'The Battle of Life' 135
A Child's History of England 134
'The Chimes' 135
A Christmas Carol 135, 136
'The Cricket on the Hearth' 135
The Haunted House 135
'The Haunted Man and the Ghost's Bargain' 135–6
Muggy Junction 134–5
Dickinson, Thorold 95
Dickson, Carter *see* Carr, John Dickson
Digby, Lady Jane 28
Disney, Walt 33–7
Dozen, Rudolf 287–90
Alone in Berlin 289
The Drinker 289
Little Man, What Now? 288
Peasants, Bosses and Bombs 288
Wolf Among Wolves 288–9
Don't Bother to Knock (film) 12
Douglas, Lord Alfred
Oscar Wilde and Myself 338
The Duke of Berwick and Other Rhymes 338
Du Maurier, Daphne 15, 134
Dubach de Revere, Aimee 28
Dumbo (film) 34
Dunsany, 18th Baron of *see* Plunkett, Edward John Moreton Drax
Dunant, Raymond 95–7
The Crazy Mirror 96

Films and Feelings 96
A Long Hard Look at 'Psycho' 97
A Mirror for England 96–7

Eberhardt, Isabelle 28
Edgar Allan Poe Award 66
Edgar Wallace Mysteries, The 326
Edwards, Amelia B. 167
'The Four-Fifteen Express' 167
Ellis, Edward
Ruth the Betrayer, or The Female Spy 328
Embrace of the Serpent (film) 313
Enchanted April (film) 26
England, Barry 233
Epicure's Almanack, The 273
Erskine, Rosalind 107–9
A High-Pitched Buzz 108
The Passion Flower Hotel 107–8
Switchboard 108
Estleman, Loren D. 99
Evans, Dr Christopher 111–12
Cults of Unreason 112
Mind at Bay 111–12
Mind in Chains 112
Everett, Mrs H.D. 167

Fallada, Hans *see* Ditzen, Rudolf
Family Way, The (film) 251
Farmer, Philip Jose
The Adventure of the Peerless Peer 99
Farrell, James 233, 290–1
'Empire Trilogy' 290
A Man from Elsewhere 290
The Siege of Krishnapur 290–1
Troubles 291
Feay, Suzi 3
Féval, Paul 315
The Black Coats 315
Fifty Strangest Stories Ever Told 356–7
Finney, Jack 113–15
About Time 114
The Body Snatchers 114
From Time to Time 114
'I Love Galesburg in the Springtime' 113
The Night People 114–15
Time and Again 114
Firbank, Ronald 116–19, 256
Caprice 118
The Flower Beneath the Foot 117
Valmouth 118–19
Fleming, Ian 105, 121
Fleming, Peter 120–1
Brazilian Adventure 120–1
A Forgotten Journey 121
Fletcher, Lucille 122–3
Eighty Dollars to Stamford 123
Sorry, Wrong Number 123
Fly, The (film) 198
Foreman, Carl 42
Forrest, Maryann *see* Hope, Polly
Forrester, Andrew *see* Ware, James Redding
Fox and the Hound, The (film) 36
Fraser, Anthea 103
Frayn, Michael 249
Freeman, R. Austin 124–6
The Eye of Osiris 124–5
Mr Polton Explains 126
The Singing Bone 125
French novels 314–18
French, Samuel 24–5
Fritzl, Josef 10
Frozen (film) 36

Gaelic language 314
Ganivet, Ángel
Idearium Español 313
Gardner, Erle Stanley 352
Gem, The 143, 144
ghost stories 167
Gilbert, W.S. 172
Ruddigore 172
Gilman, Charlotte Perkins
'The Yellow Wallpaper' 167
Gipson, Fred 34
Little Arliss 34
Old Yeller 34
Savage Sam 34
Glashan, John *see* McGlashan, John
Goebbels, Joseph 289
Gold Dagger Award 292
Golden Age crime writers 6, 7, 68, 88, 321
Golding, William
Lord of the Flies 18
Graham, Caroline 103
Graham, Harry 200–1
Ruthless Rhymes 200–1
Grand Budapest Hotel, The (film) 313
Graves, Robert 301, 302
Gravett, Paul
1001 *Comics You Must Read Before You Die* 216
Green, Michael 127–9
The Art of Coarse Acting 127–8
The Art of Coarse Moving 127–8
The Art of Coarse Rugby 127–8
Squire Haggard's Journal 128–9
Greene, Graham 63, 243

Greene, Hugh 110
Greene, Ward
Happy Dan, the Whistling Dog 37
Griffith, D.W. 56
Guthrie, Thomas 140–2
The Brass Bottle 141–2
The Giant's Robe 140
Vice Versa 140–1
'Gynaecological Gothic' 172

Haaest, Erik 149
Haggard, William 105–6
The Power House 106
The Unquiet Sleep 105–6
Hamilton, Charles 143–4
Billy Bunter books 144
Hammer Films 345
Hammett, Dashiell 104, 352
Hancock, Tony 127
Hanley, James 145–7
Boy 145–6
'The Furys' 146
Harris, Joel Chandler 34
Hassel, Sven 148–50
Hayward, William Stephens
Revelations of a Lady Detective 328
Heath, Roy A K 234–5
Armstrong trilogy 234–5
The Murderer 235
The Shadow Bride 235
Herbert, A.P. 151–3
Misleading Cases in the Common Law 152–3
Mr Gay's London 151
Herrmann, Bernard 122, 123
Herzen, Alexander 27
Heyer, Georgette 154–5
Hibbert, Eleanor 157–9
Hintze, Naomi
You'll Like My Mother 172
Hitchcock, Alfred 12, 15–16, 38, 97, 198, 229, 230, 316, 353
Hodge, Harry 160–2
'Famous Trials' 160–1
Hodge, James Hozier 160–1
Hodgetts, Sheila 163–5
Hoffnung, Gerard 285
Holding, Elisabeth Sanxay 173
Holland, Vyvyan 337–8
Hollywood 95, 194–5, 207, 208, 215, 288
Holmes, Arthur 341
Holt, Hazel 103
Holt, Victoria *see* Hibbert, Eleanor
Hope, Polly 175–9
The Immaculate Misconception 178
Us Lot 178
Hoskin, Cyril *see* Rampa, T. Lobsang
Hughes, Langston 373
Hughes, Richard 180–1
A High Wind in Jamaica 180–1
In Hazard 181
Huxley, Aldous 341

I Dream of Jeannie (tv series) 142
In Search of the Castaways 36
Inoue, Ryoki 261
Irish novels 314
Iron Gates, The (film) 230
Jackson, Shirley 173
Jansson, Tove 164
Japrisot, Sébastien 316–7
The Lady in the Car with Glasses and a Gun 317
Rider on the Rain 317
Jeffrey Bernard is Unwell (film) 333
Jeffrey, Edward 164
Johnson, B.S. 117
Jones, Craig
Blood Secrets 261
Joyce, Graham 182–4
The Facts of Life 183
The Tooth Fairy 183
The Year of the Ladybird 183
Joyce, William (Lord Haw-Haw) 162

Kästner, Erich
Lottie and Lisa 35
Keating, H.R.F. 19, 322
Kelley, William Melvin 377–80
A Different Drummer 377–81
Dancers on the Shore 378
A Drop of Patience 378
Kent, Constance 45
King, Stephen
Needful Things 260
Klane, Robert 185–7
Fire Sale 186
The Horse is Dead 185–6
Where's Poppa? 186
Kneale, Thomas Nigel 188–90
Quartermass stories 189–90
Tomato Cain and Other Stories 188
The Year of the Sex Olympics 190
Knox, Ronald 191–3
'Decalogue' 192–3
Koch-Grünberg, Theodor 313

Labour League of Youth 21
Lady and the Tramp (film) 37

Lambert, Gavin 95, 194–6
The Goodbye People 195, 196
Inside Daisy Clover 195
The Slide Area 195–6
Langelaan, George 197–9
'The Fly' 198, 199
'The Other Hand' 198
'Strange Miracle' 198
Langley, Noel 206–8
Cage Me a Peacock 206
The Land of Green Ginger 207
There's a Porpoise Close Behind Us 206–7
Larkin, Philip 239, 275
Laski, Marghanita 209–11
Little Boy Lost 210
The Victorian Chaise-Longue 210–11
The Village 210
Lawrence, Hilda 173
Lear, Edward 201–3
Lee, Harper 261
Lemarchand, Elizabeth
'Time To Be Going' 168
Levin, Ira 14
Lilliput (magazine) 62, 63
Lindsay, Cressida
'Watch Your Step' 168
Lindsay, Kathleen 262
Little Shop of Horrors 78
Lockridge, Frances and Richard 104
Lonely Passion of Judith Hearne, The (film) 242
Longrigg, Roger Erskine *see* Erskine, Rosalind; Taylor, Domini
Lopez, Maria 261
Lord, Jon 20
Lost Man Booker Prize 235
Lovecraft, H.P. 167
Lucas, George 265
McCarthy, Cormac
The Road 176
McCauley, Kirby 14, 232
MacDonald, Ross 231
McDowell, Michael 212–14
'Blackwater' serial 213
Cold Moon Over Babylon 214
The Elementals 213, 214
Gilded Needles 213–14
McGlashan, John 215–17
'Genius' 216–17
McGonagall, William Topaz 339
'The Tay Bridge Disaster' 337
Maclaren-Ross, Julian 218–19
Bitten by the Tarantula 219
Until the Day She Dies 219
Maclean, Charles
The Watcher 260
Magnet, The 143, 144
Man, Myth & Magic (magazine) 301
Manchurian Candidate, The (film) 85
Manguel, Alberto 110
Mannix, Daniel P. 36
Mantel, Hilary 134, 234
Marasco, Robert
Burnt Offerings 260
Marsh, Ngaio 6, 26
Death and the Dancing Footman 26
Marsh, Richard 220–1
The Beetle 220, 221
Martin, George R.R. 232
Marvel 215
Mee, Arthur 222–5
The Children's Encyclopaedia 222–4
London - Heart of the Empire and Wonder of the World 225
Merci pour le Chocolat (film) 13
Meyer, Gustav 226–8
The Angel of the West Window 227–8
The Golem 226–7
Meyer, Nicholas 99
Middleton, Stanley 233
Holiday 233
Midsomer Murders (tv series) 103
Millar, Margaret 170, 173, 229–31
Beast in View 230
'The Couple Next Door' 230–1
The Iron Gates 230
Mills, Clifford 236–8
Where the Rainbow Ends 236–8
Misleading Cases (tv series) 152–3
Miss Pettigrew Lives for a Day (film) 335
Mitchell, David 234
Mitchell, Gladys 239–41
Dead Men's Morris 240
Hangman's Curfew 239–40
Merlin's Furlong 240
The Mystery of a Butcher's Shop 240
Tom Brown's Body 240
Mitchell, Margaret
Gone With The Wind 233
Montgomery, Robert Bruce *see* Crispin, Edmund
Moore, Brian 242–3, 331
The Great Victorian Collection 243
Judith Hearne 242–3
The Magician's Wife 243
Moore, Roger 72

Morland, Nigel 262
Mortdecai (film) 32
Mortimer, John 162
Mortimer, Penelope
'The Skylight' 168
Morton, J.B. 244–6
The Barber of Putney 244
'By the Way'/ 'Beachcomber' column 245
A London Farrago 245

Naipaul, V.S.
In A Free State 233
Narcejac, Thomas 315–16
Les Diaboliques 316
The Living and the Dead 316
National Book Award 300
Naughton, Bill 250–1
Alfie 251
All in Good Time 251
June Evening 250–1
Spring and Port Wine 251
Neiderman, Andrew 8, 10
Nesbit, Edith 166
'Man-Size in Marble' 166
The Railway Children 166
Newby, Percy Howard 233
Something to Answer For 233
Newman, Andrea 168
'Such a Good Idea' 168
Newman, Kim 100
Newman, Paul 260
Nichols, Peter 25, 247–9
A Day in the Death of Joe Egg 247–8
Feeling You're Behind 249
The National Health 248
Passion Play 249
Poppy 248
Privates on Parade 248
Nightmare (film) 173
Nobbs, David 309
nonsense writers 200–5
Nothomb, Amélie 43

Ó Cadhain, Máirtín
Cré na Cille 314
Ogilvy, Ian 72
Old Yeller (film) 34
'One Thousand Book' authors 261–2
Orczy, Emma 252–3
The Emperor's Candlesticks 252
The Scarlet Pimpernel 253
Oswald, Lee Harvey 85
O'Toole, Peter 333

Palmer, Ray 305
Palmer, Stuart 104
Parent Trap, The (film) 35
Parry, Michael 110
Peacock, Thomas Love 256–8
Crotchet Castle 257
Nightmare Abbey 257
Pergaud, Louis 317–18
The War of the Buttons 317–18
Perrault, Charles 36
Perucho, Joan
Natural History 312
Phillips, Mike 235
Philpotts, Eden 263–4
Pinocchio (film) 36
Planet of the Apes (film) 42
Plunkett, Edward John Moreton Drax 254–5
'How Nuth Would Have Practised his Art upon the Gnoles' 255
Jorkens stories 255
Ponti, Carlo 38
Pope, Polly 175–7
Here (Away From It All) 175–6, 178
Popular Book Centres 2
Porter, Joyce
'Dover' books 266
'Eddie Brown' books 267
Pownall, David 268–70
African Horse 269
The Catalogue of Men 269
The Raining Tree War 269
The Ruling Passion 269
White Cutter 269
Price, Vincent 72
Prix du Roman d'Aventures award 316
Proctor, John 277
Psycho (film) 97
psychoanalysis 229
Pullar, Philippa 271–3
Consuming Passions 271–2, 273
pulp fiction 64–7
Pym, Barbara 274–5
Some Tame Gazelle 274, 275

Quartermass Experiment, The (TV serial) 189
Quittenton, Richard 276–7
Tim Pippin novels 276–7
Quiz, Roland *see* Quittenton, Richard

Radcliffe, Ann 167
Rampa, T. Lobsang 278–80
Living with the Lama 279
The Third Eye 278–9
Ramsay, Peggy 232
Raven, Simon 281–3

Alms for Oblivion 282
Doctors Wear Scarlet 282
The First-Born of Egypt 282
Shadows on the Grass 282
Rear Window (film) 353
Reeve, Arthur 99
Rendell, Ruth 11
Rescuers, The (film) 35
Reynolds, G.W.M. 262–3
The Mysteries of London 263
Rhodan, Perry (character) 264–5
Rice, Craig 104
Richardson, Maurice 284–6
The Exploits of Engelbrecht 285–6
A Strong Man Needed 284
Ridley, Arnold 294–5
The Ghost Train 294–5
The Wrecker 295
Rigg, Diana 239
Rinehart, Mary Roberts 171
Robbins, Tom 296–8, 304
Even Cowgirls Get the Blues 297
Fierce Invalids Home from Hot Climates 297
Jitterbug Perfume 297
Still Life with Woodpecker 297
Rogers, Deborah 232
Rohmer, Sax 56, 100, 137
Roos, William and Audrey 104
Ros, Amanda McKittrick 340–1
Delina Delaney 340
Fumes of Formation 340
Irene Iddesleigh 340
Rossi, Jeaen-Baptiste *see* Japrisot, Sébastien
Roth, Holly 169–70
The Mask of Glass 169–70
Operation Doctors 170
Rowles, Snowy 322
Rowling, J.K. 334
Rubens, Bernice 233
The Elected Member 233
Rupture, La (film) 13
Rushdie, Salman 235, 349
Rutherford, Margaret 17
Ruxton, Buck 161

Saint, the (character) 71–3
Salten, Felix 34
Bambi 34
Perri 34
The Shaggy Dog 34
Salvoni, Elena 25
Samson, Joan
The Auctioneer 259–20
Satrapi, Marjane
Persepolis 215
Saving Mr Banks (film) 33
Sayers, Dorothy L. 6
Scheer, K.H.
Perry Rhodan 264–5
Searle, Ronald 285, 355
Seberg, Jean 28
Segal, Erich
Love Story 261
Selvon, Samuel 374
The Lonely Londoners 374
Seton, Cynthia Propper 299–300
A Fine Romance 300
Severskey, Alexander P. de 35–6
Shah, Idries 301–3
'Nasrudin' stories 302
The Rubaiyat of Omar Khayyam translation 302
The Sufis 301–2
Sharp, Margery
The Rescuers 35
Shaver, Richard 304–6
Shiel, Matthew Phipps 307–8
The Last Miracle 307
The Lord of the Sea 307
The Purple Cloud 308
Sight & Sound (magazine) 95
Sillitoe, Alan 309
Simon, 'Skid' (Simon Skidelsky) 47–8
Sinclair, Mary 167
Smith, Ali 234
Smith, Madeleine 161
Smith, Shelley
The Party At No.5 172
Somerset Maughan Award 188
Song of the South (film) 34–5
Stevenson, Robert Louis 133–4
'The Bottle Imp' 134
Treasure Island 19
Stewart, Mary 170
Stoker, Bram 221
Streamer, Col. D. *see* Graham, Harry
Symons, Julian 39

Taylor, Domini
Mother Love 109
Terrail, Ponson du 314
Thief and the Cobbler, The (film) 302
Thomas, Rhys
The Ruby Slippers of Oz 208
Thomson, David 97
Tidy, Bill 268
Tinniswood, Peter 309–11
The Stirk of Stirk 310
A Touch of Daniel 309–10, 311
translated works 312–18
Travers, Pamela 33
Truffaut, François 353

Tryon, Thomas 319–20
Harvest Home 319–20
Lady 320
Night Magic 320
The Other 319
Twain, Mark
A Connecticut Yankee In King Arthur's Court 37
Tyre, Nedra 170–1
Death of an Intruder 171
'A Nice Place to Stay' 171

Unidentified Flying Oddball (film) 37
Upfield, Arthur 321–3
The Sands of Windee 322

Van Greenaway, Peter 130–2
The Crucified City 130
The Destiny Man 130–1
The Man Who Held the Queen to Ransom and Sent Parliament Packing 131
The Medusa Touch 131–2
Take the War to Washington 131
Van Gulik, Robert 137–9
The Chinese Maze Murders 139
The Chinese Nail Murders 138
Judge Dee novels 137–9
Van Thal, Herbert
Pan Books of Horror Stories 110, 168
Verne, Jules
The Castaways of the Flag 34
The Children of Captain Grant 36
Vertigo (film) 316
Victory Through Air Power (film) 35–6

Wallace, Edgar 324–6
The Four Just Men 325
King Kong 325
The Ringer 325
Sanders of the River stories 325
Ward, Arthur *see* Rohmer, Sax
Ware, James Redding 327–9
The Experiences of a Lady Detective 328–9
Waterhouse, Keith 330–3
Billy Liar 331–2
Billy Liar on the Moon 332
Jeffrey Bernard is Unwell 333
Jubb 330
Maggie Muggins 332
Office Life 332
On Newspaper Style 332
Waters, Sarah 234
Watson, Winifred 334–6
Fell Top 334
Miss Pettigrew Lives for a Day 335
Odd Shoes 335
Waugh, Evelyn 191
Weldon, Georgina 339–40
Welles, Orson 39, 123, 192
Wells, H.G. 307
Welsh novels 314
Wentworth, Patricia 102
West, Nathaniel
The Day of the Locust 195
Wharton, Edith 167
Wheatley, Dennis 343–5
The Devil Rides Out 345
The Haunting of Toby Jugg 343–4
They Found Atlantis 344
Wheeler, Terence 233
White, Ethel Lina 171–2
Some Must Watch 171–2
White, Patrick 235
White, T.H. 346–8
Farwell Victoria 348
Mistress Masham's Repose 348
The Once and Future King 347–8
The Sword in the Stone 36–7, 347
Whyss, Johann David
Swiss Family Robinson 33–4
Wilde, Oscar 162
Williams, G.M. 233
Williams, Richard 302
Willis, Ted 21
Wilson, Michael 42
Wilson, Sandy 63
Winkworth, Stephen 121
Winsor, Kathleen 349–51
Forever Amber 349–50
Star Money 351
Wizard of Oz, The (film) 207
Wood, Charles 247
Woolrich, Cornell 352–4
'All at Once, No Alice' 353
The Bride Wore Black 353
Phantom Lady 353
world authors, forgotten 312–18
Wyndham Lewis, D.B. 245, 355

Young Folks 277

Zweig, Stefan 313

Read on for exclusive paperback edition content

Where Were All The BAME Writers?

When I started this volume I didn't consider ethnicity or gender; I selected once-popular novels by the quality of the writing and the scarcity of the book. Certain patterns quickly started to appear among the authors. Many of the men had fought in a war, a surprising number had been pilots (writing and the air seem to fit naturally together) and many of the women had become disillusioned by the way they were treated by publishers and critics. A surprising number wrote to put bread on the table.

By mostly choosing authors who are now no longer with us, a time-frame emerged with a heavy concentration in the post-war 20th century, because this took in the reading of parents and relatives. Noticeable by their absence were writers of any non-white ethnicity. Had I overlooked them? I trawled through my files, then compared British publishing to its American equivalent. Stateside you're immediately led to Langston Hughes, Ralph Ellison, Richard Wright, James Baldwin and a lone female, Gwendoline Brooks.

In the UK, virtually no-one.

Of course there were always gay writers because they didn't look any different and were required to pass for straight, but the only black or Asian writers from that period that I came across on family bookshelves were VS Naipaul and Samuel Selvon, who wrote the terrific *The Lonely Londoners*, a kind of reverse Eldorado story in which a young West Indian gives up paradise to come to a dank, prejudiced London in the 1950s. This novel perfectly catches the feeling of what it's like to find yourself alone in a big city. However, Selvon penned his tale in a richly evocative patois that, although easily absorbed and understood, limited his readership at the time. Selvon had tried writing it in standard English but the words sounded wrong in the mouth of a youngster arriving into an alien culture.

The most prominent black British writers were usually university-educated and did not become populist paperback authors. The few who reached us did so after higher education. Everything becomes clear when you look at the pitiful statistics for ethnic admittance to Oxbridge. Writing about black experience in say, 1930s London would have reached a small readership.

The problem was made worse by the bigotry and nationalism that riddled much 20th century British writing, often unthinking and amiable, sometimes vicious. Even considering the social attitudes of the times, many writers are now unpublishable. I'm not simply referring to the coded digs Agatha Christie's characters regularly came out with about 'swarthy' foreigners, but jaw-dropping statements casually tossed in as if they were facts. The English were keen to categorise everyone, especially themselves.

When London's Regent Street was rebuilt in 1911, writer Shirley Brooks wondered how the removal of the grand colonnade would affect the foreigners who went there, and goes on to give outlines of national characteristics, pointing out that 'The Jews like to show themselves (as they always do) where the smart and rich people congregate'. She wrote the chapter in a jocular manner that somehow suggested amused affinity, not dislike, and this was the norm for popular writers of the time. However, some white authors became so embarrassed by the way their books dated that they subsequently withdrew them.

What chance was there that BAME authors were going to sell a book in the UK before the arrival of Monica Ali and the new wave? We think about 120 such writers were working in Britain. I knew of Francis Barber, the Jamaican manservant of Samuel Johnson who assisted in compiling his dictionary, and Andrea Levy, born to Jamaican parents, but that was about it.

Many were also committed activists, and weren't likely to end up in popular paperbacks. You quickly come to realise just how young our history of multi-culturalism is, and why there is still so much work to be done. The non-white authors who were published seemed to have been found largely by luck.

However, looking around in bookshops now, I'm immediately struck by the widening range of world authors who write about personal experience in a way that feels universal to all. In a recent survey, 81% of UK readers said that they love literature because it promotes empathy, so there's clearly a market for diverse reading. Much work is being done to recruit people from under-represented backgrounds on both sides of the fence, from encouraging careers in publishing to the creation of specific awards like the Jhalak Prize for BAME authors.

Visibility is the key; once, authors tended to be lost behind their novels, but live events and community outreach programmes now bring them into the public arena. We have crime from Abir Mukherjee and Jacob Ross, fresh history in *Black and British: A Forgotten History* from David Olusoga, Gary Younge's deeply disturbing *Another Day in the Death of America*, and Reni Eddo-Lodge's groundbreaking *Why I'm No Longer Talking To White People About Race*. There's even teen SF in *Chasing The Stars* from Malorie Blackman. Scottish books are on the list too, from *Psychoraag* by Suhayl Saadi, about a young Pakistani DJ growing up in urban Scotland, to Luke Sutherland's bleakly comic band-on-the-road saga *Jelly Roll*, although when I last looked, both were out of print.

Of the thousands of titles published in the UK last year only a tiny number were from British writers of a non-white background. It seems obvious to me that if we read to feel empathy, we'll want to read fresh stories from unheard-of voices.

Wandering the stacks in South London's Peckham Library, I watched a young West Indian boy immersed in his books and wondered, can you see something of yourself in what you're reading? How much confidence will it take to tell people you want to be a writer?

100

William Melvin Kelley

'If you're woke, you dig it.' Well, that answers the question; the word 'woke' first appeared in 1962, after William Melvin Kelley said it in a *New York Times* article that suggested beatniks had appropriated slang from African-Americans. Kelley was 24 at the time and lived 'uptown, way uptown.'

He was interested in idiomatic language, and said his grandmother had told him that 'ofay', meaning a white man, was pig Latin for 'foe', so black idiomatic language was primarily used for secrecy, exclusion and protection. Black slang, awkwardly placed in white mouths, sounds, he said, like white audiences clapping on the wrong jazz beat, first and third instead of two and four. Jazz was analogous to black writing, played first in all-black dancehalls and moving out to the white mainstream, finally reaching a point where *La La Land* could let Ryan Gosling explain a black artform to us.

Kelley sounded Bronx rather than black, and impersonated Frank Sinatra for the local kids. He set his first novel, *A Different Drummer* (which appeared less than a month after his *New York Times* article) in the recent past, having had the idea for it in high school. The book has a killer hook; Tucker Caliban, the descendant of an African chief who once decapitated his captor with his chains, burns down his homestead, kills his livestock, salts his fields so that nothing can grow, and takes off with his family for parts unknown – followed, shortly after, by the entire disenfranchised black population.

The governor is glad. 'We never needed them, never wanted them, and we'll get along fine without them.' The remaining white two-thirds are less angry than mystified. There's a callback of sorts in the aftermath of 9/11; 'Why do they hate us?' It feels like an act of natural forces, something inevitable and unstoppable. There's no anger in Tucker. 'He accepted everything almost as if he knew it was going to happen.'

So, Kelley's 24 and more than just woke, he's on fire. He writes from different perspectives, multiple voices, he's going tight into details and wide with apocalyptic events, controlled yet freeform. He's called experimental, satirical, unique. What next?

He'd grown up in a white Italian neighbourhood, the son of a former newspaper editor. Planning on a career as a civil rights lawyer, Kelley left Harvard just before getting his degree. His problem? He had trouble reading. Years later he said he'd only finished two books, James Joyce's *Ulysses* and the Bible, so I imagine they put him off.

A collection of short stories, *Dancers on the Shore*, and a second novel, *A Drop of Patience*, appeared in quick succession. *A Drop of Patience* is jazz and colour and history. Kelley is confident and in control. His writing is pleasurable, not earnest, his short story

'Not Exactly Lena Horne' is a delight and his characters slip from one book to another because like most good writers Kelley is a world-builder. Meanwhile he's hit by a series of life-changers, the assassination of Malcom X, black power, the start of the Black Arts Movement, the end of 'integrationism'.

Kelley covered the Malcolm X trial for the *Saturday Evening Post* but, disillusioned by the judicial process, he moved to Paris, then Jamaica, and eventually converted to Judaism. His third novel is *dem*, a luridly knowing soap-operatic satire that does its best to alienate readers with periodic crash-landings into wildly idiomatic language. His fourth, *Dunfords Travels Everywheres* uses an idea I'd first encountered in Friedrich Dürrenmatt's *The Visit*, in which clothes symbolise ideas. In *The Visit*, yellow shoes come to represent fascism. In *Dunfords Travels Everywheres*, segregation is based on the population's choice of clothing. This is Kelley's *Finnegans Wake* novel, and storms ahead of his readers. Very few authors apart from Gore Vidal ever cemented an enduring reputation for themselves with satire. As far as I know his final novel, *Dis/Integration*, has never appeared.

By this time the author was using a language of his own devising, part-patois, part Standard English, that had the impact of a haunting if very strange dream. When he and his family finally returned to New York, Kelley found that the reading public had forgotten him. He couldn't understand it; he knew he was a great writer producing fiction in a unique voice, so why would people ignore him?

The argument goes on. He wrote too many white characters for black readers, too much black patois for white readers, his vision of America was too bleak, his prose was too complex and fantastical.

It's more likely that times changed and while he was away new voices like Alice Walker and Toni Morrison were being heard. Readers can be disappointingly linear. Kelley was riffing on race, politics, love and life, and his audience just heard too many notes.

A NOTE ON THE AUTHOR

101. *Christopher Fowler*

A typical example of the late 20th century midlist author, Christopher Fowler was born in the less attractive part of Greenwich in 1953, the son of a scientist and a legal secretary. He went to a London Guild school, Colfe's, where, avoiding rugby by hiding in the school library, he was able to begin plagiarising in earnest.

He published his first novel, Roofworld, described as 'unclassifiable', while working as an advertising copywriter. He left to form The Creative Partnership, a company that changed the face of film marketing, and spent many years working in film, creating movie posters, tag lines, trailers and documentaries, using his friendship with Jude Law to get into nightclubs.

During this time Fowler achieved several pathetic schoolboy fantasies, releasing an appalling Christmas pop single, becoming a male model, posing as the villain in a Batman comic, creating a stage show, writing rubbish in Hollywood, running a night club, appearing in the Pan Books of Horror and standing in for James Bond.

Now the author of over forty novels and short story collections, including his award-winning memoir Paperboy and its sequel Film Freak, he writes the Bryant & May mystery novels, recording the adventures of two Golden Age detectives in modern-day London.

In 2015 he won the CWA Dagger In The Library award for his detective series, once described by his former publisher as 'unsaleable'.

Fowler is still alive and one day plans to realise his ambition to become a Forgotten Author himself.